WOMEN'S FICTION
from
LATIN AMERICA

LATIN AMERICAN LITERATURE AND CULTURE
Evelyn Picon Garfield and Ivan A. Schulman, *Series Editors*

Selections from Twelve Contemporary Authors

WOMEN'S FICTION
from
LATIN AMERICA

Edited with translations by
Evelyn Picon Garfield

Wayne State University Press   Detroit   1988

92 91 90 89 88   5 4 3 2 1

Library of Congress Cataloging-in-Publication Data

Women's fiction from Latin America : selections from twelve contemporary authors / edited with translations by Evelyn Picon Garfield.
p. cm.—(Latin American literature and culture)
Bibliography: p.
ISBN 0-8143-1858-4 (alk. paper). ISBN 0-8143-1859-2 (pbk. : alk. paper)
1. Spanish American fiction—Women authors—Translations into English. 2. Spanish American fiction—20th century—Translations into English. 3. English fiction—Translations from Spanish. I. Garfield, Evelyn Picon. II. Series.
PQ7087.E5W66 1988
863—dc 19   88-3670
                                            CIP

Grateful acknowledgment is made to the following for authorization to translate and for permission to reprint copyrighted material:

Lydia Cabrera: "The Mire of Almendares" and "Tatabisako" originally appeared as "El limo de Almendares" and "Tatabisaco" in *Cuentos negros de Cuba,* 2d ed. (Madrid: CR, 1972). Translated by permission of the author.

Armonía Somers: "The Tunnel," "The Burial," and "Plunder" originally appeared as "El hombre del túnel," "El entierro," and "El despojo" in *Todos los cuentos, 1953–67* (Montevideo: Arca, 1967). Translated by permission of the author.

Elena Garro: "The Tree" originally appeared as "El árbol" in *La semana de colores* (Xalapa: Universidad Veracruzana, 1964).

Clarice Lispector: "Love" and "Family Ties" are from *Family Ties* by Clarice Lispector, translated by Giovanni Pontiero from "Amor" and "Laços de Família" in *Laços de família* (São Paulo: Francisco Alves Editôra, 1960). Copyright © 1960 by Clarice Lispector. Reprinted by permission of the publisher, the University of Texas Press.

Griselda Gambaro: "Bitter Blood" originally appeared as *La malasangre* (Buenos Aires: Ediciones de la Flor, 1984). Translated by permission of the author.

Elvira Orphée: "Angel's Last Conquest" is the last chapter of *La última conquista de El Angel* (Buenos Aires: Javier Vergara, 1984). Translated by permission of Javier Vergara Editor, Buenos Aires. "The Silken Whale" originally appeared as "La ballena de seda" in *Su demonio preferido* (Buenos Aires: Emecé Editores, 1973). Translated by permission of Emecé Editores, Buenos Aires.

To my companion,
Ivan

Contents

Introduction   9

Acknowledgments   13

Lydia Cabrera (Cuba)   15
The Mire of Almendares   19
Tatabisako   23

Armonía Somers (Uruguay)   29
The Tunnel   32
The Burial   39
Plunder   51

Elena Garro (Mexico)   67
The Tree   70

Clarice Lispector (Brazil)   87
Love   90
Family Ties   99

Griselda Gambaro (Argentina)   107
Bitter Blood   111

Elvira Orphée (Argentina)   159
Angel's Last Conquest [Selection from the novel]   162
The Silken Whale   178

Carmen Naranjo (Costa Rica)   187
Ondina   190
Why Kill the Countess?   198

7

Contents

Marta Traba (Argentina)   211
Mothers and Shadows [Selection from the novel]   215
Conformity   226
All in a Lifetime   232

Julieta Campos (Cuba/Mexico)   239
A Redhead Named Sabina [Selections from the novel]   243
All the Roses   252

Nélida Piñón (Brazil)   265
Bird of Paradise   268
The New Kingdom   273

Luisa Valenzuela (Argentina)   279
Blue Water-Man   282
Other Weapons   288
I'm Your Horse in the Night   311

Isabel Allende (Chile)   315
Rosa the Beautiful [Selection from the novel
The House of the Spirits]   319

Bibliographies   338

Introduction

AN ANTHOLOGY of literature is by nature selective. When dealing with such a large geographic area as Latin America and with a century as fertile as the twentieth, you have two basic choices: to try to include as many authors as possible with the briefest selections in order to "cover the continents," or to limit the number of authors and represent them more fully by including more than one text or longer works. In either case, omissions would be obvious; a global representation from Latin America would be impossible; and personal preferences would inevitably prevail. I have chosen the latter option of presenting fiction by twelve authors from seven countries: Argentina, Brazil, Chile, Costa Rica, Cuba, Mexico, and Uruguay. Although some of these authors have also written poetry, literary criticism, art history, or cultural studies, in this anthology I have concentrated on prose, including nineteen short stories, a one-act play, and four excerpts from novels. I have undertaken all of the translations into English, with the few exceptions duly noted of works already in translation that I consider among the best or most important works of those authors.

One of my objectives has been to provide the reader with a representative sampling of prose fiction by some of the finest authors from Latin America in our century. When I compiled my volume of interviews with women authors, *Women's Voices from Latin America: Interviews with Six Contemporary Authors* (Detroit, 1985), I decried the neglect of works by women in traditional anthologies of criticism and literature about Latin America, in both the original Spanish and Portuguese, and in English translation. Since the early 1980s, a few anthologies have been published dedicated to Latin American literature by women authors in English translation, such as *Contemporary Women Authors of Latin America,* edited by Doris Meyer and Margarite Fernández Olmos (New York, 1983) and *Other Fires: Short Fiction by Latin American Women,* edited by Alberto Manguel (New York, 1986). These anthologies are beginning to fill the gaps in critical attention to literature written by women. However, works by the best female and male authors ought to appear side by side in the more traditional anthologies, too, in order to provide the reader with a more complete picture of Latin America's literary production.

Although variety is a key to these selections, there are several areas of interest that can be pointed out within the contexts of Latin American literature today. First, the reader may note the political commitment of certain writers. It has become a tradition among Argentineans like Valenzuela, Traba, Orphée, and Gambaro to deal with issues of political persecution, disappearances, and torture, albeit through varied expressions that may focus on the physical, the psychological, or even the mythic dimensions of such cruelty. The Chilean Allende places politics within the historical panorama of history, while the Costa Rican Naranjo winks a jaundiced and ironic eye at the hidden aspects of revolution.

Reflecting regional ethnicity or primitive roots is also a constant in Latin American literature today in writers such as Lydia Cabrera, whose tales are inspired by Afro-Cuban legends and culture, Elena Garro, whose plays and short stories reflect the indigenous presence in Mexico, and the Brazilian Nélida Piñón, whose characters sometimes explore primeval realms.

A critical view of classes in society takes place in Valenzuela's story about a village during Easter week, in Traba's evocation of the urban tenement ghetto, and in Garro's face-off between two women, a middle-class white and an Indian. But to the socially oriented, we have to add those works that cross boundaries to explore the complexities of the human psyche as it courts the unknown in Campos's fiction, in Orphée's story of a demented adolescent, in the "epiphany" that Lispector's character experiences while doing her routine chores.

Female protagonists abound in narratives of difficult and often misogynist relationships in Somers and Valenzuela, as forces of measured solidarity in counterbalance to patriarchal society in Allende and Traba, as willing or unwilling products of traditional family expectations in Lispector and Piñón, as foils for the stereotypes of legend and myth in Cabrera's black tales. The selections were not made in order to prove any kind of theory concerning the roles of women in fiction written by women. Nevertheless, the reader will find here a certain heterogeneity among works that do not shun sexual, social, and political implications of power relationships between the sexes. Of particular interest are the few works, like Allende's, Traba's, and Campos's, in which the narratives do not center on female relationships with or dependence on male figures.

The artistic styles represented here are richly varied. The straightforward plotting and musical lilt of Cabrera's tales are in stark contrast to the jagged rhythms and eruptive lyricism of Piñón's prose. Valenzuela, on the other hand, emphasizes the somatic-semantic relationship between the body and language. The dramatic expansiveness of Garro's story contrasts markedly with the intensity of Somers's tightly knit, neobaroque technique. Introspection swirls about in myriad unstable impressions in Campos or fixes on external and internal detail in Lispector. Black humor surfaces in Gambaro's play and in Somers's "The Burial." The magical transformations of everyday realities infuse both Allende's and Piñón's prose in very different ways, while Naranjo and Orphée utilize dialogue and focus in on scenes as if they were filming a movie.

The selections are presented in chronological order according to author's year of birth, and each is preceded by a brief introduction to orient the reader to the author, her work, and the selections. Unless otherwise indicated, explanatory notes are the editor's. The volume closes with a selected bibliography in which I have tried to include as many entries as possible in English, with the rest in Spanish and Portuguese. It is my hope that selections in this volume will inspire the reader to seek out further translations of literature by these and other women writers from Latin America.

11

Acknowledgments

I WOULD LIKE to thank the authors, and in some cases their families, for allowing me to include these selections in translation in this anthology. My heartfelt appreciation and admiration go to my friends and colleagues who have so patiently read these translations and given me valuable advice: author Irene Tiersten, Luso-Brazilian specialist Peggy Sharpe-Valadares, and translator Agnes Gullón.

Lydia Cabrera

Cuba

Lydia Cabrera.

Lydia Cabrera was born in Cuba in 1900 and during the 1920s studied painting in Paris, where she became interested in Oriental cultures. Influenced by ground-breaking studies that her brother-in-law, Fernando Ortiz, had done, she turned her interests toward the wealth of African cultures in her own country, Cuba, where she lived from the late 1930s until 1960, when she moved in exile to Florida.

Along with the Guatemalan Miguel Angel Asturias and the Cuban Alejo Carpentier, Lydia Cabrera was in the vanguard of what has now come to be called the style of "magical realism" of Latin American literature. These three authors lived in France and were influenced by both anthropological studies and the surrealist movement in art and literature in the 1920s and 1930s. As a result, they all became interested in the cultures of ethnic groups in their own countries, and incorporated into their fiction the perceptions of reality held by the Indian cultures of Central America (Asturias) and the African cultures of Cuba (Cabrera and Carpentier).

Cabrera, fascinated by African cultures in her native Cuba, by their poetry and primitive manifestations about to disappear, studied stories, legends, magic, rituals, ceremonies, spells, and language through the oral tradition of informants, many of whom were already old in the 1930s. But even before this concerted effort, she had already imbibed much folklore through the tales told to her by black nannies when she was a child.

Her research was published in two different though related areas: first, in her own tales based on Afro-Cuban folklore; and second, in volumes about Yoruba, Ewe, and Bantu religious traditions, rituals, and language, such as *El monte: Igbo finda, ewe orisha, vititi nfinda* (The Mountain), *Anagó: Vocabulario lucumí* (Anagó: Lucumí Vocabulary), and *La sociedad secreta Abakuá, narrada por viejos adeptos* (The Secret Society of Abakuá, as Narrated by Its Practitioners). Neither an anthropologist nor an ethnographer nor a linguist, Cabrera is nonetheless praised for these source materials on Afro-Cuban lore and its syncretic commingling with and influence on white Cuban culture and language.

In 1936, twenty-one tales were first published in Paris, in a French translation by Francis de Miomandre, as *Contes negres de Cuba,* and then in the original Spanish in Havana in 1940, with a prologue by Fernando Ortiz, as *Cuentos negros de Cuba* (Black Tales from Cuba). To those stories, mostly of Yoruba origin, Cabrera added twenty-eight more in her 1948 book *¿Por qué?: Cuentos negros de Cuba* (Why? Black Tales from Cuba). In general these collections include fables about animals, social myths, legends about the origins of man and about man's profound identification with nature and gods incarnated as natural forces. Along with abundant instances of animism and metamorphosis, the vocabulary, refrains, repetitions, and rhythmic patterns taken from African folklore or inventively modeled on it create a lyrical, musical prose.

Some of these elements can be seen in the two tales translated here, "Tatabisako" and "The Mire of Almendares" ("El limo de Almendares"). In the former, a seer undertakes a purification ritual called "ebbó" in order to placate the ire of a lagoon spirit, Tatabisako, who like other African gods is not bound by human morality and has been enraged by a lack of respect. In "The Mire of Almendares" we can see the perspective of a white author on the miscegenation ("mestizaje") of African characters, for the protagonist of this and other stories is a mulatta, rarely a central figure in African tales.

The Mire of Almendares

THE MAYOR issued a decree that nowhere in the world was there a mulatta as beautiful as Soyán Dekín.

The carriage driver, Billillo, loved Soyán Dekín but never told her so for fear of being rejected; even if she was beautiful, vain, and cunning, he wasn't just any old black man.

There was a celebration in the town hall in honor of Soyán Dekín. The Mayor was there; and Soyán Dekín, the queen, strutting about, her beauty leaving them speechless. She was dancing on and on with the Mayor.

That hurt Billillo to the quick. Unwilling to witness her vanity, for scorn takes no heed, his eyes were captivated by her glitter and sway; and he always found her with the white man, chitchatting or arm in arm.

Besides, she was affectionate.

Damn the mulatta! She must have been born to anoint herself all over with perfumes and rock herself to and fro while receiving visitors. She was a decorative trinket. And flirting with that silk shawl and the white cotton dress, the mulatta was ripe, Soyán Dekín was at her peak, just right for a gentleman's lover! And to pose as a white lily in front of the blacks!

(Billillo harbored hatred.)

He left the celebration to avoid suffering, and devils carried him along through the dark streets, while the cornet there in town hall kept vigil all night. And Billillo—God must have already forgiven him—went to the medicine man of Ceiba who dealt with death and conjured only evil spells.

Soyán Dekín used to sleep into the morning like royalty. The early morning street noises and the neighborhood racket in the communal courtyard never disturbed her sleep.

She would never think about getting up until well past eleven o'clock, and because of her pretty face, she never did anything. It was her mother—unsurpassed in ironing—who would bustle about the house and earn a living: Soyán Dekín would just sit in front of the mirror or at the window. The lazy good-for-nothing!

Soyán Dekín returned from town hall at dawn. And didn't go to bed. At the hour of fruits and meats, when the street filled with vendors' cries and the Chinese fishmonger called at the side gate, Soyán Dekín said to her mother, "Give me the dirty clothes; I'm going to the river to wash."

"Pretty face that you are and after the dance, you're washing clothes!"

But Soyán Dekín soberly repeated, as if some invisible being were commanding her, whispering in her ear, "Yes, dear mother, give me the clothes; *today* I have to wash in the river."

Accustomed to giving in to her every whim, the old woman made a bundle of all the clothes in the house and handed it over to her daughter, who left carrying it on her head.

And they say that the sun has never again seen such a shapely creature, nor more graceful, nor more lithe—the breeze blowing her dress, the morning for her halo—than Soyán Dekín that day on the road to Almendares. There's never been a more beautiful mulatta in the whole world than Soyán Dekín: a luscious Cuban mulatta from Havana, bathed in basil to drive away sorrows . . .

Where the river became a stream and the shallow waters gently played with the shore Soyán Dekín untied the bundle of clothes and, kneeling on a rock, began to wash.

Everything was green like an emerald and Soyán Dekín felt herself imprisoned, isolated within a magic circle: alone in the center of an imperturbable glass world.

Something new in that tranquility made her raise her eyes and she saw Billillo a few steps away, in the water, armed with a rifle and motionless like a statue. And Soyán Dekín was afraid: afraid of the shallow water that held no secrets, of the silence, of the light; of the mystery, suddenly so naked . . .

"What a coincidence, Billillo, to find you here! Have you come to hunt, Billillo? Last night at the dance, Billillo, Altagracia and Eliodora and María Juana from Limonar were looking for you. . . . And I thought you'd dance with me, Billillo . . . I'm not saying it to deceive you, no one can dance like you."

But Billillo didn't hear, he was in another world. He had the eyes of a cadaver, staring, immutable and glassy. Then his arms began to move slowly and mechanically; like a robot he cocked the trigger and fired into the air in all directions.

"Billillo!"

Soyán Dekín wanted to flee. She couldn't lift her feet: the rock held her fast; the river bed was sinking, so very shallow where the pebbles within reach shone like blue beads unfastened from Yemayá's* neck-lace; the clean water that before childishly played with the shore turned awesome, deep and mysterious.

The rock advanced by itself, carrying a captive Soyán Dekín with it; she found herself in the middle of a wide, turbulent river and slowly began to sink.

Billillo, so close that he could almost touch her, remained unmoved, loading and firing his rifle to the four winds; and that bottomless water didn't open at his feet to swallow him up, just her, little by little.

"Billillo," Soyán Dekín shouted. "Save me! Look at me! Have pity on me. I'm so pretty . . . How can I die?"

(But Billillo didn't hear, didn't see.)

"Billillo, evil black man, heart of stone!"

(And Soyán Dekín sank slowly, fatally.)

The water was already up to her waist. She thought of her mother and called to her . . .

---

*The goddess of water.

21

Soyán Dekín. Dekín Soyán!

Soyán Dekín, Dekín, I am suffering!

The old woman, who was skillfully ironing shirt fronts with a thousand pleats, trembled all over in anguish.

Soyán Dekín. Dekín Soyán!

Soyán Dekín, Dekín, I am suffering!

Without throwing her shawl over her shoulders, half-naked she took to the street in desperation. She went crying to seek help from the neighbors. They called an officer.

"Who has seen Soyán Dekín pass by? Soyán Dekín on her way to the river . . ."

They searched both banks of the Almendares.

The old woman was still listening to her daughter's cries, trapped in the water.

"Dekín! I am suffering! . . ."

The neighbors and officer heard her now. Everyone did except Billillo.

Now only Soyán Dekín's head was above water.

"Ay, Billillo, this is a curse! Goodbye, black man . . . I loved you, my saint, you fascinated me, black man, and I didn't let you know so you wouldn't get a swelled head. I didn't want to be turned down!"

Billillo seemed to suddenly awake from a dream. A dream that had lasted a long time or all his life.

The river had completely enveloped Soyán Dekín; her long hair floated on the gloomy, green waters.

The rock did not release its prey . . . Each of Billillo's hands grasped a lock of her hair.

For three days the women and officer searched for Soyán Dekín's body.

The Almendares River kept it forever. And they claim that in places where the river is cleaner and deeper—for Chémbe the kingfisher has seen it—a very beautiful mulatta is visible down below where her movements dilate the water's heart.

Soyán Dekín in the water's green pupil.

By night the mulatta emerges and strolls on the water's surface, never approaching the shore. On the banks, a black man cries . . .

(Soyán Dekín's hair is the mire of Almendares.)

Translated by Evelyn Picon Garfield

Tatabisako

THE WOMEN would leave very early to work the land. They planted peanuts, sesame, rice, yucca, yam, and okra. The men went to the forest to hunt.

One woman was working her field on the banks of the lagoon. She was carrying a child a few months old like a bundle strapped to her back. Arriving at the field, she untied him quickly and began hoeing. The thicket was no longer in the shade, the sun's rays began to fall mercilessly on the face of the small black child; they consumed him in heat. The mosquitoes and ants stung him. Flies got into his mouth; the wind rose up and filled his eyes with burning dust. He cried all day. The mother never interrupted her work. She didn't hear him. The Water Master of the Lagoon felt compassion for that woman's child.

One morning he called to her from the bank. He was very old, with a greenish black chest of mud; his beard spread out over the entire surface of the water. "Moana,"* he said to her, "give me your son. I am

*Woman. [Author's note]

23

Tatabisako, the Father of the Lagoon. Give him to me, Tatabisako will care for him while you work. When you finish, call me and I will rise to the surface with him."

The woman handed the child over. "Tatabisako, Tatabisako, Tatabisako, take son."

She didn't know how to speak or how to thank him as she should.

From that day on at dawn as soon as she reached the field she would show up at the banks of the still sleepy lagoon and call to Tatabisako.

Old Father Water would answer from the depths:

Tatabisako, Tatabisako, Tatabisako,
Tatabisako, Tatabisako, Tatabisako,
Tuá dila Moana a mé
Kuenda y brikuendé
Tatabisako!

Invisibly he would take the child from her arms; the woman saw nothing. Nothing more than the transparency of the colorless water; the first ripples of the smallest fish crossing in imperceptible threads along the surface.

She devoted herself to work. She used to toil tirelessly until sunset. Then at the sound of her voice Tatabisako appeared with the child. The woman would hang him on her back again and hurry off to her hut without stopping to talk to the women returning in groups from their fields.

She prepared the meal. Her husband would return from the forest. They would eat and then, worn out with exhaustion, go to sleep soundly on the bed boards.

The woman continued hoeing in her sleep. The man's spirit returned to the forest . . . An apparition on the hunting paths with his magic bow and his great knife, all night he would stalk the elongated ghosts of the fleeing animals: a vertiginous hunt from the forest to the firmament above.

When the woman sowed the seeds, she gave Tatabisako a goat as a gift. But she spoke very poorly. She didn't know how to make the offering with the proper words. She said, "eat the goat with child *tó.** And the old man retired offended to the quick.

That's why when she approached the lagoon that afternoon calling,

---

* And the child, too.

"Tatabisako, Tatabisako, Tatabisako"—thus calling many times—the old man did not respond.

The afternoon was still grand and clear, pure blue. The lagoon ceased reflecting the sky and became the menacing color of a storm. And the woman, unable to understand the water's ire, kept on shouting and becoming impatient, "Tatabisako, Tatabisako, Tatabisako."

The reeds on the banks writhed strangely, whistled and stretched out undulating, transformed into black venomous snakes; the stones advanced by themselves, enormous crocodiles with jaws agape. The gray, weeping Güijes*—children of the inconsolable rains of immemorial sadness—half feathers, half threads of feverish waters, gruffly hurled pebbles like so many pointed tears. The black lagoon boiled red with blood. Tatabisako's voice resounded like thunder:

Ungué, wó!

Ungué, wó!

And the fierce, evil night rose from the lagoon. A night of mire and blood.

The black woman found herself on the road with the other women returning from the fields. She heard one of them say, "The husband of the Moon's younger sister killed their son and gave it to him to eat."

When she reached her hut, she cut off a sheep's head and put it into a pot to cook over the fire.

Her husband showed up shortly asking for dinner, and she began to shriek and roll around all over the floor.

The man thought his wife was suffering from colic or that some rabid dog had bitten her in the stomach. He went to fetch a little water from the well to calm her down. Meanwhile she left to call the neighbors, wailing and arousing the town. When they asked her what happened, she increased her laments and cries without anyone managing to understand why she was so sorely afflicted.

Finally they discovered that the woman's husband had stuck her child into a pot and put it on the fire, assuring her that nothing bad would happen to him. When the man covered the pot, her son said,

Ungué, wó!

Ungué, wó!

---

* Dwarfs that emerge from rivers or lagoons.

like thunder . . . and what was in the pot was a sheep's head: the man was going to eat this sheep's head that was the head of his own son . . .

Listening to all that, the man also began to shriek and roll around all over the floor.

The women shouted and tore at their hair alongside the mother, who was beating her own face and breast; young and old wailed in a chorus, crying uncontrollably. The terrified children huddled against them, and the uproar increased. Sobbing, they asked that the murderer of his own flesh and bones be brought to justice. The elder men found that to be just. But the chief held that father in high esteem. He was a good hunter: he never returned empty-handed from the forest. He knew how to trap animals. He understood their language. He knew their dens, each one's hiding place, and the song that captivated them beforehand, spread upon his arrow. (And all this they say the Devil Bird of the Forest taught him in exchange for honey.) Before staining his knife with this man's blood, the chief wanted to consult with the Seer Babá. He lived alone about a league away.

Babá had an amulet that he commended to the Great Wind and a deer's horn that he commended to the Little Wind: Great Wind brought him all the words that were being said; Little Wind told him all he had seen. So that well before the messenger came for him, Babá had already begun the journey and knew everything.

"This man is innocent," the Seer said at first.

There was no way to silence the womenfolk who had covered themselves with ashes; they were seated in a circle, hands moving to their heads and waists, bodies swaying to the rhythm of their cries.

Babá commanded them to remain silent; they heard a kind of noise made by running water overflowing far off in the dark.

The Small Wind comes and goes and tells the Seer that Tatabisako is swelling and about to inundate the land, leveling the sown fields; that in his fury Old Man Water will spare no one, that all will perish by drowning because he will rise to the last branches of the highest trees. The Seer commands the Great Wind to contain the waters and to dissuade the Old Man of his resolve. He chooses a dozen billy goats and a dozen nanny goats and takes them all, men, women, and children, to the lagoon, and there they carry out "ebbó."* It is midnight.

---

* Purification. [Author's note]

Babá, naked, passes a white dove over his body, purifies himself and the others . . . Then he calls three times:

Tatabisako, Tatabisako, Tatabisako,
Tatabisako, Tatabisako, Tatabisako,
Tuá dila Moana a mé
Tatabisako, Moana tuá dila mé
Tatabisako, kuenda y brikuendé
    Tatabisako!

He set a gourd afloat toward the middle of the lagoon and there it stopped.

"Ungué, wó!"

Tatabisako answered.

The Seer sent the dozen billy goats into the water. They swam toward the middle of the lagoon and there they sank under.

"Ungué, wó!"

Tatabisako said again.

The Seer sent the dozen nanny goats; they disappeared in the same place where the billy goats sank before.

From the depths Tatabisako said:

"Tatabisako, tuá dila Moana, mé,
Tatabisako, kuenda y brikuendé
Tatabisako, kuenda y brikuendé
Kuma imbinbo yo, yo!"

Before the startled, speechless tribe, the Old Man appeared, his beard resplendent with the bright silver of live fish; because at the same time the moon shone bright.

The little black boy was sleeping on Father Water's shoulder; he was asleep cradled in the great, now tranquil night.

Tatabisako said that he considered himself appeased, that he would bring them no harm.

He held the child out to the woman, who didn't dare take him or raise her head from the ground.

The Hunter carried his son off. The little black boy was sleeping . . . And she, the woman, hiding like an animal among the shadows, went far away, forever like an animal about to die; no one ever found out where.

Translated by Evelyn Picon Garfield

Armonía Somers

Uruguay

Armonía Somers.

Armonía Somers is the pseudonym used by Armonía Etchepare de Henestrosa, born in 1920. Somers abandoned her career in teaching, in the administration of the Museum of Education, and in educational documentation and dissemination in 1972 in order to dedicate herself full-time to writing. She has received numerous literary prizes within her own country for narratives such as *El derrumbamiento* (The Cave-In) (1953) and *Un retrato para Dickens* (A Portrait of Dickens) (1969); most recently in 1986 she was honored at the National Library of Uruguay with an homage to her literary career—a celebration unprecedented in the lifetime of a writer.

Somers's literary production includes more than two dozen short stories and five novels. Although a few individual short stories have been translated into English, Somers's neo-baroque literary style defies facile translations. Her tightly knit prose, metaphorically lyrical and often viscerally repugnant, expresses the solitary nature of women and men. From her very first novel, *La mujer desnuda* (The Naked Woman), she has challenged the hypocrisy of social and religious morality, addressing topics of sexuality and eroticism, as can be seen in two of the short stories included here: "Plunder" ("El despojo") and "The Tunnel" ("El hombre del túnel"). Although humor is not one of the primary tools of her writerly craft, in her story "The Burial" ("El entierro") Somers blends a characteristic theme of hers—death—with irony and black humor. In fact, in many of her stories she explores the last few minutes bridging the lives and deaths of her protagonists.

Somers continues to live and write in the heart of Montevideo, in a high-rise building called the "Salvo Palace" amid stuffed owls, a wooden statue of an angel, and doves cooing from the windows that look out over the River Plate.

The Tunnel

A story to confess before dying

I WAS COMING OUT of that damn sewer pipe I had the courage to use in order to cross the highway—a cement tube no more than fifty centimeters in diameter—when I met him. I was seven years old then. That probably explains why someone would think of a narrow culvert as a route when you could cross the path normally. Anyway, that sacrifice was for nothing; that incredible crossing, aggravated by the curved dome, was for absolutely nothing.

As I crawled along with great effort, the putrid stench of the waste washed out and stuck to the sewer's surface penetrated every pore, but I managed to advance halfway into the tube. It was precisely at the peak of that foolish moment when sugar caramelizes that various things happened, one of them completely subjective: the thought that something horrifying could suddenly appear, like a snake or a spider when it was impossible to turn around, and the visualization of a retreat in reverse while the monster launched a frontal attack. When the curse of claustrophobia was already well established, these two slightly compensatory signs became discernible: seeing the mouth of the sewer pipe drawing closer and closer to my tongue and glimpsing the feet of a man apparently seated on the grass, given the position of his shoes.

It's clear that it didn't occur to me for even a second that I was the one who had been investigating, but rather that things were happening by themselves because I wanted them so much. (God, I never had you to hold on to, not even like a handy ring to grasp when I really needed you, not even as a provisional means for confronting fear.) So helped along by just a circular image and two strange feet, I arrived at the mouth of the culvert, and like a frog rowing on dry land, I explored the situation.

The man with the thick clumsy soles was seated, as I thought. Not on the grass but on a rock. He was dressed in black, had a drooping moustache like in old-fashioned portraits, and was holding a little green branch.

My exit from the hole didn't seem to surprise him. Even though I hadn't fully emerged, breathing wearily and tattooed with the sewer pipe's filth, I must have looked like a worm from a manure heap that was testing another creature's waters. But he didn't ask any questions and didn't bother with the usual what's your name or how old are you they pester you with when you're a kid, and there's no other way to answer except by showing your rear end in a typical gesture. If he tried anything perhaps it was a smile. But it was a honeyed smile, brimming over. He mustered it up along with the remnants of his own solitude, perhaps of his own tunnel, the way tenderness always remains virgin in this strange world of false encounters.

Then I emerged completely. That is, I stood up facing him. Again he showered me with approval, a kind of crazed collusion that soaked right through my tender skin.

I probably thought that no one had ever been capable of smiling at me that way, not only just for me like any old cheap candy, but as if a private rainbow had unfurled in a barren world. And I almost managed to reciprocate. But you suddenly become a cautious child. *A strange man. The police arresting vagrants. Never. Watch out.* They were a few laconic expressions from a basic dictionary, but they had their effect, like little tacks with their points buried in your brain and the nailheads exposed like antennas in all risky directions. So I squandered his budding attention and ran off as fast as my trembling legs would carry me.

The story babbled out in my stupid feverish state was repeated excessively. And so without anyone realizing what was happening, they taught me that in this world there is something called rape. Something terrifying, from what one could gather seeing the revulsion stuck to their faces like flies to garbage. But according to my own version of the event, if it issued from that strange man on the rock who had smiled at me, it must be a story about someone else. Rape, sweet man. They must have experienced something very dirty. But it had nothing to do with my adventure, divisible only by a unit number or itself, like those anarchic numerals in elementary mathematics that are indivisible. For I supposed that raping a little girl was like carrying her off on a mattress of clouds, high above the suspicious earth to a huge celestial farm without a roof or walls. And then come what may.

That's how my private image of the man remained incongruous, tender and withdrawn from the whole human mess that it had provoked. They arrested a few vagabonds, and that was all. My description never coincided with the rags, the lice, the long hair, the yellowed teeth. Until one day I decided to say no more. I realized they were chronic idiots, poor louts lacking adventure, incapable of deserving the grace of an angel who waits for us at the end of a culvert. And everything quieted down. But that was only the prologue. He reappeared many times, I'd say seven, enough for an entire earthly existence. And here the real story begins. About the man across the street. The only one who was present at my death. The final revelation of the void.

I lived in an attic then. I had chosen it so as to have nothing above me or beside me, a kind of unconscious liberation from the tunnel, as if psychoanalyzing oneself. Once, after a certain rather prolonged illness, I opened the window to water some plants and saw him. Yes, I saw him and he hadn't changed. So many years had passed by, yet he seemed to be the same age, wearing the same suit, with the same kind of moustache. He was standing next to a column and although no one would believe it, he was holding the same little green branch from ten or twelve years ago. Then I thought, this time he'll be mine. Except his image won't be profaned, he won't fall into the dirty annals of common crime, at least not on my account. . . . At that precise point in my thoughts, he raised his head, recognizing me, of course, and smiled at me again like at the mouth of the tunnel. ("My God, don't let him get away again," I said grabbing on to the famous ring of prayers. A few years later it wouldn't be the same. Only time enough to go down and tell him that I hadn't accused him. And not just that, but everything else, the sweet stories that his supposed rape had been capable of provoking later on in the complete solitude that You spread from the heavens when the time was right and the grapes were ripening in their true summers . . .)

I grabbed the telephone and dialed the number of the neighborhood business where he had reappeared.

"Excuse me," I said fighting back my repugnance at this kind of humiliation, "this is the student who lives on the top floor of the building across the street . . ."

"Yes . . ?"

"Well, you wouldn't understand. I simply want you to go outside and tell that man dressed in black, holding a little branch and standing near the column, that the girl who was watering the plants is the same one from the tunnel. And that she's already on her way downstairs to meet him, so he musn't get lost again just because of the five floors that separate us. Run, I beg you!"

"Nothing else, huh?" the guy dared ask.

"Go right now," I ordered in a voice that didn't seem to come from me, "I'll wait. Those same years are irretrievable, time that's lost is never recovered!"

My incoherent remarks, my craziness drumming into his ears forced him out into the street. I watched him glance toward the exact place that I had indicated, shake his head negatively, and look around. After a few seconds, while I was still watching the stranger in the same spot, the shopkeeper returned to the telephone with this stupid rendition:

"Listen, why don't you keep your jokes for someone else? There's no guy or anyone like him near the column. This is no adventure of the invisible man, damn it . . ."

"You're the one who's kidding around, not me," I shouted hysterically, "he's still there, I'm looking straight at him!"

"That's if he didn't beat it when he saw one of us about to catch him stealing my bike. Right?"

"Shut up, you fool!"

"Or crossed the street," he added confidently, "just to climb the stairs four by four up to your attic . . . Because I've been thinking that you're sleeping alone too much and anyone would gladly keep you company . . ."

I cut off his stupid, endless gushing that threatened to inundate the world. But from the experience that had slipped away between one year and another carrying off faces, I'd discovered who knows what secret link with the others. For a few minutes in reverse, I again felt the air fanned by their breath, at once like the budding of flowers, but then again just like those very flowers when they become so rotten that I would almost have bribed death to drag them away.

That's when I understood that in the future I should never share my secret with anyone. Everything was capable of being damaged on the way across the bridge being held out to me. And in a vague way I sensed that even I was capable of falling for fairy tales, that the man must be liberated from my own symbolic gift, just as vulgar as any other kind.

Well the matter was over. So while he remained in the same contemplative position, unaware that the bicycle's owner was removing it from the column and carrying it into the store, I moved toward the steps like a sleepwalker.

Perhaps I was walking along talking to myself or exceeding the normal speed or both at the same time, when the nondescript woman who was coming up the stairs, puffing along with her bag full of groceries, stepped in my way. Even before she pushed ahead, I responded to the odor of damp broom that permeated the hallway. I was imagining her on one leg, hopping off into a dark corner to hang herself from a small loop of dirty thread that she herself had tied to a groove in her neck, when she persisted in taking up the whole width of the hall. Speechless we fought for that vital space, instinctively conserving what was most dear, she her vocation as a mop, I my return to the mouth of the tunnel in search of what belonged to me. I had no other recourse but to shove her. Yes, shove, what else. You don't let anyone interfere twice, when you're balancing on the taut cord of destiny above the tiny heads of those who watch from below. And she arrived before me, of course. When I turned around to see her on the last landing among the scattered vegetables, glowering at me with glazed eyes, it was already late. The man had disappeared. I won't say forever. But from my rape to my first criminal act, then on to the other trifles of which he was also the principal witness and in which the others always acted as catalysts, his regular recurrence wrenched from me pieces of my wretched life. For years it seems you roam about thinking something's going to be taken away from you and then you end up waiting for the wine to age. So when much later I exchanged the stairs for an elevator and no one on the floor where I used to live found out about the move, I almost greeted a woman who looked like me, pushing her hair back in a hallway mirror. My God, I was about to exclaim like another time when I was under stress. But suddenly I remembered the worst and best of my tasks, neatly stealing a husband away from some unknown woman. And I decided that my lackluster hair wasn't fit for going around knocking on every door for pity.

Until a certain rainy, late afternoon, I couldn't say how long afterward, the man in the tunnel appeared again, not across the street but on the same side like a hunting dog crazed for life by the scent of his prey. I then decided that nothing in this world would stop me as I hurried to our definitive meeting. There I was without anyone between us, pushing the elevator button, when I saw the emergency ladder resting against the wall.

"That's it, as always," I mumbled, "the invincible attraction of the culvert, even though the normal path is the one that comes and goes vertically with unquestionable efficacy."

Suddenly while the elevator door opened automatically like a well-lubricated vagina, the greasy stairway banister winked at me with the guile of a fawn from behind the trees. The exact amount of time for the door to close again. And there I was losing myself astride the banister, just as someone must have invented it for incipient orgasms that later on overpower the ripe sex in bloom until it ends up contracting like a burnt rag in old age.

"Yes!" I shouted at once, completely free of all burdens, including those of others who bear their own.

That "yes," hanging in space without more meaning than its own destructiveness, remained for a few moments spinning in the stairwell's air with other smaller "yeses" that had issued forth from my entire body, accompanying me to the door. Then as dizzy as when I rode the stairs, I crossed the street unaware of the approaching tires, as if the whole world had lined up its cars in search of my guts. I was deaf and blind to all save my objective, the inseparable embrace of the man with the little green branch, standing there, ageless, ignoring his obligation to run like crazy after time. That's when I was able to see, fleetingly, how the child molester, the thief, the killer, the man who covets what isn't his, and the one who's everything else he can be from birth, opened his arms to me.

Offering, however, an unattainable haven if the car's tires reached me first. I saw him so much and so little that I cannot describe him. He was like the scenery seen through the window of an express train, with details that will never be known but all the same make the skin velvety or full of goose bumps.

"Thanks for the invention of the seven falls," I managed to say to him as I watched my tongue roll like a single petaled flower on the pavement.

That's how I entered the tunnel once again. A black hole roughly hewn in the infinite rock. And at its innumerable exits, always a stone blocking the mouth. But now without the man. Oh the consecration of the absolute, desperate void!

Translated by Evelyn Picon Garfield

The Burial

FOLLOWING HIS INITIAL SURPRISE at the trifling way the man received news of his discharge, the male nurse helped him dress and gather together his few belongings, noticing all along the man's lamentable physical condition, so very different from the festive spirit that never wavered even during his post-operation mumblings under anaesthesia. Barely managing to control his curiosity, the nurse finally returned the flask with "that thing" in it, a flask the patient had not relinquished until the very moment he was forced to put on his own shoes.

Since the first days of his stay in the clinic, attention was drawn to this patient, to his friends of all stripes concerned with his fate, and to oranges and cigarettes left in his name. One time a kind of anthology of jokes arrived at the reception desk. It was made up of all the comic strips from the weekly newspapers, with a very peculiar dedication: "To the dead man in Room 2, Honoribaldo Selva, so that by reading this he may be resuscitated. Your seven friends of THE SMALL BOTTLE TAVERN." So the matter of leaving the hospital carrying off with him is extirpated viscera, a kind of compensatory demand made by the patient upon

39

agreeing to the operation, would prove to be but one more peculiarity of a fellow whose charm had even convinced the surgeons to give him that macabre trophy as a vindication of his unquestionable rights of possession. While wrapping up the flask, he still maintained enough good humor to choose the best page from the newspaper for holding a putrid piece of flesh. Pointing to the headline, he explained to the nurse that it was in keeping with his natural repugnance toward certain human deceits. And of course, accompanied by his most loyal friends awaiting him in the street, he left that morning with the bundle tucked under his arm like a good gentleman, he said, fetching something from the market.

Faced with Selva's announcement some days before that their first outing together would be to the cemetery, one of the men hit upon the idea of renting a car, primarily because of the considerable distance that prudently separated the dead from the living. "That's the last straw," commented the cadaverous convalescent with a contagious guffaw. "I manage to survive under the knives of three doctors with faces covered like bandits from the silent screen, and you think that now I'm going to die because of three meek kilometers stretched out ahead of us beneath the trees. As for risks, some are incomparable, and the way we face them remains to be seen, even if we let them drug us till we're impotent. And now you want to protect me from an innocent stroll between heaven and earth . . ."

Then, without further discussion, he chose to walk down that long road on which tiny pieces of his wit would remain like a great bread of hilarity reduced to crumbs. Midway, because of a depression due to a ford, Honoribaldo had to slow down. Holding onto a branch to support himself, he threw a stone into the narrow stream of water at his side. But neither this first stretch nor the next one managed to daunt his spirits, despite the visible sacrifice that absurd voyage was exacting.

Finally they reached the cemetery and crossed over the chessboard of tombs where the man decided to carry out his plan right there next to the back wall. With great difficulty, he began making a hole in the earth, using the branch that had supported him. No sooner had he finished than he backed away a few steps, aimed at the hole with his package, and quickly threw it right into the center. Then he returned to the spot looking just as calm as could be, pushed the excavated earth with his foot, and began covering the thing up. He cleared his throat, straightened his tie, and awaited some taunt that never materialized for, what the devil, each of them probably had someone nearby with his mouth full of roots. He coughed, then unfurled his characteristically oblique smile that showed off a dimple in a gaunt cheek, and finally let loose with this mysterious speech:

"Future dinner guests feasting on my remains below, this package is advance payment. Besides, for after-dinner conversation I'm leaving you this newspaper open to the international page, always cheerful and rotten, to tell the truth the more cheerful, the more rotten. Enjoy! As they say here on earth above when they greet each other, until we meet again for that truly promising feast."

He coughed once more, pressed both hands against the pit of his stomach, and without further ado, rejoined the group, leaning on one of the men instead of on the green branch left poetically beside the grave.

At this point, the group's rowdy mood changed considerably, not only because of the gist of the joke but also because of the friend's calamitous appearance. Each one, shoring up his reserves, decided unanimously to end the day in a certain low-brow bar called "The Small Bottle," the only way to recuperate according to past experience. With Honoribaldo in tow, they went into that place that meant a day off to them anytime during the week, and sat down at the usual table. From then on things acquired frantic shapes. It was necessary to celebrate the main character's return to the ring. Wasn't that so? But it was second nature and urgent to take steps against a certain cold lodged in the spine for which the only sure cure was a drink. So much so that even the owner, yielding to the game, decided to medicate himself for free. That was really the beginning of the disaster, marked at the critical moment when someone suggested that the owner shouldn't bother closing the cabinets every time he took out another bottle. What need was there to wear out those beautiful old bronze handles? From then on with the self-service system, the contents began to flow without the miserable container's limitations, as someone said throwing a bottle over his shoulder.

During one late afternoon and the whole night, they finished off everything at hand until the very bottle that symbolized the bar's founding day appeared on the table wrapped in cobwebs. It was so unusual that it provoked a kind of collective panic. It was the small bottle that gave its name to the tavern and was endowed with such a mysterious survival instinct that not even the most unforgettable brawls registered in the bar's annals had succeeded in tearing it from its pedestal. Then, as with all taboos, a kind of possessive anguish broke through the first scruples. How and in the name of which unwritten law was the fascinating miniature to be saved? The table was already bristling with arms as if the men to whom they belonged had transmigrated into a kind of Brahman symbol. Immediately following a blow with the fist that made all the nearby shelves tremble, Honoribaldo Selva's voice was heard trying to rise above the group.

"Not this bottle, lads. Don't you see that it looks like an aged Lady Godiva only with ashen-colored hair?"

"La-dy what, did you say?" stuttered a thirsty fellow stretching out his hand, unsuccessfully.

"You're not going to scare me with stories about old ladies," added another one bravely. "Let the old lady show up here, because in needy cases, even a little old lady can warm the body. You can't rob them all from the cradle. Why be turned off by a few white hairs, more or less . . . !"

"You'll open that bottle over my dead body!" shouted Honoribaldo, managing to avoid the kidnappers despite his noticeable fatigue.

Perhaps it was the extreme intervention by the guest of honor defending the bottle that made the group come to its senses. Until that moment, no one had recalled either the original episode or the reason for the festivities. And therefore it didn't occur to them to observe the man's pallor, almost fading away from the world, as if squeezed and pressed inward by an imminent joke that didn't manage to surface because of its sheer weight. That pallor along with the romantic rescue soon turned the collective attention toward Honoribaldo's famous silence that usually preceded some sort of pronouncement. This time it would not be very dignified, however, due to one person who was hiccuping and the rooster crowing outside. No doubt the air was charged with a certain tension, as if the edge of an electrical storm had been touched, or more simply and humbly as if Honoribaldo had decided to die right there and then in front of them, in sweet sight of the small bottle, its virginity intact like an old button on the table. The guest of honor continued sitting there among them, but he was dead. Judging from several details, he had apparently left the hospital with a black passport. One never knows how long the mysterious cord is capable of vibrating in spite of all appearances. But man is only accustomed to calling certain states death, and nothing else.

For a long time they remained hypnotized by the corpse. Finally through the initiative of someone used to such situations or perhaps to avoid Honoribaldo's intense gaze, they decided to lay him down on the floor amid the spittle and the sawdust, the cigarette butts and the broken glasses. One person shut his eyes and mouth, another crossed his hands over his chest. Having nothing else left to offer, the owner put the disputed bottle between Honoribaldo's fingers. His oblique little smile remained fixed on his face: it never failed him, come what may.

Finally they returned to the table. And there, almost without planning it out loud, they decided to put together a coffin with whatever was at hand, bolting in search of materials like nocturnal termites. After using the wood shelving, the most active one spotted the intriguing bronze handles on the glass cases and twisted them off so that the box ended up acquiring an authentic funereal dignity, that subtle touch that was synonymous with "don't be confused, it's the real thing."

It seemed as if everything was finished, when one of the fellows, trying to surpress a sigh, let go with a cracked, drunken cry capable of moving the very heart of the deceased. "Long live the dead man, long live the dead man, I say!" That was decisive. Those who could stand up lifted the open box, and repeating "long live . . . ," carried it into the street followed with great effort by the others. They walked down the street in such a frantic state, bothering the sleepy neighbors with that cry that seemed to come from their solar plexus, until they discovered another open bar, like the one they had already sacked. So after depositing the coffin on the sidewalk, they decided to round off the posthumous honors.

"Nothing else . . . in the meantime . . . let the filthy sun . . . old buddy . . . ," clarified one of them in his circumstantial double-talk. "If it were still nighttime . . . we'd carry you inside . . . to keep on drinking . . . But the sun is going to come out, brother . . . And by daylight everything must be . . . as ordered, untamed things . . . people wanting everything in order . . . man with woman . . . right shoe and left shoe . . . the living with the living . . . the dead with the dead . . ."

Such words, equally weighted with the absurd and with common sense, seemed to awaken another individual's consciousness. Hiccuping at the same irregular rate as his buddy, as if receiving the hiccups by stealth, he managed to connect with his own ideas.

"And what about the formalities due a deceased human being?" he said. "Or do you brutes think that a dead man is a contraband bundle that can slip by without being taxed? Let's back up, I know what I'm saying; we have to do other things first . . ."

Formalities with a man who had buried his own entrails, kept on smiling in that box, and even looked better than the rest of them? That must have crossed most of their minds, for the dead man had to remain where he was, adding to the street's solitude like a valise abandoned on a railroad platform.

Burping away, more livid and bearded than when they entered, they left some hours later in broad daylight to find two surprises: a muffled noise like barricades among the clouds, making the structures below tremble as if punished by vibrations, and the robbery of the bronze handles, the coffin's only luxury. One of the staggering group, who seemed not to care about the impending rain, was the first to be terrified by that last fact, as important as a blow to the Achilles tendon, not because of the handles' functionality but because of their sumptuous nature. With his legs as twisted up as his tongue, he managed to crouch down, verifying the disaster, wherein he caught onto the idea of the unlikely guilt of the dead man in this matter.

"You're not going to fool me," he succeeded muttering in a monotone, as he was about to fall into the box, "it's you who's playing a joke on us. Now you're really dead; without handles there's no burial. Let's have a look see. Out with them if you don't want us to take them away by force . . ."

They were just about to carry out the desecration, searching the dead man's pockets, when one of them who'd vomited by a nearby tree managed to avoid the disaster, chasing off some flies that had landed on the corpse's mouth and nose. They decided to pick him up and set out again on yesterday's route.

With all this going on, the first drops could be felt, big and round as if fallen from an umbrella's ribs, albeit luckily spaced and slowly. To no advantage, for Honoribaldo Selva, at once remote and present, wasn't all there this time to make the trip seem shorter. And due to their collective drunkenness, he was shifting around in their consciousness like a reflection in the water.

So they traveled halfway to the cemetery when a certain fatalism materialized again, always occurring in duplicate—from the celebration to the death of the guest of honor, from the storm to the robbery in the street: a certain big black bird jumping from tree to tree decided to accompany them just as the downpour also joined the procession.

They had to quicken their pace, first because of the bird that was frightening them and then because of the elements. Furthermore, in spite of their mental fogginess, all of them remembered the existence of a kind of ford and how it usually swelled in such cases. Meanwhile Honoribaldo's body was jerking about up above due to the zig-zagging forced march, weighing more and more from the rain. Setting foot in the flooded road, all of a sudden they realized that a dirty trick had been played on them as usual: not only did the water reach crotch level, but it also stirred up a mean eddy in the middle, making everything dance about as it was dragged along by the water. After a quick and desperate "every man for himself," they faced the danger of landing on the lateral wire fencing that marked the current's theoretical bounds, now totally obscured by the water. Flailing about and grabbing onto each other, they had managed to dodge the small but raging whirlpool when they caught sight of the empty box floating behind them. They realized it could be useful to them as a life preserver. Restored to relative sobriety by the dunking, but still fuzzy about the reason for the crossing, they looked at the coffin almost failing to recognize it. The box went floating along like any one of the many things they clung to with all their might. Then the last man to leave the riverbed behind became Honoribaldo's choice once again to refresh their memory, for Selva was escaping between the fence wires, moving with the current. Face-up, hands crossed over its chest, the corpse rolled over three or four times and followed the current, missing a half-submerged tree, intermittently hitting another head on, but always determined by an urgency to flow on inexorably.

Very little time had transpired since the beginning of this episode. Nevertheless as is common in this kind of flood, the water was already subsiding. A fiery yellow sun appeared behind the clouds. They looked at each other like strangers, a group of half-drowned men discovered among the driftwood, with stones and pieces of shell caught in their ears and hair, but not such strangers that they were unaware that somehow they ought to remain together, even though the reason, passing from one brain to another, burst like a bubble in the air. In such a poor state of affairs, they didn't even have any cigarettes in their pockets but rather foul mixtures, extricable only by turning the linings inside out. Some time went by before anyone was able to utter a word, at least one that allowed the others to tug on the ball of twine each felt sloshing about inside him along with the dirty water he'd swallowed. One of the men, perhaps tempting fate, abruptly got up from the box that had been converted into a seat and began to examine a dead rat nearby, doubtlessly taken by surprise despite its usually formidable instincts in such emergencies. He turned it over with his foot, unconvinced that such a nervous, inaccessible, and worldly animal had fallen into the same trap. "It's a country rat," he said timidly, "you'd recognize it even on the asphalt sidewalk of a city full of skyscrapers."

Out of the corner of his eye, he looked at the group that seemed to solidify into a whole, confirmed that it wasn't worthwhile showing off his command of the subject matter, and ended up sitting down on the ground facing the others. "So?" he even managed to say, throwing to the wind the most laconic question of all for any occasion.

The adventure of speech still seemed impossible. But as if that word by its very provocative nature had introduced itself into their minds, the most miserable, small, skinny one, plagued by nervous tics, began to let loose a jumble of basic ideas similar to a bunch of tacks that were bothering him inside.

"We came to bury our friend. Isn't that so? We kept him company when he dug that damned hole, then we celebrated his return until the filthy bottle showed up, the one he baptized somehow and insisted on defending to his death. Later we made him this box with our own hands; we shouldered it halfway down the road, all along putting up with that big black bird's squawks . . ."

He looked around hoping in vain that someone would want to relieve him from going on.

". . . The water tricked us. But who's to blame for that? It's always raining and the water's always carrying off loose stuff. God's that way; he doesn't send the rain when there's a drought, but throws it down in bucketfuls if you're carrying a dead man around. He doesn't pluck out the eye of someone who's had bad luck because he'd keep on staring with the other one anyway . . ."

You could guess by his voice, progressively more choked up and confused, that he was about to do something he'd never dared to do, cry over the inexplicable matters that oppress innocent men like a punishment. When suddenly another in the group, whose worse luck was apparent from his condition, decided to take advantage of the opening left by that weakness, and after throwing up a few slushy mouthfuls, left his place to brusquely confront the others. He looked like a drowned and bearded ghost. Bluish, transparent skin showed through the holes of his shirt torn in various spots.

"If it's so," he began to say with difficulty, "he slipped away from us, better yet, he was taken from us. But remember, we were going to bury him in a specific place. So if we're not a bunch of wretches, unworthy of sharing the spit left on his glass, what we have to do now is go on polishing that box as if it were a chair in a waiting room, then hoist it onto our shoulders again and finish the burial where he left his offering, carrying out what we all witnessed, his last wish."

He was spitting out more dirty water each time, waiting for an answer. Until one of them, like a sort of mentally retarded mongoloid child, looked both ways and asked:

"You said to carry on the burial anyway? How? A funeral, I believe, requires a dead body on a stretcher or something like that. Without a corpse there's no ceremony . . ."

"What do you mean 'how'? However we can!" the man shouted, blue from more effort than his mud-filled lungs seemed to allow. He continued, controlling his voice with great sacrifice. "Honoribaldo always used to say that the most serious matters, the ones that turn out best, aren't thought about a lot but simply surface at the last moment. And if he thought that way, it was for a good reason. I never heard him utter a senseless word. Why do you think we're his friends? Let's see, can someone explain it any other way?"

The little man with the tics began to shout, "Long live the dead man, long live the dead man! Didn't I say that from the start." He stood up, arms flailing about.

They had to force him to be seated, holding his legs down and placing a knee on his stomach. The crisis past, the small madman looked at them one by one and calmly chewed them out.

"You animals can't understand the human soul. While you're holding a makeshift funeral, you get to thinking that somebody's crazy just because he's discovered something in life but can't find the words to express it. I have a three-week-old kid, you know, and that's why I have the right to shout 'long live the dead man' as many times as I like. Because if it hadn't been for something that simply happened without much thought, like Selva used to say, the baby wouldn't be here, and I'd be nothing more than the smut that's left when rain washes off a rear end. We have to look for him," he shouted, becoming agitated again, "and if you're still afraid of that big black bird, I'll go by myself. Let go of me, you fags, let go!"

They had to pin him down again. He let them do it after all because, if you think about it, it was important to know just what would happen in the last instance, the one always foreseen by Selva.

"All right, let's carry on," said the man who pointed out that there's no funeral with an empty coffin. "But we'll have to throw something in, even though it's that dead rat, to weigh it down and get some flies to follow. Because first it was a box without handles, then without a corpse, but damn it, there have to be flies!"

One fellow tried to argue in a sober voice that the business with the rat was an insult, an offense to human dignity. They were already bending to the usual impulses despite having been schooled in Honoribaldo Selva's influential and captivating immorality. But at that very second, and as if Honoribaldo himself had chosen him as his representative in that tournament, one man joined the polemic with the following thoughts:

"An insult to human dignity, you say? Don't give me that . . . I was once a ship's stoker. What do you think of that? And there's where I saw a lot worse done by the Americans, who are really somebody you know, because whatever you say, they're important all right . . ."

He was going to reach for his cigarettes but discovered the jacket lining was turned inside out and chose to continue in a suspenseful tone:

"One day an official died on board. A dispatch was sent to his country's embassy in the nearest port. A group of local high officials met on board and the crew gathered to honor him before a coffin just like this one, only draped with a flag. Afterward, everyone was satisfied. But those of us who were down below knew otherwise; you see the body was really in the cold storage room, and they had honored a box full of spare parts. Nevertheless, the dead man was so grateful they hadn't let him rot that he spent the rest of the voyage without one single nighttime trick, like leaving the refrigerator for a minute to stroll around on deck at dawn as he would have done had he been offended. Because as someone who knows more than me explained, what's symbolic is symbolic and ought to command everyone's respect."

48

The anecdote was so clear to everyone that it seemed to convince the group. The man who'd discovered the rat grabbed it by the tail and threw it into the box. They immediately set out again. That stormy late afternoon, a strange sun beat down on their backs, making a sort of cauldron's steam rise from their sopping clothes, chilling their shivering bodies as the clouds again covered the heavens. They finally reached the cemetery. The gravedigger saw the procession arrive shouldering the burden, but because of professional indifference, he didn't even notice their physical state. By chance or mysterious design, they once again took the same route of the day before, though this time sinking ankle-deep into the mire. And luck would have it that the excavated grave was right next to Honoribaldo's buried innards. The stick was still there, oblivious to all and fresh as a kiss in the rain. By some common stroke, all eyes were riveted to that trivial object, a simple green-leafed stick, and not even where they were going to unload their burden. But the gravedigger's knowing glance convinced them the critical moment had arrived. In turn the pallbearers looked about as if asking the others for help. They weren't there to joke around, everyone knew that. The dead man had so rigorously drawn a dividing line between their last minutes together and the gray, empty hours, that each one had a semiconscious premonition about his imminent future, a sort of sentence to live by, without resorting to Honoribaldo's tender, universal soul. Each lost spirit fighting to stay afloat in his own solitude was becoming a mere shadow of himself, like a tree uprooted from the earth.

Finally coming to their senses, the two who were carrying the box decided to lower it. That's when it was seen for what it was, empty. Not even the rat's corpse lost in one corner served to maintain the lie.

After watching with distrust, the gravedigger looked up at the group, then at the sky which had clouded over again. Finally he observed each man, figuring that somebody's always ready to pull a fast one. So these scoundrels must be pulling his leg, holding the dead man up on his feet between them so that he would strike up a conversation with a corpse. At that very moment, thunder clapped against the stone wall and the gravedigger glanced toward the heavens, inspected the group one by one, then faced the bluish-looking man whose chin was splattered with muddy spittle from his last vomiting spell. The gravedigger grabbed him by his skinny arm, brutally threatening him.

"Hey you, fresh corpse, what do you say we finish this off now? Or are you waiting for it to rain so you can drown again without being buried?"

As the man, more rigid and blue than ever, lifted his foot to get into the box, the first swollen drops began to fall from the sky, huge and promising like the morning rain. For once and for all, the burial must go on, he thought, feeling his life ebb away.

Translated by Evelyn Picon Garfield

Plunder

I
The Spider

HE FLED THE FARM at dawn, as soon as the boss's loud coughs were barely audible. His truly propitious sign had been that violent hack, more so than the reddish sky intensified by the mooing, the clucking and the barking below.

He touched his body anxiously. His irreplaceable flute was luckily still there. He was escaping from the farm the way he had arrived, master of body and soul, with but a few more calluses on his hands from the damn wood and the damn water and the eternally damned man who coughed at dawn, not from illness but from the mere bestiality of his guts.

He slithered along a while in the wheat field, kissed all the dogs that had followed him there as if helping him to track something down. Then he threw a stone over his shoulder to chase them off and finally began to swim alone on the cutting edge of the wheat field's tide. He had heard that

51

once, but what's said hardly ever counts for much. It seemed you had to slash yourself open, to insert that experience into the flesh in order to realize it, and in addition be burdened down by crawling on all fours.

When he stood up again, the boss's cough had stopped forever, and his whole farm weighed him down. The main thing was to be completely sure of the event. By cursing a man in the midst of the sharp wheat fields, you ended up imagining him that way, lying face up with his arms and legs spread open. Since he has to support the farm on his chest and stomach, his dung-covered boots no longer kick anyone's ass. His eyes, yes, those eyes, are the same as before, they stare at him with the same intensity. Every time they looked his way on the farm, he felt himself seized by the silent passion of something bound to happen. Now it had been revealed, so that's why he could take stock of himself again. Anyone who has seen a man crushed that way by a roof or a train, or whatever, knows very well what those eyes are saying. The eyes bulge more and more from their sockets ("get it off of me, get it off of me"); then the plea is transformed into what is ineffable, only understood by others in the same situation. Someone is suddenly suffering, giving birth to his eyes, and the others, unaware, won't understand until it happens to them. Unfortunately, he's aware of the others' ignorance, but he can't yell at them either, because on top of it all he's vomited up his tongue. Suddenly, as if pushed from within by displaced viscera, the poor bloody eyeballs surprisingly end up wrenched from their sockets and remain riveted in the distance, no longer exacting anything.

But there's a terrible mystery to all that, despite the happy ending. Could the events have coincided? Because certainly sometimes curses fall on an unfortunate wretch many years later, when the spell no longer matters. He has no doubt but that the other man will lay crushed under the farmhouse. That violent dream is more necessary to him than his own breath. But he would like the eyes to be wrenched free at the moment that he's sucking on the palms of his hands full of blood mixed with earth, when he's lost all sense of time in the wheat field.

Suddenly his kidneys made him jump like a kneecap under a hammer. Yes, it had to have happened there, far away.

He poked around again anxiously. It was there, thank God, it was always there even if he jumped in to swim completely dressed. Nevertheless, he was unable to overcome the fear of losing it. He took it out, looked at it, shined it up on his jacket and put it to his lips without interrupting his journey across the open fields. He never knew what would emerge from that carved wood, never said, I'll do this or that. He just let go and the music flowed by itself, unhindered, free like the pleasure of peeing in the fields. But it was precisely then that the avoidable occurred to him. Sure, the farm had remained on the other side of the wheat field, and there, he thought, he had also left the man's wife buried, burning and luminous, the woman he had secretly made love to for exactly four months. But it was clear that he shouldn't even think about the perfectibility of things. She had come to him, after him or from within, he didn't know how. She emerged unexpectedly from the music, beheld the air in fear, as if she had to breathe it for the first time, and then returned to the instrument's perforated shelter with the speed of a white snake. From that point on, he was unable to emit even one single note that was not made of her flesh. He blew hard at first, then furiously, as only a man is capable of doing to rid himself of love. Until she had to come forth, violating every orifice, to retreat in time, to drag her husband out from under the farmhouse, put his eyes back into the sockets, listen again to his morning cough and, finally, remain lying in the same bed, her back to her victimizer while making love to another man without moving a muscle, as if she were dead.

Because that's how it had been, even if no one believed it, not that he needed to tell anyone about it to achieve credulity more convincing and powerful than his own experience.

Now he sees the husband again without the farmhouse atop his belly, but it doesn't matter anymore. He is about to deceive him as soon as the farmer closes the door and puts the enormous key under the pillow, exactly where he rests his head all night. Now he's sitting on the edge of the bed taking off his boots and flinging them away like all his clothes that are thrown helter-skelter through the air. Then inevitably, he'll touch his filthy toes, flexing them one at a time; afterward, he'll blow out the light and jump into bed, weighing it down almost as if he were breaking it. Finally, no longer a living man, just an assuring gurgle that will take shape in time.

It is clear that these are different times, and that waiting lasted longer and was more anguishing than remembering it. He would have to return to the terrifying moment in order to once again feel gooseflesh, his barely contained breathing, his wretched blood beating like muffled trip-hammers, and even his miserable intestines inventing angelic choirs below the domes. A certain night, the husband turned the light on again, took hold of a box and began to count money. He seemed full of arms like an octopus. The furniture had grown in the shadows on the wall and his hands had to expand disproportionately to maintain their relative size. But the man is an exhausted beast; he falls back again and sleeps like a log.

It is then that the other man emerges from behind the chest like a moth. The piece of furniture is as long as his body, and she's put things on top to conceal the hiding place. He comes out of there half suffocated, with creaking joints, his heart in his mouth. He drags himself along gasping, constantly pricked by some splinter on the floor, but finally touches the hand she reaches out to him in the shadows. With energy equal to that of the man's eyes rejecting him by day, and of his snoring bubbles by night, the woman herself helps him up like a feather onto the bed to make love to her the same way (inexplicable now) in a sort of bodily evaporation. She had an unusual way of falling asleep on his chest afterwards, her hair thick with the salt she couldn't get rid of even by weeping. He had learned how to move that head and place it on the pillow. Of course he had to get off the bed at once, hide behind the chest and wait, all senses alerted for the cough at dawn, the boots, the key in the lock. When he left on the husband's heels, he could barely stay awake. But he had to drag along until siesta time, his great loafer's siesta from which he was awakened many times by the toe of the boss's boots . . .

The man changed his tune by blowing violently. What difference did they make, those wasted dreams in the shed since he had full possession of the night? Just from remembering it he was feeling the sweet, bland moisture of his penis, the only thing that retained the farm's smell and sweat. But that part of the farm was stuck to his body that moved on, and whatever walks in that direction, he mused, feeling the wind in his hair, doesn't stink like the people who remained in the past: "Rot, rot now that I'm moving on."

. . . Until a certain terrible night, the last one, just a few hours ago. She had been ravished by her husband only once in all that time, and he, the other man, had been to blame, by moving about clumsily behind the chest, dislodging a piece of wood. The brute turned on the light, listened for a moment. He was about to get up, about to crush the dirty rat that had moved inside the piece of furniture. The shadow cast by his raised head suddenly filled the room, began to move on the ceiling and along the walls like a runaway spider. That's it, too: a man doesn't even know how small he is until he's hidden away in a miserable hole and sees his enemy's shadow climbing up the walls.

Suddenly the hairs on the ceiling descended brusquely, and a powerfully rhythmic neck began to be projected up above. The spider had descended onto the woman and was devouring her, ravishing her body.

No, he never again thought about the first knot in the floor that savagely pierced his knee. He would abandon all that the next day. He was going to tell her at once, to whisper in her salty ear. But when he reached her side, he understood why certain things are done without prior explanation. The woman had completely dissolved. She was a viscous mixture, warm and salty, of tears, mucous, anguish, semen. And like that, totally dissolved, she penetrated his blood like a virus for the rest of that sort of unsung shipwreck in which both anticipated their loss. When he tried to pull free, she held tight as never before, almost suffocating him. He had to shove like a crazy man to return to the chest. He reached it trembling, almost at the edge of the husband's coughing spell.

Yes, he would leave the farm, would bury it in the past forever. No one would know how to find it. Who was he to them? Why, he hadn't even given his real name. "I am love," he said conceitedly. He was a little embarrassed to hear himself. He knew he was commonplace and clumsy, with black eyes she said were beautiful and a dark curl falling onto his forehead. But what if he were love after all?

Love . . . And he had left her alone at the farm, perhaps the farmhouse had not collapsed on the man. The vision of the nocturnal spider is about to dispense with the idea of moving forward. But suddenly he realizes how ridiculous his thoughts are. What is a woman, one single woman who's going to die being a woman, if all of them are to die the same way? Night after night they're devoured in silence, mounted like her. It's just that out there nobody knows about it, no one's hidden behind a chest watching the enlarged Chinese shadow figures on the wall, so different from what the farmer had promised her. Hadn't he also taken advantage of the gratuitous feast?

Suddenly in a powerful final revelation, he began to feel that the spider and he had really been lovers in the shadows, forming a close-knit group around the victim. Each one plundered her in his own way, that was all. And she, poor thing, choosing the greater deceit, the sweeter one.

It was precisely that, knowing that he loved the man, confessing that man only loves himself and his fellow man, that made him discover something new in his music, a kind of strong, primitive note, devoid of womanly softness, that began to harden the bones beneath his flesh. That would suffice for a seven-hour journey, at least.

II
The Rape

She advanced with difficulty because of the disheveled bundle of bread that seemed to spring from the air. A young redheaded girl and a cat, also the color of tree bark, gripped by the same kind of drowsiness, sleeping on a pile of empty sacks.

"Sixteen years old," the man muttered, excluding the cat, but always seeing them as one entity. From their tiny, open mouths the bumblebees of superficial snores emerged, weaving a braid with the flies in the air. "But I've come for the bread, and it's much better to be a bread thief than a killer . . ." She was dressed in a nondescript color, very like the earth. "Yes, it's much better, you know, you always know . . ." Upon reaching the waist, the colorless dress clung tight as if breaking the body in two.

It is precisely at that point when the breads you could steal begin to offer themselves up, so abundant that you don't know which is best, the one that isn't misshapen, or too burned, or doesn't have a fleck of charcoal stuck in the middle. If he could at least have a drink before deciding. Even though perhaps he didn't need that either. It was more as if he were aching from something, from something other than his own body, more like part of the girl's waist, a pain that she communicates to him without moving a muscle. First he felt it in the lining of his jacket. From two or three holes in the worn-out material, certain wads of stuffing poked through, digging savagely into his flesh, into the same body that he had forgotten about. That is, he had a body that felt itself punished by those irremediable holes. ("But I was coming for the bread, I insist that I had to eat or collapse.") Now his skin rebels from within. The girl and the purring cat are heating him up inside from his ankles to his neck in a sort of monstrous upheaval that extends all over and presses until it skins him alive. Enough fighting. He resisted until then, but he knows now he will never escape. When he breathes deeply the first few times and feels blood rush to his brain, thought is still possible. But he has already exhausted that recourse. His last inspirations remained stuck fast like a sun in his kidneys.

The girl's spittle had condensed in the corners of her mouth. It dripped like honey from a fig, and with some monosyllables and all kinds of facial gestures, she finally let out a sort of corraled anguish like a transparent hiccup that didn't even manage to wake up the cat. It would always be better this way, although perhaps she ought to scream like all the others so he would exchange her for a loaf of bread and leave without living that adventure. "As long as she doesn't yell, my God. Get it off of me. Get it off of me." The man with the farmhouse on top of him; he remembered it again . . . She had no time to get up, he was already halfway there, and never felt such a fierce desire to annihilate someone and such complete helplessness to defend himself from his own desire. It's clear that the worst part is the unfortunate circumstance of having to be so quick, of not being able to confide in the impunity of the events. "And I was coming for the bread, you know, you little bitch, I was coming . . ." He hears a liquid gurgling from inside the squashed bowels, and that submerged answer brings with it much more force than the poor words with which he tries to justify his actions. It's her intestines that are fabricating bubbles bursting under his pressure; it's also the bread she'd eaten in the morning that he's crushing under his weight. But in her bulging eyes a supplication flounders about, unlike the others. She desired this at some point, and doesn't now, she'd want it again as soon as he took his violent weight off of her.

It was all different with her, from the absurd mixture of those bread and cat odors to the resistance of her flesh inside. For a nauseating second, the smell of all the women he had abused in his life joins the whirlpool that wafts under his nose, as if they were pushing him into a garret, suffocating him with soiled clothes. Then after struggling unsuccessfuly to get a reaction out of the little girl, he wanted to wallow and splash about again in the others. But there was no longer time to even yearn for the easy slide into the married woman, from whose bed emanated the smell of the husband's confidence in her. That fury is necessary even in exchange for forgetting other things. He despises her as he rapes her, hates her each time more deeply, he's going to pierce her vertebra and pin her womb to the sacks.

But what has she done to him? It was at the end of that question that he looked at her face. The small flowers from before had evaporated and instead there was only a tenuous layer of floating freckles that seemed to have descended from her rebellious hair like small lice of the same rust color. "Damn it," he muttered with a final, weak shudder, "damned if it had to happen." He tried unsuccessfully to revive her with his vulgar resources. Then quickly, the way all that must have happened, he slid down and began to kiss her violated rose with all the ardor he could painfully muster in that exhausted state. Until she showed signs of becoming aroused. Only at that moment would she come to know something of her part in all this. The other, the terrible ripping asunder, kept her nails riveted to the sacks. She had only experienced shreds of herself. But her love, her image of love, with honey-colored hair and blue eyes, was stopping her. Now she knew everything, and besides she was looking at a ceiling much higher than she imagined. There were a lot of things together to know in so short a time, things she wished to say to him without suspending satisfaction.

At that moment someone's heavy wooden shoes were heard dragging along on the flagstones out back. The man jumped up like a spring. "Now's when they shout, when they remember to do it." The danger had passed. Through the wall he could almost see the heels of the thick shoes change direction . . . "And then there's no choice but to strangle them." The noise of an oven door brought the odor of hot bread. "But this one's different, she's from a hot-blooded race, the kind who die without causing a scandal. If a small bitch like this could be carried hidden between the legs, if she wouldn't hang onto us later and get fat on our account . . ." He still saw the unlikely waist, the childish arms that had just fallen lifeless at her side. For a stupid moment, she waited for him to sit down on the edge of the sacks, not to abandon that bread under his arm or leave like a dirty beggar closing up his fly with a free hand. The man felt all that behind his back as if she had thrown desperate splinters at him for every thought. She was innocent like flour, he mused. But he could see a poplar-lined road in the distance so adventures go to hell. He needed to harden his bones again, to reach the shade as soon as possible.

He was feeling a metallic taste under his tongue and a certain thick moisture on his lips. He wiped his mouth with the back of his hand and saw the blood offering. "What do they feel when they give that up, what must they think when they've lost it?" Just then he realized what had happened. She had remained with all the bread on top of her. This time the eyes weren't bulging and broken but seemed like damp violets. And besides, someone had left a waist in his hands. That sensation of carrying a flower by the stem began to pursue him, to move ahead of him like the insistent circles of a bumblebee as he walked along with the girl's waist in small circles up front, intercepted by the rays of light penetrating the trees. But no more than just that. No one's going to prosecute you because of one virgin more or less, if at the end of the same day all humanity must be tending towards that same experience. On the contrary, it is man who will always carry the burden, he, for example, and the damned waist offered up to him. "They're not content if they don't throw us something, whatever it may be," he said quietly. He had already sucked up all the girl's blood and began to feel the need to spit with his own saliva, to see it outside of himself in a small blob on the ground.

A blue sky, barely cottony with clouds, spread out over the poplars. Without lowering his gaze, by the very noise of his footsteps, he knew he was crossing a small bridge and went down under it to drink his fill. But his body resisted getting up from the ground. While staring at the stones holding fast like scabs to the streambed, at last he was able to recognize his own exhaustion. He took the bread from his pocket and began to chew on it slowly until he tasted its sweetness, like the thighs of the young baker girl he had raped.

The colors of the wheat, the bread, the cat, her hair, all the same terrible thing. That color would be embedded forever in his bones, in the destiny of the bones that inhabited his flesh. He had once made love to a woman with yellow eyes. He had a kind of repressed obsession and didn't let her close them. He was terrified that she might fill the moment with someone else's image so he forced her to vibrate with her eyes wide open, staring without respite. One night of lovemaking, after having possessed her that way under intense light, he ended up asking her to stop looking at him. She couldn't. He had to lower her eyelids with his fingers and tie her jaw with a handkerchief. Three eyelashes remained on his fingertips. The woman had escaped from him through who knows what mysterious door. What do you do with three golden eyelashes, put them back, throw them in the fire? Even when they leave us that way, he thought, they insist on leaving something. But at least that one is a blessed memory. It always came to him just when he was about to fall asleep (the baker girl's waist), glimpsed among the last wakeful images (the waist expands, disappears) which is the best way to evoke those terrifying eyelashes. (They beat her but she doesn't answer. Then her breasts swell, she becomes enigmatic, enormous and painful like the full moon. Perhaps her bones are too narrow, and she, too, ends up in their arms, with hardened eyes, without asking for anything. But how is he to blame for all that, so far away, after so much time?) And now he'll fall asleep eating bread, he'll go away chewing until the end of his conscience.

III
The Accused

"Hey, you, kid, do you want to hitch a ride on the hay?" The man awakened to another color sky above him. Seen from way down below it seemed higher and rounder, the real height and roundness of the sky. And what if he had been crushed by that sky? He refused to keep thinking about it, avoiding death would always be a victory.

A peasant woman was pushing a small cart along the poplar road following the slope that he would take. At the same time, with that need they have to take advantage of their energy, she had fastened to her waist the end of a rope whose other extremity was tied to a cow. The peaceful scene didn't fail to comfort him. The road had a sad and unin-habited air as if it led where feet never tread upon the grass. "But she's not dead," he said, taking the ants off the remaining bread and saving it in his pocket, "she's the most real thing that could ever happen to me." He stretched his legs, stood up and climbed onto the path. When he was near the trees again and standing tall, the absurd nature of the proposi-tion moved him to laughter. But he took to looking at the peasant woman again. Her offer remained firm, she awaited him. A woman of indefinite age, like the fields, her youth stemmed more from her rich vitality than from her appearance. She emanated rusticity and energy from her skin to her clothes and hair.

The man tried to smile at her several times but made no impression on her. Finally he had to climb up on the cart. He lay down on his back face up, pulled in his legs as much as he could and folded his arms under his neck. When he saw the sky and trees begin to move backward, he decided to accept things the way they were happening. He really couldn't hope for anything better than all that, slipping away without knowing where, to the squeak of an ungreased pulley in his stomach, all doubled up like a spring. He closed his eyes and allowed himself to be invaded by a new lethargy.

Until the cart stopped again. They had arrived at thick woods that kept them from advancing. To the left of that path cut off by the dark trees, another one opened up, perhaps the one that led to the woman's house, for you could see smoke rising from a roof in the distance.

Now he didn't want to move from his new position. It seemed he could remain hidden like a grasshopper in the hay, and she would have to go off with her cow in the direction of the smoke. He would watch with only one eye until the human shape and the animal would evaporate into the sky, he would be capable of extending them that kindness. But as always, the opposite was to happen. She not only failed to leave but was crying over his head. The woman had kneeled down behind, between the two handles on the cart, and while he was dreaming about his abandon she continued to close in around him with her fence of tears, more meaningful and real than her own body. What was it they felt when they cried that way? His long experience had never reached so far into the depths of that hidden liquid state of those women who wept in silence. But lo and behold, he saw how the woman got up and led the cow to the edge of the road, and how the animal lay down in the grass as if it were ordered to do so. But something else still perplexed him. The strange creature finally approached the cart, took up an armful of hay, deposited it near the grass and prepared two pillows.

All her movements had been mysterious, full of philosophy and destiny, as if shifting about in a ritual atmosphere that followed like a halo around her body. But what was she doing, where was she going with all that? It was inconceivable that she wanted to make love, at least in its common guise. There was such an infinite sadness about her that he, being who he was, came to sense the profanation that desire could represent at that moment. Finally leading him and handling him like a little boy—he again felt her tears—she laid him down carefully on the ground. Then she stretched out on his right side with only her weeping as an introduction; this seemed to excuse her from the equivocal gestures.

Now the man could see her entire face close up. She had blue eyes and dry strawlike hair from living out in the country. But when he was able to examine her in more detail, he was suddenly bewitched. The woman was undoubtedly about to open her dress. There are things done only one way that can happen only in their most simple form. She began with one of the middle buttons that fell off into her hand, a thread hanging from it in the air. She threw it aside, brusquely ripped open the others and ended up exposing her entire breast. It was an incredible breast, too white for the rest of the skin, at least the weathered skin on her face, neck and arms, and it didn't seem to belong to her body. The blond woman's nipple was slightly cracked with a chaste, smooth aureola. And no sooner had it escaped from the bodice, it began to grow, to harden, excited by some secretly submerged wave. Nor was there any doubt in the man's mind about that trivial event. But he had fallen into negating his habitual actions, as if his will had dissolved into the woman's as he awaited what she was about to deliver. First, she passed her arm under his neck, made him turn over until she held him sideways and put her breast to his lips. There was no longer anything more to do then, except what has always been done out of necessity or custom. A sweet, smooth stream began to enter his body.

The man swore not to swallow it. Then having no choice, he thought of rejection. But with the milk warming his throat, he understood it was no use. How was he to deny something that was being offered to him so differently from the usual way, without any warning? Besides, she held the breast in her hand, squeezing with each suck, as if wishing to empty it. If he chose to drink, he would have to do it at the same rhythm. And then no more resistance, but rather endless forgetfulness that is so different for each of them and never to be shared.

Only in midstream when she gently switched him over to the other breast, could he begin to bear witness to himself. A man is wrenched from his sleep under a bridge, the deepest possible sleep on earth. Then without time to even grow accustomed to the light, they tell him he's a little boy, oblige him to cuddle up atop a pile of hay, lull him to sleep again, push him who knows where, invade him, penetrate him . . . But certainly the grass is too soft to hurt. And besides, he had forgotten the sweet click of really sucking, an excess of liquid in the corners of the lips and the rhythmic urge to sink mouth, nose and hands into that boneless mass that seemed like an enormous, stranded mollusk. But she, so still, so blind, how was she involved? It doesn't really matter to him. If she had lemon-colored eyes, he couldn't allow it to happen. Nevertheless, the loss of a blue-eyed woman doesn't anguish him. Besides, he thinks himself sole master of the moment, and also the only one who could satisfy her that way, leaving her without a drop to offer to anyone else.

In the midst of that fabulous possession, he noticed his leg on top of the peasant's warm thigh, and both were sweating through their clothes, exchanging bodily messages. He left her at that. There was no danger. Neither of them were vibrating below the waist. Strange, they seemed to have died down there, while their lives existed and throbbed up above, joined by milk and tears. How mysterious and sweet. A breast not pursued, surrenders. But who could have discovered it before for it to swell so? Sure, all of them had that under their blouses, he thought. When you brush against their dresses, you can feel the undeniable roundness like apples in a bag. Of course their fruits are different from apples, they have vital warmth, and that heat burns the cloth, sticks to the fingers and irremediably penetrates man's sinking fatality. But who could have discovered that breast, so very different from her outward appearance? In the light his fingers ran along her fine veins like fantastic trees beneath the snow. That meant this rustic woman, suffering and loveless, also nurtured blue trees discovered by someone more penetrating than he, who had let her pass by a thousand times without a pang of desire. He felt violence surge inside and unexpectedly bit her nipple. Her entire body shuddered then from her roots, communicating the shock to him. But he didn't want that to happen again. He didn't want to vibrate with that woman who had immersed him in milk and tears.

She seemed to recover her own tranquility with the man's moderation. Her sobs began to cease. On his chest he had gathered together the ever-widening distances that stretched between one sigh and another.

And so when he senses her complete relief, he will ask her the unavoidable question. And not in order to know things that to a certain extent are none of his business. It's just that in that milk there has to be more than a dead child. Why doesn't she do something about it? Why does she weep instead of trying to make love again?

He began to forget about his mouth on the nipple, as if he had fallen asleep. All of that was really like sleeping through a kind of dream, like a return to the intrauterine shadows, to a hidden splashing about that evoked all the odors and softness of that forgotten mating. But how would he ask about it? The difficulty lay not with words but with the need for a voice. He was afraid to hear himself, to rend the air that had covered them.

But suddenly, he found himself saying what he didn't want to say, could not say.

The woman was startled. That return of the human voice must have sounded clumsy to her, too. From then on, he seemed to be considering innumerable answers, even though the question could have no more than one presumably simple reply, like the way she opened her dress would have allowed for nothing but suckling. Everything about her was so deliberate and so hidden away inside that he stopped urging her.

"You're asking about the child," the woman said in a neutral voice after a long silence.

"Yes," he nodded secretly, continuing to caress her breast.

"Well, if you want to know," she continued in the same tone, "I don't have one, never had one nor ever felt one in my womb for a single day . . ."

Through his pores the man gathered up what she had just said. Her revelation took the shape of her secret abundance, unique in itself, different from the rest of her body.

"And this?" he asked amazed, squeezing out a bit of milk and holding it out to her on his fingers.

"It happened from wishing it," the woman answered, sinking more and more into herself. "One night they hurt and began to ooze. . . ."

He raised himself up halfway leaning on an elbow. With the other hand he kept on squeezing her breast, as if he were about to tear it to shreds. A kind of perverse victory had warmed his breath and spilled over onto the peasant's face as he looked her in the eye.

"You mean then that they never discovered you either, that they never made love to you?" he said, his words tripping over one another.

But there was no time in the air to recover yesterday's face. As if she had just realized that she had nursed a man, she looked at him with violent hatred.

"They don't know, they can't know," she answered severely, withdrawing her breast from him and hiding it.

He felt then that his heart was about to shrivel up, to harden like a nut losing its pulp. And he wouldn't be able to detain that process, at least the sensation of that process, not by repeating the delicate task of suckling nor even of forcing himself upon her. There was only one sure thing: a solitary udder, humble and meek, secretly filled up by itself, and he, the accused, the criminal of that unheard-of lost cause, had just received the best part.

The woman finally got to her feet, helped him to get up and then

64

recovered the button lost in the grass. That's it, he thought. Her obscure ritual finished, she would go off. Anyway with her breast hidden away she was no longer the same. And besides, she was leaving. That also entered into the order of things that cannot be done any other way, going off, carrying a small hump of rancor and sadness. Women always left the same way, he observed, slam a door in their face or let them go off into the fields.

The man watched her move away alone toward the dawn, the cart before her, the cow behind, as he had met her. He was struck with uncontainable repugnance for what she had just done to him. For finally she had gone away without exacting anything more. One night she would drown in her own white stream—he almost saw her crushed by her breast—and without the cowardly "get it off of me" like the others, of that he was sure. But why should her death matter to him? Besides, all that was too nebulous, as if it had never happened. He was so acclimated to vulgarity that during his lifetime he had denounced the marvelous as ridiculous daydreams.

He touched his body, terrified. No, it hadn't been left on the bridge or in the hay. That flute was loyal to him like his penis. He coaxed a vulgar melody from it to recover its tone, and began to calculate the time it would take to get to the damned cemetery.

"You never pass through there completely calm," he mumbled, with night already upon him and his leaden feet weighing him down.

Walking along he felt rigid like an uprooted tree. By now he would like to have been assured safe-conduct. Those miserable women had changed him in so many ways. Those women . . . He wanted to think back on all of them again, ever since his first desire in life. But at that moment his flute slid down alongside his thigh and fell dully onto the grass.

"Strange, I don't want to, I can't lift it up. And nevertheless, with or without it, I must go on . . . Solitude, my dear child, shall we keep going?" he said, clenching his teeth.

He was truly a vulgar guest for death. He still had the earth and the dung from the farm under his nails.

Translated by Evelyn Picon Garfield

Elena Garro

Mexico

Elena Garro.

Elena Garro was born in Puebla, Mexico, in 1920, but has spent much of her adult life in Spain and France, where she now resides. While living in Mexico she published criticism and essays for the newspaper *La Cultura en México*. Although she began her literary career as a dramatist, producing a dozen one-act plays, it was her first novel about life in the small town of Ixtepec during the late 1920s that won her the coveted Xavier Villaurrutia Prize. *Los recuerdos del porvenir*, which appeared in English translation by Ruth Simms as *Recollections of Things to Come*, has taken its place among the best novels of the Mexican Revolution by authors such as Mariano Azuela, Martín Luis Guzmán, Agustín Yáñez, Juan Rulfo, and Carlos Fuentes. It is a chronicle of collective fear embodied in the townspeople's passivity during the brutal occupation of Ixtepec by General Francisco Rosas at the time of the Cristero Rebellion (1926–29). Three other novels and two collections of short stories complete her works, some of which have been translated into English, French, Swedish, and German.

In her narratives, Garro often denounces social and economic exploitation of certain groups in Mexico such as the Indians, and exposes the victimization of women in her society. Loneliness, alienation, a fascination with time and myth underly her narratives and plays. Provincial legends, colloquial expressions, and popular language are converted in her drama into metaphors and dreamlike dialogues. In 1963, before the term "magical realism" was popular in Spanish America and used to describe novels like *One Hundred Years of Solitude* (1967) by García Márquez, Garro's *Recollections of Things to Come* had already infused fiction with the magical transformations of everyday existence and the mythical dimension of indigenous legends.

"The Tree" ("El árbol") was written as both a play and a short story. We have translated the latter for this collection. Rather than exploring the close ties between white and Indian women, who in some of Garro's other works endure similar fates, the author in this story deals with a basic duality of Mexico's two cultures: urban, European, and educated; rural, Indian, and uneducated.

The Tree

On Saturday Gabina left at three o'clock in the afternoon. It was her day off and she wouldn't return until Sunday morning. Marta watched her go and retired to her room, alone. She looked at the untouched perfume bottles and porcelain figurines on the dressing table. Her house of rugs and thick curtains isolated her from the noises and lights in the street; silence weighed her down, she felt its abandon. There were untouched beds, some windows no longer opened and the only ceremonies she attended were farewells: burials and weddings. The sound of the doorbell wrenched her from her thoughts. Cautiously she traversed the house and approached the door.

"Who's there?" she asked before deciding to open.

"It's me, Martita," came the childish voice from beyond the door. "Luisa? . . ."

Marta opened to let the Indian in. The woman's gloomy, dark shape quickly slipped by toward the living room; she entered like a flash of lightning, avoiding the furniture and watching Marta out of the corner of her eye. In the shadow created by the silk curtains her angular face was

70

barely distinguishable. She let herself fall into the easy chair, then waited. A noxious odor emanated from her body. Marta looked at her blackened, bare feet, worn from prolonged walking.

"What's going on, Luisa? What brings you to Mexico City?"

Luisa bolted upright, lifted her slip and uncovered an enormous black and blue mark on her bare thigh; then convulsed, she pointed to her bruised nose and ear from which a stream of half-coagulated black blood was oozing.

"Julian!"

"Julian?"

"Yes! Julian beat me."

"That's not true, Julian's a good man." And Marta remembered Gabina's words: "A bitch of a woman is a good man's lot." Luisa was a bitch, she pursued her husband to distraction. The Indian woman looked her in the eye, arms crossed over her chest.

"He's always beating me, Martita! . . . Always!"

Her voice squeaked like a rat's. Marta was sure she was slandering her husband. She had known the couple for many years. Used to see them whenever they went home to the countryside, to the town of Ometepec. When she met them, she thought that Luisa was a child bride; it wasn't until much later that she noticed her laughter and conduct were not just strange but evil. She lost all affection for her and found opportunities to treat her harshly. That woman who followed her husband with such stupid tenacity angered her. She continually pestered him; wherever he was going, she went along smiling wickedly. Everyone liked Julian; on the other hand no one ever asked for Luisa. He put up with her. The Indian woman burst out laughing and looked at Marta maliciously as if she could guess her thoughts.

"Don't laugh," Marta abruptly commanded.

"Julian's bad, Martita, very bad!"

"Shut up already, don't talk nonsense!"

She would have liked to tell the Indian she was odious and that if Julian had hit her she deserved it, but she controlled herself.

"He's bad, he makes me cry!"

"Look, Luisa, you're easily prone to laughing and crying. And you know what I say? If Julian hit you, you deserved it."

"I don't deserve it. He's bad, very bad . . ."

She insisted on accusing him. Her misery inspired nausea. Her odor was filling the room, seeping into the furniture, sliding along the silk curtains. "Just smelling her is punishment enough," Gabina had said, and it was true. Marta looked at her in disgust. Luisa jumped up and as usual began to shower her with kisses. Then she stopped and returned to the sofa. Marta saw dirty tears running down her cheeks, but felt no compassion. The Indian wiped the tears away with a dirty finger, crossed her arms like a small monkey, looked at Marta suspiciously and added, "He always hits me, always. He's bad, very bad, Martita."

The two women remained silent looking at each other with hostility. Marta turned to the mirror to observe her well-combed hair. She was upset by the Indian's repugnance. "My God! How can You allow human beings to assume such shapes and ways?" The mirror reflected the image of a lady dressed in black, wearing pink pearls. Dazed by the Indian's wretchedness, Marta was embarrassed in front of that unfortunate woman, who was devoured by centuries of misery. "Can she possibly be human?" Many of her relatives and friends maintained that the Indians were more akin to beasts than to man, and they were right. Her nausea intensified. Why did she have to listen to that woman? It was already late, she was in her living room and hadn't the courage to throw her out in the street. She sensed Luisa crying behind her back. She would give her something to eat since she couldn't offer her affection. It was impossible to leave her sitting there on the sofa miserable, helpless and ugly.

"Luisa, do you want something to eat?"

"Don't bother, Martita, let Gabina give me something."

"She's not here, it's her day off."

"Then don't bother, Martita."

Without listening, Marta went to the kitchen. Luisa followed her, sat near the window and waited. As the afternoon light shone on her face, she became more horrible: her face was like a trampled piece of fruit; the dry blood mixed with the fresh blood that oozed from her ear was soaking her matted black hair. Her stench seeped into the aluminum pots, the sink, the blue chairs, the corners. Marta served her hot coffee, some pieces of chicken and bread. Then she approached the door to escape from the smell that was beginning to make her dizzy. When Marta looked at the Indian angrily, Luisa shrank into the chair, and burst out crying.

"I left my kids . . . !"

"Bitch! How dare you talk to me about your children? Poor kids!

72

Always crying, 'Mama, leave my father alone, stay at home . . .' And what do you do as soon as they're born? You take to the street in pursuit of Julian. Don't tell me you're crying for them."

"Yes, Martita, I'm crying for them."

"Well your tears don't move me. Why do you run after Julian? The poor man complains that you don't even leave him alone when he goes to the bathroom."

Marta remained silent and looked at the Indian in anger. The other woman smiled gently.

"Things are different there, Martita, there we go in the gully."

"What does the gully have to do with what I'm saying?"

Marta stamped her foot; the Indian's guile made her blush with anger.

"The gully's very dark, Martita, very dark . . ."

Luisa's voice sounded strange in the bright kitchen. Marta remained silent and looked at her attentively. The woman burst into tears and brusquely pushed the plate away.

"You don't know what darkness is like, Martita, here there's lots of light, but there it's dark, very dark . . . and darkness is very ugly, Martita."

She seemed like a corraled animal. Marta felt compassion for that creature who was only capable of understanding fear.

"Yes, I know, Luisa. Be happy, here there's lots of light. If you like, stay a few days with me. Where are you going to go anyway? No one wants you."

"It's true, Martita, no one wants me."

Who could want that woman? Marta again felt the repulsion she experienced a few minutes before. The stench invaded her house, seeped into her nostrils, turned the air sticky. She went to her room to breathe the perfume contained between her walls. How could she tell Luisa to bathe? The whole house was about to become contaminated by that stench of rancid bile, blood and sweat. She searched around in the closet and found some very worn clothing. On that pretext she would tell her to bathe and the old woman would gladly accept the order and the gift. She returned to the kitchen and found her staring at the plate.

"Luisa, now when you've finished eating, go bathe. You look very tired."

Luisa jumped to her feet and opened her eyes wide. She approached Marta and took her hand.

"Where, where, Martita?"

"Where, what?"

"Where do I bathe, Martita?"

"Wait, don't rush, when you've finished eating . . . And look, put on these clean clothes. . . ."

"Thanks, Martita, thanks, God bless you. I brought my clothes, I kept them with me, I left home and was alone in the middle of the world . . . with nowhere to go. I was walking, walking and suddenly, in the middle of the field Martita appeared before me and I said to myself I'll go with her, she's so good! . . . And that's how I came here with Martita's face before me guiding my steps . . ."

As she was talking, she untied one of the corners of her shawl and took out some old, clean clothes. She shook them in front of Marta, "Look, there's no color left."

Marta hid the clothes she held in her hands and didn't know what to say.

"I'd better bathe now, Martita, so I don't make you sick."

While saying those words, she stared at Marta; she seemed ashamed and seemed to want to shame Marta, too.

"Sick? . . . Luisa, my God, don't say that!"

"Yes, Martita, I say it because it's true. Where do I bathe?"

Marta blushed. The Indian woman had realized how repugnant she was.

"Where, where?" she insisted maliciously.

Marta gave in to Luisa's demanding voice and, dominated by it, took her to the door of the yellow bathroom.

"I'm going to show you how to use the shower . . ."

"I know, Martita, I know!" replied Luisa, pushing her out of the room.

"How do you know? In your village there aren't any bathrooms . . ."

Luisa closed the door without answering.

"Stupid old woman, you're going to scald yourself!" Marta shouted angrily, banging hard on the door. But the Indian woman had locked it. A resigned Marta returned to her room. She would have to wait until the woman came out of the bathroom: she'd probably break everything and burn herself. She was a savage who was ignorant about modern improvements. Luisa took so long to bathe that Marta fell asleep in the easy chair. In her sleep she heard someone talking on the telephone.

"Martita is asleep in a chair . . ."

She awoke startled and went to the next room where she found Luisa, receiver in hand. Seeing her, the woman hung up and smiled at her. The Indian's hair was loose and damp and she was wearing a clean dress. The odor had dissipated.

"How annoying you are! Why did you grab the telephone if you don't know how to use it?"

"I do know how, Martita, I do!"

Marta didn't want to contradict her. How was she to know if in Ometepec there wasn't even any electric lighting? She was crazy. She had heard the bell and out of curiosity grabbed the receiver; upon hearing a distant voice, she began to converse with it like a crazy woman and now there she was, hair loosened and eyes full of malice, looking at Marta complacently.

"I'm going to finish eating, Martita."

It was already nighttime and Luisa had turned on all the lights in the house. Marta noticed the time; it was eight o'clock. She went toward the kitchen to prepare some dinner for herself and found Luisa crying over the plate.

"He's bad, Martita, bad!" she again insisted.

"Shut up already, you're the one who's possessed!" Marta answered violently.

"Possessed, Martita?"

"Yes, possessed. Why do you run after Julian?"

"I don't run after him, I take care of him because he's a coward."

"A coward? Now you're slandering him. Julian should do what his children tell him: go far away and leave you."

"Go far away? Leave me?"

From a corner Luisa's tiny eyes watched her for a brief moment. She seemed scared and no longer felt like slandering.

"Yes, leave you, because you're possessed."

"Possessed? But I only saw him twice!"

"Who?"

"The 'Evil One,' Martita!"

She had seen the devil twice. If she became scared of the 'Evil One,' death and the hereafter, maybe she would behave better.

"Ah, so you already saw him twice! Well watch out, the day you die, the devil is going to pursue you the way you pursue Julian."

75

Luisa looked at her angrily. She shrank down in her chair and moved the plate away. Marta observed her ill humor out of the corner of her eye, placed the dinner on a tray, and got ready to leave. She wanted to let Luisa reflect alone. Fear would alter her behavior.

"What you owe in this life you pay for in the other. So think about what I'm telling you, and when you return home, behave."

She thought she was going to burst out laughing and hurried to reach the door. Luisa remained silent and cast a gloomy glance in her direction. To dispel the poor impression before leaving, Marta added, "Be good!"

In spite of herself she burst out laughing. She always laughed with the Indians. They were like her, they liked to laugh and when she would arrive in Ometepec, they used to receive her with a chorus of laughter that she shared.

"Go on, Martita," Luisa answered somberly.

Marta kept on laughing in her room. Poor old woman, what a scare I gave her! It was easy to handle the Indians: you only had to name the devil in order to do anything with them. She finished dining but didn't feel like returning to the kitchen. Suddenly it seemed to her that there was something strange about the woman: her odor had dissipated and in its place the heavy air had left the curtains and furniture immobile. In fact, she didn't know how she could have felt like laughing. She couldn't put her finger on the reason for Luisa's strangeness. She remembered the Indian woman cornered in the kitchen, looking at her with tiny tenacious eyes. For years she had considered her the village idiot; when she scolded her, Luisa used to laugh and then kiss Marta so passionately that she seemed crazy. Many times she had felt that her scolding filled Luisa with anger and that her apparently childish kisses were filled with hatred. "Crazy people are evil, they believe that everyone's after them and that's why they're after everyone and Luisa is a crazy woman, Ma'am," Gabina used to repeat while she gave her the bath salts and towels perfumed with rosemary. And it was true, Luisa was unusual, above all that night. It was as if all these years of misfortune began to take shape and were embodied in that shadowy being. Marta became alarmed by her own thoughts and looked around her to verify that it was fear that made her think of such nonsense. The tightly ordered room restored her tranquility. "She slanders her husband because she's so very miserable; I'm not going to let myself get scared over such trifles."

She interrupted her thoughts upon hearing vaguely audible barefoot steps pressing down on the hall rug. She remained still. Luisa appeared at the doorway, small, emaciated, her exceptionally white teeth in an ambiguous smile.

"Martita!"

"Yes, Luisa . . ."

"The first time I saw the 'Evil One' was before . . ."

"Before what, Luisa?"

"Well, before I killed the woman."

A long, surprising silence ensued. Luisa had killed a woman? Where, when? And she was saying it so calmly in that childlike voice? Marta felt she had to answer so as to keep the Indian from staring at her while the same fixed smile hung from Luisa's lips.

"You killed a woman?"

"Yes, Martita, I killed a woman."

"Ah, what things you say, Luisa!"

She wanted to pretend that it seemed normal to have killed a woman. The Indian continued observing her, chuckling to herself with only a grimace of laughter as if she were busy listening to something that Marta didn't hear."

"Martita, I hear your thoughts . . . ," she said in her same childish singsong. She advanced rapidly toward her and noiselessly sat on the rug at her feet.

"Fear is very noisy, Martita," she added. And then she remained silent. The two women discovered themselves face to face in a lonely house isolated from the world by walls covered with silk tapestries and rugs that muffled all noise.

"The first time I saw the 'Evil One' was before I married my first husband."

She had had another husband! Marta discovered that she knew nothing about the woman seated at her feet.

"When I saw him, he was in the corral at my house. He was a cowboy breathing fire; he didn't wear boots, only horse's hooves that threw off sparks when he walked. He carried a whip in his hand and hit the stones with it, and the stones gave off sparks, too. It was four o'clock in the afternoon and I began to shout, 'There he is! There he is!' 'Who?' my parents answered because they didn't see him. The 'Evil One' I heard myself shout as he was approaching me, his eyes like fire. 'There he is!

There he is!' I was shouting. 'Who?' my parents answered because they didn't see him. And the 'Evil One' began to whip me before I said his name. . . . Later I still trembled with fear. At that time my first husband arrived and asked for me and my parents gratefully gave me away to him to see if he could relieve me. So we came to Mexico City . . ."

She had lived in Mexico City and Marta was unaware of it. Luisa stared at her. She seemed very conscious of Marta's surprise, it amused her. Seated on the floor, curled up like a small animal, she lowered her eyelids to hide the malicious sparks that her eyes gave off.

"I lived in Mexico City here in Tacubaya . . . and here I had child. But I became completely swollen, Martita, and three days after I gave birth, my husband took me to the village and left me in my parents' house. 'You didn't receive her all swollen up, why are you returning her this way?' they said to him. 'Go to hell,' he answered them and left, and I never saw him again. But my parents didn't find that out. After a while I said to them, 'Look, papa, I'm going out to look for my husband.' And my papa broke down crying. 'Leave the child with us!' he begged. 'Of course! Do you really think I'd take her away?' And that's how I came back to Mexico City and returned to Tacubaya where I lived . . ."

Luisa stopped talking to watch the other woman. Not knowing how to respond to that glance, Marta lowered her eyes and waited. Luisa raised her skinny arm, "I lived here!"

And she pointed to a place in space as if Tacubaya were inside the room. Marta remained silent, confused. She sensed that the Indian woman confided in her for reasons she wasn't managing to figure out. She had to prevent her from continuing the story.

"Luisa, don't tell me any more, it's better to forget . . ."

"No, Martita, you mustn't forget. Here's where I lived and here's where I met the woman!"

She paused again; Marta felt unable to say a word; Luisa's voice and the silent house overwhelmed her. What did Luisa want from her? Why was she looking at her this way? She was a fox!

"And here's where I killed her!"

When saying this sentence, her voice and face acquired childish features. She killed her and was saying it innocently. Marta repented for having been gentle in her dealings with the Indians: seated at her feet was proof of that mistake. The old creole repugnance toward everything indigenous violently welled up inside. They deserved nothing but lashes! She looked at the Indian and felt assured, entrenched in her principles.

"And why did you kill her?"

"Because she was going around saying things . . ."

"What things?" she asked again harshly.

"Just things . . . that I was fooling around with her husband, and I didn't even know him . . ." Her tiny eyes shone as she said this; like most women she lacked feelings of guilt. She was innocent before Julian, the dead woman and the dead woman's husband. Marta was furious with her.

"I didn't even know him! . . . I never saw him and she was saying things . . . ," Luisa declared, scratching her head to convince herself of the words' veracity; then she raised her index finger, " 'Look, woman, don't go around talking or my knife will silence you!' That's what I said to her, and she paid no attention. Do you think, Martita, that she didn't understand me? So I went to look for her in the marketplace at the hour that we all go shopping. And it was so lovely! Full of nice onions, coriander and limes. I stood alongside the women who sell tortillas; they were kneeling, so I saw her coming. The old hag was walking along swinging her basket full of fruit and I said to myself: 'Now you're going to shut up, little turtle dove' . . . and I sank my knife into her." Luisa stopped talking. Marta was sure that her silences were premeditated. Frightened, Marta breathed the heavy air accumulated above their heads by Luisa's words.

"Ay, Luisa, how did you have the courage to do such a horrible thing? How can you knife someone? . . ."

"In the belly, Martita, where else is it surer and softer than in the belly?"

With a brusque movement, Luisa took out an enormous knife that she was carrying hidden under her blouse and made a gesture of sinking it into an imaginary stomach. Marta barely had time to stifle a cry of terror that almost escaped from her chest. Mute, she watched Luisa disembowel a nonexistent being. The Indian had forgotten her childish ways, her deluded eyes shone.

"Like this, and this!" repeated Luisa, panting as she kept on stabbing at the air.

"And I left her there and ran away . . ."

"You ran away . . ."

And Marta imagined her running off among the people in the marketplace with her hair afire and her cruel eyes, like now, knife in hand. The others let her pass by and later took off in pursuit.

"To kill must be terrible, perhaps even impressive," Marta said to herself.

"And I fled from the market and ran down the street . . . I still had the knife in my hand when I went into the house where they caught me. I was drenched in blood!"

"You didn't leave the knife stuck in her?"

"No, Martita, I took it out because it was mine. And it sure was full of blood! . . . Martita, do you think I got splattered? . . ."

With her fingertips she caressed the blade and raised her eyes to meet Marta's. She scratched her head as if to rid herself of a thought and stroked the knife again, lost in memories.

"We have too much blood . . . we're fountains, Martita, beautiful fountains . . . That's how she ended up like a fountain one morning in the marketplace . . . You see, Martita, one morning in the marketplace with its beautiful fountain? . . ." Her voice once again hid beneath the childish tone. She smiled affably.

"And who was she?"

Marta wanted to know who that woman was who remained wasted in the remote marketplace morning with her overturned basket and her fruit mingled with blood; by her side the vendors' shouts and the smell of coriander.

"Ah! It's anybody's guess . . ."

"What was her name?"

"It's anybody's guess!"

Luisa realized she was interested and didn't want to share her dead woman. She jealously guarded her for herself and hid her name and face. Marta became irritated.

"What do you mean, it's anybody's guess?"

"Yes, Martita, it's anybody's guess. She was just the woman who said things; that's why I stabbed her with this knife . . ."

Luisa placed the knife at her feet and looked at it passionately. Marta saw it was useless to ask about the woman and observed the shiny weapon that had entered the taut skin of an unknown woman's stomach.

"With that knife?"

"Yes, Martita, with this knife. They took it away from me when they caught me, only later I cried so very much that they gave it back with my freedom."

Marta had the impression that the Indian woman was lying to her. It wasn't probable that they had returned the murder weapon. Luisa had wanted to scare her because she had defended Julian. Besides being envious, the Indian was shrewd. Marta felt ridiculous believing those stories. She saw herself through the eyes of a third person: two old women spying on each other, scaring one another in the shadows of a room, a knife lying on the rug. She burst out laughing and contemplated Luisa mockingly; she was a scoundrel.

"And they took you off to jail?"

"Of course, Martita! They locked me up, they took away my freedom. And that's where I saw the 'Evil One' again . . ."

Once more the "Evil One" appeared; there was some logic to her story, what she was telling was true. Marta discovered that she had provoked her confidence by saying she was possessed. She had wanted to scare her and the only thing she achieved was to open the floodgates for her devils to escape. She began to worry.

"Yes, Martita, I saw him again. He was painted on the wall, like this, my size! And he was both woman and man. They gave me the job of whipping him and they gave me the whip, too. Every day I whipped him and whipped him until my hand trembled. And when I had just finished beating him and could no longer move, a friend would say to me, 'Hit him some more for me!' And I would whip him again, because you don't deny a favor to a prisoner just like you. When they set me free I never saw him again."

"Never? How wonderful, Luisa! You must be happy to see yourself free of the devil and jail."

"No, Martita, life with the prisoners wasn't bad: we got up at four o'clock in the morning and started to sing; then we ground the maize for the other prisoners; later we bathed. That's why I told you I knew about the bathroom. You see, Martita, see how I didn't lie to you? The prison baths were just the same as yours, only not yellow."

She was talking softly now and the words "prisoner" or "friend" were said with passionate tenderness. Her eyes had filled with nostalgia. She remained sad, the knife shining uselessly at her feet. She looked at Marta sweetly.

"The work was never done: we cleaned the pots where they cooked the prisoners' meals . . . we washed the clothes, the steps, the hallways . . ."

"And how long were you there, Luisa?"

"Who knows! I've even forgotten the street. I was only there with the prisoners, my friends. There I found a home and never suffered. I grew so fond of it that the days and nights flew by. If we got sick, there were two doctors, two, Martita! And they took care of us. I stayed there for so long that I had no other home . . ."

She looked at Marta sadly and remained silent. Now her pauses were involuntary. It was strange to see her so melancholy, evoking her time in the penitentiary. "I used to answer the telephone. See how I didn't lie to you, Martita?"

"It's true, Luisa, you didn't tell me lies."

Suddenly she livened up and began to laugh.

"At night there were dances in the corral. The prisoners took out their mandolins and guitars and we'd dance and dance. I'd never danced before, Martita! The life of the poor is no dance, only long walks over stones and hunger. My friends taught me some steps; they put my braids on top of my head and said to me, 'It's so you'll look less like an Indian.' And we danced and danced . . ."

She became gloomy again and Marta felt uneasy.

"When they told me they were going to give me my freedom, I didn't want it. 'Why, Sir? Where do you want me to go?' So I stayed there. But they told me again that I had to be given my freedom. A lady said to me, 'Take it, Luisa, take it!' And even though I didn't take it, they forced it on me. 'And now what do I do, Doctor? I no longer know the streets and I don't have a cent.' The street is money, Martita, money. The doctor gave me enough for my trip and the lady who told me to take my freedom came to wait for me at the door to the world; and when I found myself in the street, the train took me to my parents' house . . ."

Upon saying this she became somber and burst out crying inconsolably. She looked very old, her face furrowed with wrinkles, her skin dried out from the sun and the dust. Marta remained silent.

"But I didn't recognize it, Martita! 'Ay, Luisa, this is no longer your home!' And I could only sit there thinking about my friends and what they were probably doing . . ."

Her voice broke into sobs.

"How long were you there, Luisa?"

"With the prisoners? . . . Who knows! But it was a long time, didn't I say I'd forgotten about the streets and the world? When I reached my parents' home, my child was so big."

Luisa lifted her arm and drew a ten year old's height in the air. She remained suspended, lost in her memories; for her, prison meant gratifying years. She spoke of it the way others speak of palaces, riches or lost youth. Now that her thoughts brought her home, her face had grown hostile. She stopped crying.

"And what did your parents say to you?"

"Nothing! 'How are you, child?' "

"No, what did they say to you about your time in prison?"

Luisa jumped to her feet in a flash, put up her guard and stared straight at Marta.

"About prison? Nothing! They never found out. No one ever found out! They thought that I'd lived in Tacubaya with my first husband."

"But didn't your husband return to the village?"

"No! I was lucky that one of the prisoners who got out of jail killed him. So he never ever went back to the village to tell on me. There are things, Martita, that no one should know. No one knows that I was in prison; not my parents who are dead now or even Julian. When he came to ask for me, I didn't tell him anything; I acted like a widow and that's what I am."

She curled up in a ball again and looked at Marta. The two remained silent. Why was she telling her this story? They looked one another in the eye, spying on each other's thoughts. The little gold clock on the chest made a quick noise; time made itself felt, pouncing on them with unaccustomed speed. Luisa straightened up a little.

"Before leaving prison, my friends, who loved me a lot, said, 'Look, Luisa, don't ever tell anyone that you killed the woman. People are bad, very bad.' That's what they said. 'We already know that you're going to be tempted to tell. They make you confess your sins, your own sins. You have your own and they're for no one but you; and besides you have the dead woman's sins and together they're going to weigh you down.' You know, Martita, we're weighed down with the sins of the dead people we kill. That's why you see those men so stooped over by the weight of two or three they've killed. 'But don't tell anyone, Luisa, don't tell anyone where you've been these years!' That's what they told me and that's what I did, Martita, I haven't told anyone but you. 'But look, Luisa,' my friends told me, 'if some time you feel that those sins are doubling you over and emptying your stomach, go to the fields, far from people; look for a leafy tree, hug it and tell it everything you want to. But only when you can't stand it anymore, Luisa, for you can only do it once.' And that's how it was, Martita; time went by and only I knew about my life. Until my legs began to give way and I couldn't hold food down, because my sins and the dead woman's, even worse than mine, were sitting in my stomach. And so one day I said to Julian, 'I'm going to cut some wood!' And I went to the hills and found a leafy tree and did what my friends told me. I hugged it and said, 'Look, tree, I've come to confess my sins to you, so please take them away from me.' And there I was, Martita . . . and it took me four hours to tell the tree what was inside me . . ."

Breathless, Luisa stopped telling he story and looked slyly at Marta, who was very pale. Where was the Indian woman heading with all that? Marta felt her heart racing but didn't dare lift her hand to her breast. Motionless, she awaited the end of the story.

"I went back home and didn't visit the tree for a while but when I did . . ." Luisa remained silent and stared at Marta.

". . . I found it all dried up, Martita."

Silence fell between the two women and the room filled with beings that were rending the air with tiny knives made of dry wood.

"It dried up?" murmured Marta.

"Yes, Martita, it dried up. I laid my sins on it . . ."

The dry tree entered the room; the entire night dried up within the walls and the desiccated curtains. Marta looked at the clock; it was drying up on top of the chest. She searched her memory for a banal gesture to make toward Luisa who was watching her; the Indian woman was deluded and petrified by her own words.

"Luisa, when I said that you were possessed, I was kidding, calm yourself! The past no longer exists. We can never return to what we were." The Indian remained motionless, staring at her from far back in time. Marta felt fear.

"Don't be scared, Luisa, we two are happy here and what happened is over. Never to be recovered . . ."

"It dried up, Martita, it dried up . . . ," Luisa repeated.

"You already told me, Luisa, don't repeat it anymore. Go to bed in peace! We're both safe here far from everything . . ."

"How very alone we are, Martita! . . ."

"Why do you say that, Luisa?" Marta asked in a voice drained by fear, conscious of the immobile silence of her furniture and curtains.

"Because Gabina doesn't come back until tomorrow . . ."

"Luisa, go to sleep . . . you already know where your room is . . ."

Marta wanted to be alone, to break the spell. Luisa smiled and took the knife. Marta shouted, "Leave it!"

"Why, Martita, if it's mine?"

And with a gentle motion she made it disappear under her shirt. Slowly she abandoned her mistress's room. All remained still. Marta waited a few minutes; nothing was stirring in the house. She got up and moved the perfume bottles on the dressing table, dropped the hairbrush. But the noise didn't assuage her fears; from the shadows they were spying on her movements and laughing at her; they were swinging in the empty space. She began to undress. From within a black tunnel they were roaring with inaudible laughter. She jumped into bed; she wanted to deceive her enemies, make them believe she wasn't afraid. And turned out the light. Why had she told the woman she was possessed? She had restored her to her past. How strange that she had been so happy in jail! There she had been like the others. What could she be doing now? She would have liked to spy on her, was sure that she wasn't sleeping either. Luisa was afraid, too. She spied on Julian out of fear; she was afraid he would leave her; the countryside has no doors and so she couldn't lock him up. She was frightened by her own freedom and that of others. Stupid old woman! She was the same as all the Indians. Marta didn't like them and only accepted those who flattered her like Gabina. Sometimes she was inadvertently nice to them but deep in her heart there was an incurable callousness. In jail Luisa had found her equals and had learned to dance. Out in the world, she had returned to her place and had confided only in a tree . . . "and it dried up, Martita, it dried up . . ." Luisa's voice reached her repeating the same sentence from within an infinite tunnel. Marta found herself in a cold sweat and switched the light on. She looked at the turned down sheets with her embroidered initials. She was sorry she had no gun; I'd kill her like a rat! "If she appears at the door, I'll say to her: you see, Luisa, I'm praying, and she'll begin to pray with me." Crime is a solitary act . . . She listened again. No noise reached her ear; perhaps the Indian woman had already fallen asleep. Where could she have put the knife? She never let it out of her sight. It was the key that had opened her door to equality, dancing and happiness. It was her talisman. The silence convinced her that while she was brooding, the other woman was fast asleep. She glanced at the clock, 2:00 A.M. She yearned for the dawn. In the future she would be harsher with the Indians. Suddenly the little hands raced frantically and made a deafening noise. From within that noise, Marta heard barefoot steps pressing down on the rug.

"Luisa! . . . Luisa! . . . Luisa! . . ."

No one answered her calls, the telephone was in the other room. The steps stopped halfway down the hall. That wouldn't give her time enough to reach the door and lock it. She would jump at it like a wild cat.

"Luisa! . . . Luisa! . . . Damned Indian!"

Again she heard the footsteps. She hid her face in her hands.

Gabina returned to her mistress's house at six o'clock in the morning. It wasn't until eight o'clock that she noticed something strange had happened. She found Mrs. Marta in her room; she had been dead for more than five hours. The police found Luisa and the bloody knife hidden at a neighbor's house. They took her to the Tacubaya jail.

"None of my friends are here any more!" Luisa said after searching the cells and the patios. Then she sat down to cry bitterly. She had forgotten that more than a quarter of a century had transpired between her release and her return. Martita was right: the past is never to be recovered.

Translated by Evelyn Picon Garfield

Clarice Lispector

Brazil

Clarice Lispector.

Clarice Lispector was born of Jewish parents in Tchetchelnik, Ukraine, USSR, in 1925. When she was only two months old, the family moved to Brazil, first to Alagoas in the northeast and then to Recife, where Lispector spent her childhood. Later she was to graduate as a lawyer and become editor of the news agency, Agencia Nacional, one of Brazil's first female journalists, and the only one on the staff of the newspaper *A Noite*. She also wrote weekly columns for the prestigious *Jornal do Brasil*. Lispector spent most of her life in Rio de Janeiro, where she died of cancer in 1977.

She has won several literary prizes for her work, which includes nine novels, six collections of short stories, and four children's books. Her narratives are basically philosophical and psychological portraits of an existential nature, which reveal the inner world of her characters in contact with their surroundings. Self-realization and the authenticity of being preoccupy her characters in painful and complex interior monologues and quests during which sudden moments of revelation dominate, rather than external actions. Her literary style is hermetic, rich in imagery and nuances, ambiguities and intense detail.

Her reputation rests on her short stories rather than her novels, although novels such as *A maça no escuro* (1961), translated into English by Gregory Rabassa as *The Apple in the Dark*, definitively brought Brazilian literature onto the sophisticated international scene, away from the traditional regionalist novel of the land into the self-consciously introspective novel of language and the universal human condition.

Two of her most famous short stories are presented here in Giovanni Pontiero's translations. In "Love" ("Amor") and "Family Ties" ("Laços de família"), the frequent female protagonists of Lispector's fiction bare their inner psychological dramas to the reader: in "Love," Anna's heightened awareness bursts upon her everyday routine, while in "Family Ties," the double-edged sword of generational relationships affects an individual's freedom.

Love

FEELING A LITTLE TIRED, with her purchases bulging her
new string bag, Anna boarded the tram. She placed the bag on her lap
and the tram started off. Settling back in her seat she tried to find a
comfortable position, with a sigh of mild satisfaction.

Anna had nice children, she reflected with certainty and pleasure.
They were growing up, bathing themselves and misbehaving; they were
demanding more and more of her time. The kitchen, after all, was
spacious with its old stove that made explosive noises. The heat was
oppressive in the apartment, which they were paying off in installments,
and the wind, playing against the curtains she had made herself, re-
minded her that if she wanted to she could pause to wipe her forehead,
and contemplate the calm horizon. Like a farmer. She had planted the
seeds she held in her hand, no others, but only those. And they were
growing into trees. Her brisk conversations with the electricity man were
growing, the water filling the tank was growing, her children were growing, the table was growing with food, her husband arriving with the
newspapers and smiling with hunger, the irritating singing of the maids

resounding through the block. Anna tranquilly put her small, strong hand, her life current in everything. Certain times of the afternoon struck her as being critical. At a certain hour of the afternoon the trees she had planted laughed at her. And when nothing more required her strength, she became anxious. Meanwhile she felt herself more solid than ever, her body became a little thicker, and it was worth seeing the manner in which she cut out blouses for the children, the large scissors snapping into the material. All her vaguely artistic aspirations had for some time been channeled into making her days fulfilled and beautiful; with time, her taste for the decorative had developed and supplanted intimate disorder. She seemed to have discovered that everything was capable of being perfected, that each thing could be given a harmonious appearance; life itself could be created by Man.

Deep down, Anna had always found it necessary to feel the firm roots of things. And this is what a home had surprisingly provided. Through tortuous paths, she had achieved a woman's destiny, with the surprise of conforming to it almost as if she had invented that destiny herself. The man whom she had married was a real man, the children she mothered were real children. Her previous youth now seemed alien to her, like one of life's illnesses. She had gradually emerged to discover that life could be lived without happiness: by abolishing it she had found a legion of persons, previously invisible, who lived as one works—with perseverance, persistence, and contentment. What had happened to Anna before possessing a home of her own stood forever beyond her reach: that disturbing exaltation she had often confused with unbearable happiness. In exchange she had created something ultimately comprehensible, the life of an adult. This was what she had wanted and chosen.

Her precautions were now reduced to alertness during the dangerous part of the afternoon, when the house was empty and she was no longer needed; when the sun reached its zenith, and each member of the family went about his separate duties. Looking at the polished furniture, she felt her heart contract a little with fear. But in her life there was no opportunity to cherish her fears—she suppressed them with that same ingenuity she had acquired from domestic struggles. Then she would go out shopping or take things to be mended, unobtrusively looking after her home and her family. When she returned it would already be late afternoon and the children back from school would absorb her attention. Until the evening descended with its quiet excitement. In the morning she would awaken surrounded by her calm domestic duties. She would find the furniture dusty and dirty once more, as if it had returned repentant. As for herself, she mysteriously formed part of the soft, dark roots of the earth. And anonymously she nourished life. It was pleasant like this. This was what she had wanted and chosen.

The tram swayed on its rails and turned into the main road. Suddenly the wind became more humid, announcing not only the passing of the afternoon but the end of that uncertain hour. Anna sighed with relief and a deep sense of acceptance gave her face an air of womanhood.

The tram would drag along and then suddenly jolt to a halt. As far as Humaitá she could relax. Suddenly she saw the man stationary at the tram stop. The difference between him and others was that he was really stationary. He stood with his hands held out in front of him—blind.

But what else was there about him that made Anna sit up in distrust? Something disquieting was happening. Then she discovered what it was: the blind man was chewing gum . . . a blind man chewing gum. Anna still had time to reflect for a second that her brothers were coming for dinner—her heart pounding at regular intervals. Leaning forward, she studied the blind man intently, as one observes something incapable of returning our gaze. Relaxed, and with open eyes, he was chewing gum in the failing light. The facial movements of his chewing made him appear to smile then suddenly stop smiling, to smile and stop smiling. Anna stared at him as if he had insulted her. And anyone watching would have received the impression of a woman filled with hatred. She continued to stare at him, leaning more and more forward—until the tram gave a sudden jerk, throwing her unexpectedly backward. The heavy string bag toppled from her lap and landed on the floor. Anna cried out, the conductor gave the signal to stop before realizing what was happening, and the tram came to an abrupt halt. The other passengers looked on in amazement. Too paralyzed to gather up her shopping, Anna sat upright, her face suddenly pale. An expression, long since forgotten, awkwardly reappeared, unexpected and inexplicable. The Negro newsboy smiled as he handed over her bundle. The eggs had broken in their newspaper wrapping. Yellow sticky yolks dripped between the strands of the bag. The blind man had interrupted his chewing and held out his unsteady hands, trying in vain to grasp what had happened. She removed the parcel of eggs from the string bag accompanied by the smiles of the passengers. A second signal from the conductor and the tram moved off with another jerk.

A few moments later people were no longer staring at her. The tram was rattling on the rails and the blind man chewing gum had remained behind forever. But the damage had been done.

The string bag felt rough between her fingers, not soft and familiar as when she had knitted it. The bag had lost its meaning; to find herself on that tram was a broken thread; she did not know what to do with the purchases on her lap. Like some strange music, the world started up again around her. The damage had been done. But why? Had she forgotten that there were blind people? Compassion choked her. Anna's breathing became heavy. Even those things which had existed before the episode were now on the alert, more hostile, and even perishable. The world had once more become a nightmare. Several years fell away, the yellow yolks trickled. Exiled from her own days, it seemed to her that the people in the streets were vulnerable, that they barely maintained their equilibrium on the surface of the darkness—and for a moment they appeared to lack any sense of direction. The perception of an absence of law came so unexpectedly that Anna clutched the seat in front of her, as if she might fall off the tram, as if things might be overturned with the same calm they had possessed when order reigned.

What she called a crisis had come at last. And its sign was the intense pleasure with which she now looked at things, suffering and alarmed. The heat had become more oppressive, everything had gained new power and a stronger voice. In the Rua Voluntários da Pátria, revolution seemed imminent, the grids of the gutters were dry, the air dusty. A blind man chewing gum had plunged the world into a mysterious excitement. In every strong person there was a lack of compassion for the blind man, and their strength terrified her. Beside her sat a woman in blue with an expression which made Anna avert her gaze rapidly. On the pavement a mother shook her little boy. Two lovers held hands smiling. . . . And the blind man? Anna had lapsed into a mood of compassion which greatly distressed her.

She had skillfully pacified life; she had taken so much care to avoid upheavals. She had cultivated an atmosphere of serene understanding, separating each person from the others. Her clothes were clearly designed to be practical, and she could choose the evening's film from the newspaper—and everything was done in such a manner that each day should smoothly succeed the previous one. And a blind man chewing gum was destroying all this. Through her compassion Anna felt that life was filled to the brim with a sickening nausea.

Only then did she realize that she had passed her stop ages ago. In her weak state everything touched her with alarm. She got off the tram, her legs shaking, and looked around her, clutching the string bag stained with egg. For a moment she was unable to get her bearings. She seemed to have plunged into the middle of the night.

It was a long road, with high yellow walls. Her heart beat with fear as she tried in vain to recognize her surroundings; while the life she had discovered continued to pulsate, a gentler, more mysterious wind caressed her face. She stood quietly observing the wall. At last she recognized it. Advancing a little further alongside a hedge, she passed through the gates of the botanical garden.

She strolled wearily up the central avenue, between the palm trees. There was no one in the garden. She put her parcels down on the ground and sat down on the bench of a side path where she remained for some time.

The wilderness seemed to calm her, the silence regulating her breathing and soothing her senses.

From afar she saw the avenue where the evening was round and clear. But the shadows of the branches covered the side path.

Around her there were tranquil noises, the scent of trees, chance encounters among the creeping plants. The entire garden fragmented by the ever more fleeting moments of the evening. From whence came the drowsiness with which she was surrounded? As if induced by the drone of birds and bees. Everything seemed strange, much too gentle, much too great.

A gentle, familiar movement startled her and she turned round rapidly. Nothing appeared to have stirred. But in the central lane there stood, immobile, an enormous cat. Its fur was soft. With another silent movement, it disappeared.

Agitated, she looked about her. The branches swayed, their shadows wavering on the ground. A sparrow foraged in the soil. And suddenly, in terror, she imagined that she had fallen into an ambush. In the garden there was a secret activity in progress which she was beginning to penetrate.

94

On the trees, the fruits were black and sweet as honey. On the ground there lay dry fruit stones full of circumvolutions like small rotted cerebrums. The bench was stained with purple sap. With gentle persistence the waters murmured. On the tree trunk the luxurious feelers of parasites fastened themselves. The rawness of the world was peaceful. The murder was deep. And death was not what one had imagined.

As well as being imaginary, this was a world to be devoured with one's teeth, a world of voluminous dahlias and tulips. The trunks were pervaded by leafy parasites, their embrace soft and clinging. Like the resistance that precedes surrender, it was fascinating; the woman felt disgusted, and it was fascinating.

The trees were laden, and the world was so rich that it was rotting. When Anna reflected that there were children and grown men suffering hunger, the nausea reached her throat as if she were pregnant and abandoned. The moral of the garden was something different. Now that the blind man had guided her to it, she trembled on the threshold of a dark, fascinating world where monstrous water lilies floated. The small flowers scattered on the grass did not appear to be yellow or pink, but the color of inferior gold and scarlet. Their decay was profound, perfumed. But all these oppressive things she watched, her head surrounded by a swarm of insects, sent by some more refined life in the world. The breeze penetrated between the flowers. Anna imagined rather than felt its sweetened scent. The garden was so beautiful that she feared hell.

It was almost night now and everything seemed replete and heavy; a squirrel leapt in the darkness. Under her feet the earth was soft. Anna inhaled its odor with delight. It was both fascinating and repulsive.

But when she remembered the children, before whom she now felt guilty, she straightened up with a cry of pain. She clutched the package, advanced through the dark side path, and reached the avenue. She was almost running, and she saw the garden all around her aloof and impersonal. She shook the locked gates, and went on shaking them, gripping the rough timber. The watchman appeared, alarmed at not having seen her.

Until she reached the entrance of the building, she seemed to be on the brink of disaster. She ran with the string bag to the elevator, her heart beating in her breast—what was happening? Her compassion for the blind man was as fierce as anguish but the world seemed hers, dirty, perishable, hers. She opened the door of her flat. The room was large, square, the polished knobs were shining, the window panes were shining, the lamp shone brightly—what new land was this? And for a moment that wholesome life she had led until today seemed morally crazy. The little boy who came running up to embrace her was a creature with long legs and a face resembling her own. She pressed him firmly to her in anxiety and fear. Trembling, she protected herself. Life was vulnerable. She loved the world, she loved all things created, she loved with loathing. In the same way as she had always been fascinated by oysters, with that vague sentiment of revulsion which the approach of truth provoked, admonishing her. She embraced her son, almost hurting him. Almost as if she knew of some evil—the blind man or the beautiful botanical garden—she was clinging to him, to him whom she loved above all things. She had been touched by the demon of faith.

"Life is horrible," she said to him in a low voice, as if famished. What would she do if she answered the blind man's call? She would go alone. . . . There were poor and rich places that needed her. She needed them. "I am afraid," she said. She felt the delicate ribs of the child between her arms, she heard his frightened weeping.

"Mummy," the child called. She held him away from her, she studied his face and her heart shrank.

"Don't let Mummy forget you," she said. No sooner had the child felt her embrace weaken than he escaped and ran to the door of the room, from where he watched her more safely. It was the worst look that she had ever received. The blood rose hot to her cheeks.

She sank into a chair, with her fingers still clasping the string bag. What was she ashamed of? There was no way of escaping. The very crust of the days she had forged had broken and the water was escaping. She stood before the oysters. And there was no way of averting her gaze. What was she ashamed of? Certainly it was no longer pity, it was more than pity: her heart had filled with the worst will to live.

She no longer knew if she was on the side of the blind man or of the thick plants. The man little by little had moved away, and in her torment she appeared to have passed over to the side of those who had injured his eyes. The botanical garden, tranquil and high, had been a revelation. With horror, she discovered that she belonged to the strong part of the world, and what name should she give to her fierce compassion? Would she be obliged to kiss the leper, since she would never be just a sister?

96

"A blind man has drawn me to the worst of myself," she thought, amazed. She felt herself banished because no pauper would drink water from her burning hands. Ah! It was easier to be a saint than a person! Good heavens, then was it not real, that pity which had fathomed the deepest waters in her heart? But it was the compassion of a lion.

Humiliated, she knew that the blind man would prefer a poorer love. And, trembling, she also knew why. The life of the botanical garden summoned her as a werewolf is summoned by the moonlight. "Oh! but she loved the blind man," she thought with tears in her eyes. Meanwhile it was not with this sentiment that one would go to church. "I am frightened," she whispered alone in the room. She got up and went to the kitchen to help the maid prepare dinner.

But life made her shiver like the cold of winter. She heard the school bell pealing, distant and constant. The small horror of the dust gathering in threads around the bottom of the stove, where she had discovered a small spider. Lifting a vase to change the water—there was the horror of the flower submitting itself, languid and loathsome, to her hands. The same secret activity was going on here in the kitchen. Near the waste bin, she crushed an ant with her foot. The small murder of the ant. Its minute body trembled. Drops of water fell on the stagnant water in the pool.

The summer beetles. The horror of those expressionless beetles. All around there was a silent, slow, insistent life. Horror upon horror. She went from one side of the kitchen to the other, cutting the steaks, mixing the cream. Circling around her head, around the light, the flies of a warm summer's evening. A night in which compassion was as crude as false love. Sweat trickled between her breasts. Faith broke her; the heat of the oven burned in her eyes.

Then her husband arrived, followed by her brothers and their wives, and her brothers' children.

They dined with all the windows open, on the ninth floor. An airplane shuddered menacingly in the heat of the sky. Although she had used few eggs, the dinner was good. The children stayed up, playing on the carpet with their cousins. It was summer and it would be useless to force them to go to sleep. Anna was a little pale and laughed gently with the others.

After dinner, the first cool breeze finally entered the room. The family was seated round the table, tired after their day, happy in the

absence of any discord, eager not to find fault. They laughed at everything, with warmth and humanity. The children grew up admirably
around them. Anna took the moment like a butterfly, between her
fingers before it might escape forever.

Later, when they had all left and the children were in bed, she was
just a woman looking out of the window. The city was asleep and warm.
Would the experience unleashed by the blind man fill her days? How
many years would it take before she once more grew old? The slightest
movement on her part and she would trample one of her children. But
with the ill will of a lover, she seemed to accept that the fly would
emerge from the flower, and the giant water lilies would float in the
darkness of the lake. The blind man was hanging among the fruits of the
botanical garden.

What if that were the stove exploding with the fire spreading through
the house, she thought to herself as she ran to the kitchen where she
found her husband in front of the spilt coffee.

"What happened?" she cried, shaking from head to foot. He was
taken aback by his wife's alarm. And suddenly understanding, he
laughed.

"It was nothing," he said, "I am just a clumsy fellow." He looked
tired, with dark circles under his eyes.

But, confronted by the strange expression on Anna's face, he studied
her more closely. Then he drew her to him in a sudden caress.

"I don't want anything ever to happen to you!" she said.

"You can't prevent the stove from having its little explosions," he
replied, smiling. She remained limp in his arms. This afternoon, something tranquil had exploded, and in the house everything struck a tragi-
comic note.

"It's time to go to bed," he said, "it's late." In a gesture which was not
his, but which seemed natural, he held his wife's hand, taking her with
him, without looking back, removing her from the danger of living.

The giddiness of compassion had spent itself. And if she had crossed
love and its hell, she was now combing her hair before the mirror,
without any world for the moment in her heart. Before getting into bed,
as if she were snuffing a candle, she blew out that day's tiny flame.

Translated by Giovanni Pontiero

Family Ties

THE WOMAN and her mother finally settled back in the taxi that would take them to the station. The mother counted and re-counted the two suitcases, trying to convince herself that they were both there. The daughter, with her dark eyes, to which a slight squint gave a constant gleam of derision and indifference, assisted.

"I haven't forgotten anything?" her mother asked her for the third time.

"No, no, you haven't forgotten anything," her daughter replied, amused but patient.

She still retained the impression of the almost farcical scene between her mother and her husband at the moment of departure. During the older woman's two-week visit, the two of them had barely endured each other's company; the good-mornings and good-evenings had resounded constantly with a cautious tact which had made her want to smile. But suddenly at the moment of departure, before getting into the taxi, the mother had changed into the exemplary mother-in-law and the husband had become the good son-in-law.

"Please forgive anything I might have said in haste," the older woman had said, and Catherine, with some enjoyment, had seen Tony, unsure of what to do with the suitcases in his hands, stammer—perturbed by his role as the good son-in-law.

"If I laugh they will think I am mad," Catherine had thought, frowning.

"Whoever marries off a son, loses a son, but whoever marries off a daughter gains a son," her mother had added and Tony took advantage of his cold to be able to cough. Standing there, Catherine knowingly observed her husband as his self-assurance disappeared to give place to a slightly built man with a dark complexion, forced into being the son of that grey-haired little woman. . . . It was then that her desire to laugh became stronger. Fortunately she never in fact laughed when she felt the urge: her eyes took on a knowing and restrained expression, they became more squinted, and her laughter showed in her eyes. It always hurt a little to be capable of laughing. But she could do nothing about it: ever since she was a little girl she had laughed through her eyes, and she had always had a squint.

"I still think the child is too thin," her mother said, resisting the bumps of the taxi. And although Tony was not present she was using the same tone of challenge and accusation which she adopted in front of him. So much so that one evening Tony had become exasperated.

"It's not my fault, Severina!" He called his mother-in-law Severina because before the marriage it was decided that they would be a modern mother and son-in-law. Right from her mother's very first visit to the couple, the word Severina had become awkward on her husband's lips, and now, despite the fact that he addressed her by her Christian name, it did not prevent. . . .

Catherine watched them and smiled.

"The child has always been thin, Mother," she replied. The taxi drove on monotonously.

"Thin and highly strung," her mother added decisively.

"Thin and highly strung," assented Catherine patiently.

He was a nervous and distracted child. During his grandmother's visit he had become even more distant and he had started to sleep badly, disturbed by the excessive endearments and affectionate pinching of the older woman. Tony, who had never really given much attention to his son's sensibility, began to make sly digs at his mother-in-law, "for protecting the child. . . ."

"I haven't forgotten anything . . ." began her mother again, when a sudden slamming of brakes threw them against each other and sent the suitcases toppling.

"Oh! Oh!" the older woman exclaimed, as if overtaken by some irremediable disaster. "Oh!" she said, swaying her head in surprise, suddenly aged and poor. And Catherine?

Catherine looked at her mother and the mother looked at her daughter. Had some disaster befallen Catherine too? Her eyes blinked with surprise, and she quickly rearranged the suitcases and her handbag in her attempt to remedy the catastrophe as quickly as possible. Because something had, in fact, happened and there was no point in concealing it. Catherine had been thrown against Severina with a physical intimacy long since forgotten, and going back to the days when she belonged to a father and a mother. Although they had never really embraced or kissed each other. With her father, certainly, Catherine had experienced a much closer relationship. When her mother used to fill their plates, forcing them to eat far too much, the two of them used to wink at each other in complicity without her mother even noticing. But after the collision in the taxi and their composure had been restored, they had nothing further to say to each other—both of them feeling anxious to arrive at the station.

"I haven't forgotten anything?" her mother asked with a resigned note.

Catherine neither wanted to meet her eyes again nor make any reply.

"Here are your gloves!" she said, picking them up from the floor.

"Oh! Oh! my gloves!" her mother anxiously exclaimed. They exchanged another glance only when the suitcases had been lifted onto the train and they had exchanged a farewell kiss: her mother's head appeared at the window. It was then that Catherine noticed that her mother had aged and that her eyes were shining.

The train was still waiting to depart and they both lingered without knowing what to say. Her mother took out a mirror from her handbag and studied her new hat, bought from the same milliner patronized by her daughter. She studied herself, putting on an excessively severe expression that betrayed a certain satisfaction with her own appearance. Her daughter observed her with amusement. "No one else can love you except me," thought the woman with a smile in her eyes; and the weight of responsibility put the taste of blood into her mouth. As if "mother and daughter" meant "life and repugnance." No, no, she could not say that she loved her mother. Her mother distressed her, that was it. The old woman had put the mirror back into her handbag and looked at her affectionately. Her face, which was lined but still very expressive, seemed to be forcing itself into making some impression on the other passengers, and here the hat played its part. The station bell suddenly sounded, there was a general movement of alarm, and several people began to run, thinking that the train was already pulling out.

"Mother," said the woman.

"Catherine!" said the old woman. They exchanged frightened glances—a suitcase carried on a porter's head interrupted their view and a youth running past caught Catherine by the arm as he went, disarranging the collar of her dress. When they could see each other again, Catherine was on the point of asking her if she had forgotten anything. . . .

"I haven't forgotten anything?" her mother asked. Catherine, too, had the impression something had been forgotten, and they looked apprehensively at each other—because, if something had really been forgotten, it was too late now. A mother dragged a child along the platform and the child was crying. Once more the station bell sounded. . . .

"Mother," said the woman. What had they forgotten to say to each other? But now it was too late. It seemed to her that the older woman should have said one day, "I am your mother, Catherine," and that she should have replied, "And I am your daughter."

"Don't go sitting in a draught," Catherine called out.

"Now dear, I am not a child," her mother shouted back, still obviously worrying about her appearance. Her freckled hand, somewhat tremulous, delicately adjusted the brim of her hat and Catherine felt a sudden urge to ask her if she had been happy living with her father.

"Give my love to Auntie!" she shouted.

"Yes, yes."

"Mother," said Catherine, because a prolonged whistle could be heard and the wheels of the train were already moving.

"Catherine!" said the older woman with a gaping mouth and frightened eyes, and with the first jerk the daughter saw her lift her hands to her hat: it had fallen forward covering her nose, so that only her new dentures were showing. The train was already moving and Catherine waved. Her mother's face disappeared for a second and now reappeared, hatless, the topknot on her head undone and falling in white strands over her shoulders like the tresses of a madonna—her head was leaning out and she looked serious, perhaps no longer even able to perceive her daughter in the distance.

Amidst the smoke, Catherine began to walk back down the platform, her eyebrows drawn in a frown and in her eyes the shy look of those with a squint. Relieved of her mother's company, she had recovered her brisk manner of walking; alone it was much easier. Some men were watching her, she was sweet, her body a little on the heavy side perhaps. She walked confidently, looking modern in her outfit, her short hair tinted a reddish brown. And things had disposed themselves in such a way that the sorrow of love seemed to her to be happiness—everything around her was so tender and alive, the dirty street, the old tram cars, orange peel on the pavements—strength flowed to and fro in her heart with a heavy richness. She was very pretty at this moment, so elegant: in harmony with her time and the city where she had been born, almost as if she had chosen it. In her eyes anyone would have perceived the relish this woman had for the things of the world. She studied people with insistence, trying to fix on those inconstant figures a pleasure still moist with tears for her mother. She avoided the cars and managed to approach the bus, circumventing the queue and staring ironically; nothing would prevent this little woman who walked swaying her hips from mounting one more mysterious step in her days.

The elevator droned in the heat of the beach. She opened the door of her apartment with one hand while extricating herself from her little hat with the other; she seemed disposed to take advantage of the largesse of the whole world—a path her mother had opened and that was burning in her breast. Tony scarcely raised his eyes from his book. Saturday afternoon had always been "his own" and, immediately after Severina's departure, he returned to it with pleasure, seated at his low desk.

"Has *she* gone?"

"Yes, she's gone," replied Catherine, pushing open the door of her little boy's room. Ah yes, there was her child all right, she thought with sudden relief. Her son. Thin and highly strung. Since the moment he had found his feet, he had started to walk steadily; but, now nearly four years old, he spoke as if verbs were unknown to him: he observed things coldly, unable to connect them among themselves. There he was playing with a wet towel, exact and distant. The woman felt a pleasant warmth and she would have liked to fasten the child forever to this moment; she drew the towel away from him in reproach.

"What a naughty boy!" But the child looked indifferently into the air, communicating with himself. His mind was always somewhere else. No one had yet succeeded in really catching his attention. His mother shook the towel in the air, screening off the view of the room.

"Mummy," said the child. Catherine turned round quickly. It was the first time he had said "Mummy" in that tone without asking for something. It was more than a verification: "Mummy!" The woman continued to shake the towel vigorously and asked herself whom she could tell what had happened, but she did not find anyone who might understand what she herself was at a loss to explain. She stretched the towel out neatly before hanging it up to dry. Perhaps she might be able to tell if she were to change the form. She would relate that her son had said, "Mummy, who is God?" No, perhaps, "Mummy, child wants God." Perhaps. The truth could only be captured in symbols, and only in symbols would they receive it. With her eyes smiling at her necessary lie and above all at her own foolishness, escaping from Severina, the woman unexpectedly laughed in fact at the child and not only with her eyes; her whole body laughed, broken, her exterior breached and a harshness appearing like a fit of wheezing.

"Ugly," the child then said, examining her.

"Let's go for a walk," she said, coloring and catching him by the hand. She passed through the room, without stopping she advised her husband, "We're going out," and she slammed the apartment door.

Tony had barely time to lift his eyes from his book, and, surprised, he surveyed the room that was already empty.

"Catherine!" he called after her, but the noise of the elevator descending could already be heard. "Where were they going?" he asked himself perturbed, coughing and blowing his nose. Saturdays were "his own," but he liked his wife and child to be at home while he pursued his private occupations. "Catherine!" he called impatiently, although he knew that she could no longer hear him. He got up, went to the window and a moment later spotted his wife and child on the sidewalk.

The two of them had stopped, the woman perhaps deciding which direction to take. And suddenly she was off.

Why was she walking so fast, gripping the child by the hand? From the window he saw his wife holding the child's hand with force and walking quickly, her eyes fixed straight ahead of her; and, even without looking, the man could see the hard expression on her lips. The child—who knows by what dark understanding?—was also staring fixedly ahead, startled and ingenuous. Seen from above, the two figures lost their familiar perspective; they seemed to be flattened to the ground and darker by the light of the sea. The child's hair was blowing in the breeze.

Her husband repeated the question which, even beneath the innocence of a commonplace expression, disturbed him. "Where are they going?" Preoccupied, he watched his wife leading the child away and he feared that at this moment, when they were both beyond his reach, she might transmit to their son . . . but what? "Catherine," he thought, "Catherine, this child is still innocent!" At what moment was it that a mother, clasping her child, gave him this prison of love that would descend forever upon the future man. Later her child, already a man, alone, would stand before this same window, drumming his fingers on the windowpane: imprisoned. Obliged to respond to a dead man. Who would ever know at what moment the mother transferred her inheritance to her child. And with what morose pleasure. Now mother and son were understanding each other within the mystery they shared. Afterward, no one would know on what black roots man's freedom was nourished. "Catherine," he thought, enraged, "the child is innocent!" They had, however, disappeared along the beach. The mystery shared.

"But what about me?" he asked in alarm. The two of them had gone away on their own. And he had stayed behind. Left with his Saturday. And his cold. In the tidy apartment, where "everything worked smoothly." Who knows, perhaps his wife was escaping with her son from the room, with its carefully selected pieces of furniture, its curtains and pictures? This is what he had given her. The apartment of an engineer. And he knew that if his wife had taken advantage of his situation as a young husband with a promising future, she also despised the situation, with those cunning eyes, escaping with her thin, highly strung child. The man became distressed. Because he would not be able to give her anything more except—greater success. Because he knew that she would help him to achieve it and at the same time would hate what they achieved. Such was the nature of that serene woman of thirty-two who never really spoke, as if she had lived since the beginning of time. The relationship between them was so tranquil. At times he tried to humiliate her by entering the room while she was changing her clothes, because he knew that she detested being seen in the nude. (Why did he find it necessary to humiliate her?)

Meantime, he knew all too well that she would only belong to a man so long as she was proud. But he had got used to making her feminine in this way: he humiliated her with tenderness, and now she was already smiling—without rancor? Perhaps from all this their peaceful relationship had grown, from those quiet conversations that created a family atmosphere for their child. Or this irritated the child at times. At times the child became irritated, he stamped his feet and shouted in his sleep because of some nightmare. From where had that vibrant little fellow emerged, unless from that which his wife and he had cut from their daily life? They lived so tranquilly that, if a moment of happiness approached, they quickly looked at each other, almost ironically, and their eyes said mutually, "Don't let's waste it, don't let's stupidly throw it away"—as if they had lived forever.

But he had watched her from the window, he had seen her walk quickly away, holding the child by the hand, and he had said to himself, "She is taking her moment of happiness—alone." He had felt frustrated because for some time now he could not live with anyone but her. Yet she was able to find her own moments—alone. For instance, what had his wife been up to between the station and the apartment? Not that he suspected her of anything, but his mind was troubled.

The last light of evening fell heavily on the objects in the room. The parched sands cracked. The whole day had languished under the threat of irradiation which did not explode at this moment, although it became more and more deadened and droned in the uninterrupted elevator of the building. When Catherine returned they would dine, warding off the moths. Their child would cry out before falling into a deep sleep and Catherine would interrupt her dinner for a moment. . . . Wouldn't that elevator halt for even a second? No, the elevator would not halt even for a second.

"After dinner we'll go to the cinema," the man decided. Because after the cinema it would be night at last, and this day would break up like the waves on the rocks of Arpoador.

Translated by Giovanni Pontiero

Griselda Gambaro

Argentina

Griselda Gambaro.

Griselda Gambaro was born in Buenos Aires, Argentina, in 1928. She has won several literary awards for her prose fiction—*Madrigal en ciudad* (City Madrigal, 1963) and *El desatino* (The Blunder, 1964)—and for her play, *El campo* (The Camp, 1968). A frequent visitor to the United States, Gambaro was a Guggenheim fellow and is often invited to lecture at universities on Latin American theater and to attend international drama festivals. Her plays have been adapted for radio in Sweden and France, and have been staged in Argentina as well as in Italy, Germany, Poland, Mexico, Venezuela, Uruguay, France, and the United States. In the 1986 theater season in Buenos Aires, four of her plays were staged, including one debut performance.

Although Gambaro is best known as one of the most important dramatists in Latin America today, she has also continued to write novels, including an original and humorous parody of the erotic novel genre, entitled *Lo impenetrable* (The Impenetrable), in which eroticism does not depend on a sadomasochistic relationship or sexual victimization. This novel and several recent plays point to an evolution in Gambaro's characterization of humankind. For a trademark of Gambaro's work has been her insistence on cruelty in human relationships at all social and political levels: family, friends, acquaintances, social and governmental institutions. Her main characters are victims and victimizers who play out insidious authoritarian scenes in theater of aggression and passivity, of subjugation and lack of freedom. Only black humor draws a fine line between the despair depicted in a minor key and the grotesque scenes. In her earlier works, the victims passively accepted their lot, whereas in her latest works, such as the play *Bitter Blood* (La malasangre), they have begun to protest.

The grotesque element in her plays is rooted in two principle influences: first, the grotesque theater in Argentina, a tradition stemming from a dramatic form called the "sainete" in which caricatures, exaggerations, and black humor are the norm; and second, the French theater of cruelty as defined by Antonin Artaud. As in the latter, Gambaro emphasizes theatrical elements—properties, costume design, makeup, movements, facial gestures, and off-stage sounds and smells—rather than relying primarily on literary ones, i.e., words. She carries this technique of the theater of cruelty one step further by juxtaposing a dispassionate verbal system with menacing dramatic elements; the latter contradict the former, thus producing the cornerstone of her theater: duplicity.

These exaggerations, caricatures, and grotesque scenes are apparent in the one-act play *Bitter Blood*, set during the time of Juan Manuel de Rosas, one of Argentina's more brutal dictators (1835–52). Staged for the first time in Buenos

Aires in 1982, the performance had to be suspended when someone in the audience stood up to shout that the actors were insulting his grandmother (referring to the Rosas family); a commotion ensued. Sentiments concerning authoritarian regimes and their excesses run high in Argentina, and so this play set in 1840 has a striking impact on audiences some 140 years later.

Bitter Blood

Characters

Dolores*
Raphael
Father, also known as Benigno**
Mother
Fermin
Juan Pedro

Scene I

A drawing room in Argentina, ca. 1840, walls covered in garnet red. The characters' costumes are also in various shades of red. A large, bare, lustrous oak table, a sofa, three high-backed chairs, and a heavy piece of furniture, a sideboard or chest of drawers with a candelabra. A piano to one side. Two side doors and at the back, a window with curtains. The

---

*In Spanish means "suffering, pain."
**In Spanish means "kind, gentle, merciful, humane."

father, dressed in a red that verges on black, is standing with his back to the audience, completely immobile, looking through the window at the scene down below. After a moment, Mother enters. She is carrying a tray with a crystal decanter and two glasses.

Mother: Here's the wine. (*Smiling timidly*) I wanted to bring it myself.

Father: Thank you. (*Pauses. Dryly*) Why are there two glasses? Who's joining me?

Mother: I thought . . .

Father: Better not think. (*Mother leaves the tray on top of the table. Father looks out the window again, sour-faced and in a bad mood*) I don't like any of them. None of them. Not even one is worthwhile. They think all they have to do is show up and I'll be struck dumb and deaf.

Mother (draws near and looks with him): The third one . . .

Father (coldly): What about the third one?

Mother: He seems nice.

Father (gloomy): Yes.

Mother (feeling insecure): He's going to stay here in the house.

Father: Yes. So what?

Mother (timidly): It's better if he's nice. Right?

Father: Yes. And he seems intelligent, too, (*mimics her*) right?

Mother (insecure): I don't know.

Father: And what other qualifications does he have? (*He touches her breast in a vulgar way*) My wise little wife.

Mother (pulls away): Benigno, please.

Father (puts his arm around her, makes her look through the window. Sweetly): Let's look together. Two heads are better than one. What else do you see?

Mother: He seems . . . (*stops abruptly*)

Father: Yes.

Mother: He's quite a dandy.

Father: You mean good looking!

Mother: No. I mean he's well dressed. With gloves . . . red ones.

Father: How perceptive! What else do you see? I was right to ask you to look with me.

Mother (insecure): Well . . . I don't see anything else.

Father: Yes, you do. You like his face! (*He shoves her brutally*) Get out!

112

Mother: But why?

Father: You're only supposed to look at me, you whore!

Mother: I *am* looking at you, stop insulting me!

Father (as if he misunderstood, cups his ear. Looks around, amused): What? I give the orders here. And the compliments. The insults, too. I meant what I said, and I repeat. (*Very softly*) Whore.

Mother: I asked you not to insult me.

Father: Why?

Mother: Out of respect.

Father (as if playing along, alarmed): And they can hear!

Mother: Yes.

Father: No. I said it very softly. But I can shout! No one hears what I don't want them to. They hear, but they don't understand. Go on, get out of here!

Mother (moves away toward the door, then turns. Calmly): I hate you.

Father (turns toward her): What?

Mother: I didn't mean to say it.

Father: What? (*He takes her by the arm as if wanting to caress her. But after a pause he twists it*) What did you say? I don't understand what I don't like to hear. (*He twists her arm more*) What?

Mother (bearing the pain, then): I love you.

Father (sweetly): After so long? Again . . .

Mother (remains silent a moment, then, since father increases the pressure): I . . . love you.

Father (lets her go, kisses her on the cheek. As if nothing had happened): Thank you, dear. Now leave. It's cold on the patio. They must be freezing. I don't want them to wait any more. (*Mother leaves. Father rings the bell. Looks out the window. Fermin appears. He's tall and robust. A certain understanding between him and the father is noticeable, a certain tacit agreement about their respective roles*)

Fermin: Sir?

Father (looks out the window): The third one goes. It's cold.

Fermin: Yes, sir.

Father: Fermin! If he dallies, you can push him.

Fermin (as if playing along): How do I know if he's dallying? Should he run? (*Father shrugs his shoulders childishly. Fermin smiles*) I'll take care of it, sir. (*Exits*)

Father (looks out the window): You caught cold for nothing. You'll look at yourself in the mirror and lose faith in your good looks or your grimy nails hidden in those gloves. (*Turns around. Childishly*) What did I do? What did I do? Why are you throwing me out? I was standing in line like a good boy! And I bought red gloves! (*He looks*) Not so brusquely, Fermin! What a brute. (*Laughs convulsively, chokes. Bitterly*) None of them serves my purpose. The first one's too proud, the second too tall, the third is gone, the fourth . . . And that one who's getting out of line, how dare he? Did *I* say they could jump around like kangaroos to warm up? (*Sees something that surprises him, turns around*) Oh! Oh, oh my God! (*Laughs convulsively with joy. Rings the bell*) My God, I thank you. I thank you for answering the wishes of a sinner. (*Hums*) The mother gets hot on me, the daughter gets seduced . . . (*Fermin appears*) The one who's turning around . . . The one who looks the worst . . .

Fermin: Kick him out?

Father: No! Bring him here.

Fermin: And the others?

Father: Let them wait. The cold is healthy. It takes them down a peg. (*Fermin leaves. Father serves himself some wine and drinks. Content*) Let's see if the same thing happens with this one. (*Laughs convulsively. Hums*) The mother gets hot on me, the daughter gets seduced . . . (*Fermin opens the door for Raphael, who enters and bows. He wears a suit made of lightweight material; he's purple from the cold. He has a very handsome, serene, and gentle face. His back is deformed by a hump and he walks bent slightly forward*)

Father (*smiling cordially*): Come in. (*Moves toward Raphael. Doesn't offer him his hand. Walks around him and looks at his back. Laughs convulsively*) Yes . . . you're a hunchback . . .

Raphael: Sir . . .

Father: You'll like it here. As you can see, I'm good-natured. (*Raphael sniffles*) It was cold outside. Wasn't it? The bed was so warm I got up late today. That's why you all waited so long. But here it's not cold. Right?

Raphael: No . . . No, sir, it's not cold.

Father (shyly): I want to ask you . . . (*He stops*)

Raphael: What?

Father: Don't take it the wrong way. I'm curt with people, no one loves

me, but you can't ask people to love you. If there's no interest . . .
You *are* interested.

Raphael: Yes, sir.

Father: Well . . . I don't mean love, but you'll understand.

Raphael (doesn't understand): Yes, sir.

Father (in an outburst): Well then, I'm asking you! (*Remains silent, immobile. Then walks around nervously. Stops, looks at Raphael as if waiting for something*)

Raphael: At your service, sir.

Father: That's what I wanted to hear! Afterward don't complain! (*Laughs nervously and convulsively. Pauses. Then tenderly and almost lasciviously*) Get undressed.

Raphael: What?

Father: You said yes, you said yes!

Raphael (backing off): No . . .

Father: Come on . . . Between us men. My wife wanted to stay but I threw her out.

Raphael: Why?

Father: Why did I throw her out?

Raphael: No. Why do you want to . . .

Father: I've never seen one before! (*Laughs, chokes*)

Raphael (humiliated): I'm not a freak.

Father: Me neither. And I get undressed. Only when I bathe. (*Tenderly and confidentially*) In the dark. The other stuff we do in the dark. Through a hole in the nightgown. (*Laughs, covers his mouth embarrassed*)

Raphael: I can't (*Bows and moves off toward the door*)

Father: Sir! (*Raphael turns around*) Do you see how many are waiting in the patio?

Raphael: Yes.

Father: A long line. Freezing to death. They know I'm wealthy, and that I'll treat them well. And I looked at them, for some time now I've observed them, and when you showed up I said: that one. That's the one.

Raphael: Why?

Father (mockingly): Why, why? Because of your pretty face. (*He approaches and walks around him*) You're clean. (*Brushes Raphael's cheek with his thumb*) Shaven. (*Points to the hunchback*) But this! Can I . . . touch it? It brings luck. (*Laughs*) Fortunate man!

Raphael (pale and humiliated): I'm a good teacher.

Father (gently): We'll see. (*Anxious*) May I?

Raphael: No.

Father (approaches the window, separates the curtains and looks out): It's raining. And they're not leaving. They don't even seek cover under the eaves. Disciplined and in line. They write well. They know opportunities exist for those who write well. (*Turns toward Raphael*) But I've already chosen. You.

Raphael: I'm a good teacher.

Father (indulging): That matters, too. Get undressed. (*Laughs*) Just to the waist. That's all. (*Touches his clothes*) Clean but worn out. Lightweight. Shaven, but gaunt. That's called hunger. And not everyone in this city (*laughs*) wants to have a hunchback at home. But I do. And you won't be a servant. You'll have your own room. You'll sit with us at the table. And you'll eat well. We'll treat each other as equals.

Raphael: Thank you.

Father: Leave if you want to. (*Silence. Sound of rain*)

Raphael: I don't want to go.

Father: It's a deal! I'll have the others leave. It doesn't make sense to have them wait around. (*Rings the bell*) It's raining hard and the job's filled.

Fermin (at the door): Sir?

Father: The job is filled.

Fermin: I'm glad, sir. (*Pause*) Do you need something?

Father: Me?

Fermin: You rang, sir.

Father: I did? I don't remember why. What did I want?

Fermin: We already took in the bird cages.

Father: Oh! That's it! It's raining so hard!

Fermin: You know I take care of the birds. You shouldn't worry, sir.

Father: Thank you, Fermin. (*Fermin withdraws. Father smiles at Raphael*) I should ask you what you teach.

Raphael: French and Latin, sir. Botany, mathematics.

Father: Mathematics, too? Fantastic! You'll teach me mathematics, the girls only need to know that two and two make four. (*Vaguely lascivious*) And . . . my request? (*Softly*) Get undressed.

116

Raphael: Why?

Father (joking): To see if it's true.

Raphael: It's true. (*Smiling nervously*) I've been a hunchback since childhood. Perhaps my father was also a hunchback . . . No one's been able to tell me how it happened. If you want, you may touch it.

Father (brusquely): Not through your clothes.

Raphael: I . . . can't.

Father (sweetly, anxiously): I want to see it. Please.

Raphael (stares at him. Then slowly undoes his tie, takes off his jacket and shirt)

Father (draws near and observes with curiosity as if Raphael were a strange creature): I've never seen one before. Is it a bone?

Raphael (mortified): Flesh and bone.

Father: It's very smooth.

Raphael: Yes, very smooth.

Father (repulsed, reaches out, barely touching it): It's the first time I've seen one, touched one. It's disgusting. Strong, compact. Isn't it heavy? Poor thing, it must weigh you down. Like carrying around a sack of rocks. All the time. When you sleep and eat and walk. And . . . make love.

Raphael: No.

Father (anxious): You don't make love?

Raphael: No, it isn't heavy.

Father: The genes mated wrong. (*Enticed. Laughs convulsively*) What a whim! (*Stretches, straightening up*) Cover yourself up. You'll catch cold! (*Laughs*) Let's toast. I accept you. (*Rings the bell. Pours two drinks. Holds one out to Raphael who is dressing clumsily. Waits, glass in hand. Smiling*) Quickly . . . No one keeps the boss waiting. (*Raphael takes the glass, nervously, tries to drink, spills it. Father watches him, laughs*) Almost perfect. (*Hums*) The mother gets hot on me, the daughter gets seduced . . . (*Fermin entered somewhat before, responding to the ring. He has observed Raphael's clumsy movements with mocking curiosity*)

Fermin: Your tie, sir, shall I make a knot?

Raphael: No, thank you.

Father (to Fermin): Call for the ladies. The professor is here. (*Fermin leaves*) You never thought you'd have such luck . . . I'm not even asking for references. Luck. Huh? Why?

Raphael: I don't know, sir. I appreciate it.

Father: Your hunchback! Boy, it brings you luck! (*Laughs*)

Raphael: Yes, sir.

Father (looks out the window): It's raining. They say that in times like these no one is capable of persisting at anything. (*Laughs*) But those down below! They're made of good stuff! Necessity breeds persistence . . . They're waiting unconvinced . . . that they've already been forgotten! (*Dolores and Mother enter. Dolores is a pretty girl, twenty years old, lively and passionate, with a sort of fragile quality that is overcome by pride and an arrogant disdain*)

Father: My wife, my daughter Dolores. (*To Raphael*) What's your name?

Raphael: Raphael Sanchez.

Father: Raphael, let's say. (*To Dolores*) He'll teach you Latin and French. Botany. Do you know what botany is?

Dolores: Yes.

Father: What the little leaves and trees and birds are like. (*Insinuating*) Did the other one teach you that? (*Dolores turns her back on him*) And drawing. (*To Raphael*) Do you know how to teach drawing?

Raphael: Yes, sir.

Father: A gem! Dolores, you may welcome him. (*To Raphael*) She was very attached to her old teacher. Well, not so old. Right?

Dolores (looks at him defiantly): No.

Mother (timidly): He wasn't here very lo . . .

Father (glowering, shuts her up): That's the danger. If they're old they're decrepit, and if they're young, they take advantage. But some are born with crooked feet or backs, (*celebrates the comment giggling, covering his mouth*) and they're not dangerous at all. (*To Mother*) Bring your needlework and sit down over there. (*Points to the sofa*) But you can leave at any time. (*Laughs convulsively and leaves*)
(*Dolores looks at Raphael, gravely and with hostility*)

Mother (smiles clumsily): Welcome. You'll be comfortable with us. Dolores is . . .

Dolores (brusquely interrupts her): The way I am.

Mother: Sit down.

Raphael: Thank you. (*But he doesn't sit down since Dolores and Mother remain standing*)

Dolores (looks at him. After a pause): It's better to die of hunger than to accept what we don't deserve.

Raphael: I'm a good teacher.

Dolores: Or what we merit because of physical defects.

Mother (confused): Don't pay attention to her. Sit down. (*She sits down. Raphael does the same*) Will you dine with us? (*Fearing she's talked too much. Gets up. Raphael does the same*) Or . . . perhaps with the servants. But the food is good. It's the same. Only without wine.

Raphael: I'll dine with you, madam. Your husband was so kind to arrange it.

Dolores: How extraordinary! Papa is too good-hearted. (*Smiles grimacing*) You'll see. Overflowing with goodness like a river . . . (*smile disappears*) that drowns. Mama, weren't you told to go look for your needlework. And you're still here. Get going, little puppy.

Mother: Dolores!

Dolores: Come back later, there's no danger. Papa said so, (*looking at Raphael*) and that's for sure!

Mother (clumsily to Raphael): I'll be right back. If you want to start . . . (*Leaves*)

Dolores (furious, goes to the sideboard, opens a drawer. Takes out notebooks, books, a portfolio with drawings. Throws everything on the table): Come over here!

Raphael: I didn't know you had another teacher. Let's continue then . . .

Dolores: With nothing! I had another teacher with a straight back! (*Pause*) Excuse me. I meant to say . . . who didn't grovel.

Raphael: I don't either. (*Pause*) Or maybe I do. (*While she looks mockingly at him*) There are no clear limits, miss.

Dolores: For some. (*Opens the portfolio*) Come here. This is what I draw. Not bad, huh?

Raphael (looks): No. It's very good.

Dolores: I'm talented.

Raphael: I'd say so.

Dolores (laughs): My teacher did them. My hands shake. I hate drawing.

Raphael: I'll make you like it.

Dolores: Really? (*Slowly*) No one makes me like anything. No one makes me like anything!

Raphael: I mean . . .

Dolores: I'll make your hair turn gray.

Raphael: Why?

Dolores: Because my father chose you.

Raphael: He chose the other teacher, too.

Dolores: I chose the other one. Without giving it too much importance, of course. He lasted fifteen days. To me he was an old man, but to my father he seemed good-looking. Father was suspicious. (*Laughs bitterly*) Not only of me, but of mother, too.

Raphael (meekly): He won't be suspicious of me.

Dolores (looks at him): No. That's obvious.

Raphael: Don't attack me.

Dolores: Me? I wouldn't bother. Because of your nature you already feel attacked. (*Since Raphael is about to speak*) Don't answer. Would you like some wine?

Raphael: No.

Dolores: How can you have wine anyway without permission? *I* can. (*She takes some and raises the glass to Raphael. With icy fury*) A toast to you. Welcome to this house. (*Drinks. Throws the glass against the wall. Mother enters. Looks surprised. Dolores, with hypocritical sweetness*) The glass flew out of my hand, mama. I wanted to serve the teacher and the glass flew out of my hand.

Scene II

Raphael and Dolores in the drawing room. They are studying, seated on the same side of the table strewn with books and notebooks. Silence. Mother appears. Dolores looks at her coldly.

Mother (smiling uncomfortably): Is everything all right?

Raphael: Yes, ma'am. (*About to get up*)

Mother: No, no, I'm going. I just wanted to see if you needed anything.

Dolores (venomously sweet): No, mama. Such concern moves me deeply. We're studying. See?

Mother: Yes, yes. (*Clumsily*) Keep studying. See you later . . . (*Leaves*)

Dolores (imitates her with a crooked smile): Keep studying . . . I have a headache. (*Raphael is silent, his eyes on the book*) One says

"I'm sorry" or asks if it hurts a lot. One must be polite. My head aches.

Raphael (without looking up, in a monotone voice): A lot?

Dolores: Yes. So much that I can't write.

Raphael: You're coming along very well.

Dolores: I'm intelligent. (*Throws her pencil down*) I'm not in the mood! (*Sound of a cart and horses' hooves on the cobblestones. Both listen. Dolores*) Every morning it goes by. But in deference to my father, many times they don't shout . . . "melons."

Raphael (without looking up from his book): Let's continue. If you try . . .

Dolores: I said I'm not in the mood!

Raphael: The suffix "or" is added for the comparative. For example, "prudenti, prudentior" . . .

Dolores (gets up and faces him on the other side of the table. Emphatically): I don't care. I do *not* care.

Raphael (without looking at her): Your father said to spend the morning learning Latin.

Dolores: My Father's an idiot! Latin! In an uncivilized city. The best head is a severed one. The best noise is silence. And he wants me to learn Latin. You'd have to be an imbecile!

Raphael (looks at her): If you refuse to study, I'll have to tell him.

Dolores: Around here everyone's a tattler. One more won't make any difference. (*Father appears. Quickly, Dolores picks up a sheet of paper and then she and Raphael remain silent as if concentrating. Father looks at them and laughs convulsively. Raphael nods to him and is about to get up. Father gestures him to remain seated, laughs and goes off*)

Raphael: I ought to tell him . . .

Dolores: So why didn't you? (*She imitates him*) I ought to tell him . . . And what do you suppose my father will do? Will he make me do penance? (*Shakes her head no and smiles mockingly*) He'll reprimand you. That's what he's paying you for.

Raphael: Sit down, please. (*Dolores looks at him, finally sits down in her place*) And the superlative is formed by adding "ssimus," "prudenti, prudentior, prudentissimus." (*Dolores ostensibly indifferent, hums a tune*) Pay attention to me. You're making my job difficult.

Dolores: That's what they're paying you for.

Raphael: They pay me to teach you. Not for you to make fun of me.

Dolores: Yes, to make fun of you. That pleases my father. (*Fermin enters. He is carrying a garnet-red bag, holding it away from his body*)

Fermin: Excuse me, miss.

Dolores (sees the bag, gets up with a start): What's that, Fermin?

Fermin (smiling): Melons! (*Sticks his hand in the bag, then takes it out covered with blood*)

Dolores (pale): Take that away! (*Covers her mouth with her hand*) It stinks! Why . . . ?

Fermin (smiling): They went by and so I bought some! I thought, Miss would like it. (*Rummages around in the bag*)

Dolores: No, no!

Raphael: Leave!

Fermin (smiling gloomily): Don't raise your voice to me, sir. Watch out. (*To Dolores*) Miss, what do you think? I went shopping at the slaughterhouse. On the way, the cart passed by. Look. (*Takes out a melon*) It's a melon. Pure honey. I said to myself, Miss will go crazy over the melons . . .

Dolores: But I never . . . never again ate . . . ! (*She composes herself*) What a stupid joke! I'll tell my father! Brute, disgusting beast!

Fermin (very pleased): Miss! But it was your father's idea. He said to go amuse the girl and the hunchback. They're studying so much! (*Laughs*) Don't you want it?

Dolores: No! (*Turns her head away*) Raphael, let's go on with the lesson. Where were we?

Fermin (smells his hand, dries it on his clothes): I bought rotten meat. To scare you. But it was the master's idea!

Raphael: It's all right, Fermin. Tell him thank you.

Fermin (puts the melon on the table among the books): I'll leave it here. You can eat it. (*Vindictive*) I'm going to tell the master that you weren't amused! My young mistress believes that we shouldn't cut off the heads of those filthy, disgusting beasts. She's too kind.

Raphael: No. Your young mistress believes in justice. (*Doloress lifts her head, looks at him. Raphael returns her glance*). God will forgive the weak.

Dolores: But I won't forgive myself.

Fermin: Are you going to eat it or not?

Raphael: Later.

Fermin: It's not ripe! (*Laughs*) Pure honey! In winter! (*Leaves*)

Raphael (*takes the fruit and puts it on top of the sideboard*): Let's finish the lesson.

Dolores: Thanks. (*Pause*) But you don't need to speak for me.

Raphael: I won't do it again. (*Leafs through the book*) Here we are. "Prudenti, prudentior, prudentissimus."

Dolores: I said I had a headache. And now it hurts more. (*Tenderly mocking*) "Prudentissimus" Raphael.

Raphael: Please, let's go on. You're lying.

Dolores: I never lie!

Raphael: "Veritas odium parit."

Dolores: What's that? Don't you ever look me straight in the eye?

Raphael (*lifts his head and looks at her*): Truth engenders hatred.

Dolores (*laughs, then*): You're wrong. When I look at your face it seems . . .

Raphael: We haven't made any progress.

Dolores (*softly*): Have you ever had a woman?

Raphael: We haven't . . .

Dolores: We haven't to hell! (*Softly*) Have you ever had a woman? (*Raphael remains tense and silent*) No? (*Raphael shuts his eyes*) Who's going to love you? Right? That's why my father chose you. He's saving me for someone like him. Richer. I'd rather kill myself. But no, I don't like the idea of death. Do you?

Raphael: What?

Dolores: Death, dummy!

Raphael: No.

Dolores: Then we like the same things. (*She strokes the back of his hand with her finger*) What a beautiful little hand!

Raphael (*draws his hand away*): Leave me alone.

Dolores: I'll leave you. (*She moves to another spot*) You know from the front, you're not bad looking. Look at me. (*Raphael lifts his head and looks at her. Dolores, sincerely*) You have lovely eyes. Too tender. (*Awaits a comment or reaction. There is none*) When I look at you it seems to me you don't have . . .

Raphael (*finishes the sentence for her*): A hunchback? Well I do, miss.

Dolores: That relieves my father. But he's wrong. When he denies me fruit, I want to eat it all the more. Do you understand?

Raphael: No. And I don't want to.

Dolores (sweetly): Shall I explain?

Raphael (tense): No.

Dolores: There are women who . . . who can fall in love with cripples . . .

Raphael (tense): And cripples who luckily don't fall in love with imbeciles!

Dolores (laughs): Ah, so you *can* fall in love!

Raphael: Like any other man. Let's go on. The verb ending varies,
"Petrus amat . . ."

Dolores: And did they fall in love with you?

Raphael (more and more tense): "Petrus amat, Petrus . . ."

Dolores (cold and authoritarian): I asked you a question. Answer me.
Here the servants answer when they're asked something.

Raphael: Have you recovered from the scare? I'll answer the questions
that have to do with the lesson. I'm not a servant.

Dolores: Who said I was frightened? It'll take more than a stupid joke.
And yes you *are* a servant because they leave you alone . . . with
me. (*Exasperated, Raphael abruptly closes the book. Dolores smiles
sweetly*) Are you mad?

Raphael: No, miss. (*He controls himself, opens the book*) Let's go on.

Dolores: Lovely eyes . . . Tender and eager. Look at me.

Raphael: I'll never look at you.

Dolores (convincingly): No?

Raphael: You're confused.

Dolores: About what?

Raphael: The object of your . . . (*About to say something irreparable, he
controls himself*)

Dolores (coldly): Finish.

Raphael: I want to teach you what I know and that's all. It's my job and
I'll do it conscientiously. Don't flirt with me. It won't work. I'm your
teacher and you ought to obey me . . .

Dolores (laughing, then sweetly): Lovely eyes . . . eager. (*Brief pause*)
But it would be so hard to embrace you! (*Makes an offensive gesture
as if her arms don't reach around him*)

Raphael (gets up suddenly): Shut up, damn you! You hateful, spoiled
brat!

Dolores: Groveler.

Raphael: Groveler? How stupid! You haughty young lady with a full stomach!

Dolores (confronts him up close): Gro-ve-ler! (*Raphael slaps her. Dolores touches her cheek in disbelief, torn between humiliation and crying, recoils in anger*) I'll tell my father! You dare strike me! (*Rings the bell frantically*). No one has ever struck me and certainly not a . . . ! I'll tell him! He'll throw you out in the street! Hunchback!

Raphael: Don't do it!

Dolores: He'll have you jailed!

Raphael: I'm asking for your forgiveness!

Dolores: Not if you got down on your knees! (*Fermin appears*) Call my father.

Fermin: What happened, miss?

Dolores: Call my father! (*Fermin leaves*)

Raphael: Forgive me, please! You shouldn't have offended me!

Dolores: Me? There's no one here to offend!

Raphael: Don't say that. The most miserable creature can be offended.

Dolores: It's a good thing you know your place. I'll show you who obeys whom! My father will show you more quickly!

Raphael (shrugs his shoulders, sadly): As you like.
   (*Father enters*)

Father (smiling): Children?

Dolores (throws herself into his arms): He hit me!

Father: Who? Him?

Raphael: Sir . . .

Father (embraces Dolores. To Raphael, sadly): Why?

Dolores: I didn't draw well. (*Separates from him, opens the portfolio of drawings, looks for one*) You'll see papa. This drawing!

Father (sadly): It's very lovely . . .

Dolores (returns to his arms): Isn't that so, papa? Dear papa.

Father (looks at her face): He left his handprint . . . (*Caresses her gently*) So what shall we do, Dolores? What shall we do with him?

Dolores: Get rid of him.

Father: You'll be without a teacher. You'll be dumb, a little dummy. Like your mother. So if a Frenchy comes you won't know how to even say "hello." What shall we do with him?

Raphael: She's lying, sir.

Father: Shut up! (*Sweetly to Dolores*) What do you want us to do? Fermin told me he didn't like the joke. Maybe he thinks we shouldn't cut off the heads of those swine. (*To Raphael, over Dolores's shoulder*) Maybe you think that.

Raphael: No, sir. I don't think that.

Father: But this isn't solving anything. You hit my little girl. (*To Dolores*) What do you want us to do?

Dolores: Throw him in jail, beat him, throw him out . . . (*Cries*)

Father: Oh, no, no. Those pretty little eyes . . . Well, papa will do something his little girl will like. Stop crying. (*Dries her tears*) It breaks my heart. I'll buy you a dress. We'll have a party!

Dolores (hugs him, coyly): Thank you, papa. (*Hiccups*) But he hit me!

Father: Yes, he hit you. That's bad! Papa isn't forgetting.

Raphael: She provoked me, sir.

Father (looks at him and answers with a convulsive laugh. Stops laughing): Papa is good, but he gets very angry when his little girl cries. (*Sits down and puts Dolores on his knee*)

Raphael: I'll leave, sir.

Father (pays no attention to him): Here, like when you were little. (*Bounces her up and down*) Horsey! Let's play riddles. All right?

Dolores (coyly): Yes.

Father: Let's see if you guess the first one. (*As if playing a children's game*) Who is the strongest servant?

Dolores: Fermin.

Father: Who has the broadest waist?

Dolores: Fermin.

Father: The strongest arm?

Dolores (laughs): Fer-min!

Father: And the thickest back?

Dolores (naughty): Raphael (*Raphael backs up until he bumps into the chair*) He got scared! (*She gets up*) He got scared, papa! (*Goes toward Raphael*) Hit me again! Hunchback, lackey. Groveler! Isn't that the word that offended you? Groveler! (*Terrified, Raphael moves her aside and makes for the door. When he opens it, Fermin stands in the doorway, and grabs him*)

Raphael: Let go of me! (*He struggles uselessly. Father looks on and laughs convulsively. At that moment Dolores understands that the game is over, becomes frightened and bursts out crying in anguish*)

126

Scene III

Morning. Dolores and Mother in the drawing room. Books and folders on the table.

Mother: You shouldn't have done it.

Dolores: He shouldn't have done it.

Mother: Your father is harsh.

Dolores (guilty but proud): No one raises a hand to me.

Mother: Yes. But there are many ways to strike out.

Dolores (mocking): What a wise woman. Too bad you don't use that wisdom to your own advantage. They hit you in many ways, but none irritates you enough. (*Mother looks at her and moves toward the door*) Mama! (*Begging*) Stay.

Mother: No. I have to see about lunch. I hope you eat a little . . . today. (*Vindictive*) This isn't the way to win his forgiveness.

Dolores: His forgiveness? *Me* win *his* forgiveness?

Mother: No, of course not. So then eat. (*Pause*) And sleep at night.

Dolores: You're spying on me.

Mother: I'm taking care of you.

Dolores: Oh, so that's what you call it!!

Mother: Pride doesn't mix well with repentance.

Dolores: Yes it does! If not, it's useless. (*Proud, but on the verge of tears*) I tell you, no one strikes me. I'm not like you!

Mother: I'll go see about lunch.

Dolores: Mama! (*Her voice cracks*) Stay.

Mother: No. (*Leaves*)

Dolores (agitated, leafs through the folder. Sound of a cart going by. Dolores remains still, pays attention. Sound of a vendor shouting something indistinguishable. When he stops, Dolores slams the folder shut, strikes it with her fist. Raphael enters, walking more bent over than usual. They look at each other long and hard. Then, suddenly, Dolores offers him a chair): Sit down. (*Raphael keeps on staring at her. Dolores, uncomfortable*) How . . . are you?

Raphael: All right . . .(*adds*) miss. (*Stares at her*)

Dolores: Why are you staring at me?

Raphael (turns away): Excuse me.

Dolores (now she looks at him in another way, guilty, sadly, and with feeling. After a silence): Look at me.

Raphael (raises his eyes to her, indifferent): Let's go on . . .

Dolores: You said you would never look at me.

Raphael (indifferent): I was wrong. Let's go on . . .

Dolores: I don't want to. In three days I've forgotten everything.

Raphael: We'll review.

Dolores: Nothing you teach me is useful. Did you hear them shout "melons" today?

Raphael: No.

Dolores: Lucky you. They went by twice. The first time they left a head on the corner.

Raphael: I didn't see anything.

Dolores: You got up late.

Raphael: Perhaps. I didn't feel . . . well.

Dolores (softly): I know. I want to tell you . . .

Raphael: Never mind. They pay me to teach you.

Dolores: I told you those things are useless.

Raphael: Useless or not, I have to teach you. They're paying me. Salary, room, and board. With the family.

Dolores (looks at him. Suddenly): Let's begin! (*She sits down. Raphael does not*) Sit down.

Raphael (suffering from the beating): I feel better standing.

(*Fermin comes in carrying a tray with one cup and a pitcher of hot chocolate*)

Fermin: Excuse me, miss. Madam told me to serve you some hot chocolate. Do you remember when I used to bring it to you in bed?

Dolores (abruptly): I don't remember that.

Fermin: Oh, how we used to laugh! (*Serves*)

Dolores: Not any more.

Fermin (holds the cup out to her): I used to bring you gifts. What did you bring me, Fermin? you used to say. Don't let it get cold.

Dolores (angry): For me? Just for me? Don't you see I'm not alone?

Fermin (mocking): Yes, miss.

Dolores: Well?

Fermin: Some company doesn't count. (*Looks at Raphael with mocking superiority. Smiles*)

Dolores (furious): Who told you to smile? Who gave you permission? Did I? Did I crack a joke? Are we in on something together?

Fermin: No, miss.

Dolores: Then wipe that grin off your face, lackey! And get rid of this! (*Takes the cup and puts it on the tray*) There are two people here!

Fermin: Your mother . . .

Dolores: My mother doesn't run this house! I told you to take it away! (*Grabs the tray and throws it violently against the door*)

Fermin (humbly, bends down, picks up the pitcher and the pieces of broken cup): Excuse me, miss. You shouldn't get mad at me. (*Leaves. Silence*)

Raphael (barely smiling): It's not enough.

Dolores: What's not enough?

Raphael: You know.

Dolores: Don't think just because I'm defending you . . . ! (*Raphael laughs bitterly. Dolores, angrily*) Don't laugh!

Raphael (stops smiling): No, I won't laugh either unless you give me permission.

Dolores: What's not enough?

Raphael: You know.

Dolores: Stop repeating yourself.

Raphael: And you?

Dolores (in an outburst): I can . . . ! (*Controls herself. Painfully humble*) Please.

Raphael: What do you want now? It was time for French and botany. But we can do something else. If your father doesn't find out. (*Changing the tone of his voice*) What do you want?

Dolores (looks at him. Painfully humble): For you to forgive me. (*Draws near*)

Raphael: Me? . . . What for?

Dolores: Forgive me. (*Draws near*)

Raphael (moves away): Miss, someone could come in and we're not working.

Dolores: You're forgetting to add that I might get you involved. Don't be . . . (*stops*)

Raphael (meekly): Don't get me in trouble.

Dolores (scornfully): You're all lackeys!

Raphael (explodes, angrily): All right! What do you want from me? Forgiveness? Are you asking my forgiveness? Mine? If that makes you happy, you're forgiven. You can commit all kinds of insults and you'll be pardoned.

Dolores: Not like that!

Raphael: Yes, like that! So beautiful, the society lady and her powerful father, yes, like that! How else do you want lackeys to forgive? We pardon like lackeys! Now let's begin! Sit down! (*He grabs her violently by the shoulder to seat her*)

Dolores (resists. Lifts her head and looks at him close up. Both remain motionless. Dolores, as if discovering him): I love you . . .

Raphael: Be still.

Dolores (terrified): I love you . . . I love you with your angry eyes . . .

Raphael: Be quiet!

Dolores (leans against him. Impulsively): I love your nose, your legs, your teeth, your tongue.

Raphael: I hate you. (*Pushes her away*)

Dolores (pays no attention. Anxious and sweet): Didn't you hear me? Didn't you hear what I said?

Raphael (in suspense. Very softly, as if someone else were talking): If . . .

Dolores (pressing): Yes, what?

Raphael: Yes . . . Dolores . . .

Dolores (pressing): Dolores, what?

Raphael: Dolores . . . my happiness.

Dolores (pressing): Am I?

Raphael (for a moment it seems he's going to say yes. Then, decisively): No.

Dolores: You said yes!

Raphael (moves away): Get away. (*Vindictive*) Did you amuse yourself like this with the other guy?

Dolores: What other guy?

Raphael: The teacher your father threw out!

Dolores: I didn't even look at him!

Raphael: No? But a little flirting with a lackey can distract you, it kills time.

Dolores: Don't you understand anything? Don't you know anything about repentance? (*Draws close to him*) Hit me!

Raphael (quietly): And you won't cry groveler? You won't call your father? What a temptation!

Dolores (beats his chest with her fists): How can *you* reject *me?* What must I do? How must I talk to you?

Raphael (motionless): Just like that. Now I recognize you.

Dolores (lowers her arms): Forgive me.

Raphael: You shouldn't excuse yourself. I understand your fits, miss.

Dolores: Please . . .

Raphael (slowly): Leave me alone! I don't want to be anyone's plaything, and least of all yours! If I were . . .

Dolores: What you're not. Taller, more handsome, straighter, I wouldn't love you. (*Draws close and stretches her hand out toward Raphael's face*)

Raphael: You're forgetting about me. (*He lowers her arm*) Whom should I love, miss? You, the way you are?

Dolores (humble): Me . . . the way I am.

Raphael: You're asking a lot.

Dolores: No. (*Laughs trembling*) You said . . . Dolores my happiness.

Raphael: Because . . . (*searches for the word*) it sounded good. Even if it wasn't true. (*Recovers his anger*) And you don't deserve forgiveness either! My back hurts! He beat me right on my hump!

Dolores: Forgive me. I ask your forgiveness!

Raphael: I said I forgave you! If someone is forgiven everything it means he doesn't deserve forgiveness at all. Like forgetfulness, miss! If you forget everything, you bury it, you decapitate your memory. Is that the kind of forgetfulness you want? Do you need to clear your conscience? Well, I give you my permission! Now leave me in peace!

Dolores: No. I won't leave you alone. I want you to hate me . . . for what I did to you . . . and to forgive me.

Raphael: You have my hatred. (*Laughs*) And forgiveness!

Dolores: I love you.

Raphael: What do you know about that?

Dolores: I know I love you.

Raphael (mimics her bitterly): "I know I love you." You're aroused too quickly, don't you think? You're just a silly child. "I know I love you!" I'm not just a nobody. I eat with you people. I have my own room. "I know I love you!" (*Laughs*) You love a servant! A lackey, as you say.

Dolores: No!

Raphael: Yes, a servant who can be punished with impunity. Do you know what my hunchback is full of? Humiliation! A servant's humiliation, of course.

Dolores: No one ever humiliated you. I'm the one who feels humiliated because I had you . . .

Raphael (smiling sarcastically): Punished? No, miss, it's not the same. Don't worry. I'm a servant. They always serve me last, I only speak when spoken to, and I must say, yes, sir, yes, miss. And in my wonderful room my hunchback bumps up against the walls!

Dolores: I love you!

Raphael: You love me? Yes, sir! (*Laughs, catches himself*) Yes, miss! Your father's going to be delighted!

Dolores: Don't talk to me about my father!

Raphael: He'll dance a jig when he finds out! And then do somersaults!

Dolores (embraces him): Don't punish me!

Raphael (vindictive): But I'm not punishing you! I'll go to bed with you and make you a hunchbacked child. We hunchbacks can make children! Did you think of that? It will be amusing!

Dolores: No, no!

Raphael: No, no? Yes! We'll laugh together, you and I!

Dolores (hides her face on his shoulder): Don't punish me, Raphael!

Raphael: Your father's little grandchild! With a twisted neck, and if we're lucky, a hump bigger than mine because of his young flesh.

Dolores: I love you!

Raphael (pushes her away): Be still! (*Sound of the cart passing by*) Do you hear? It keeps going by. Your head will be there, too. And mine! It's not worth it, miss! It's not worth it to me! (*Dolores turns her back to him and muffles a sigh*) Now come the tears. Young ladies cry when they don't get their way.

Dolores (dries her tears. Faces him, proudly): Who's crying?

Raphael: I like you better this way. (*They look at each other from a distance, like two enemies. Fermin enters, observes them, mockingly suspicious. Again he's carrying a tray with a pitcher and one cup*)

Fermin: By mistake the professor was served in his room. The servants are very busy now. And I have an urgent message from the master. (*Serves the hot chocolate*) Drink it while it's hot. Study a lot. (*Goes toward the door*) And don't get mad at me, miss. I can make mistakes, too. (*At the doorway, as if by chance, by insinuation, he puts both hands on his broad belt. To Raphael*) You're not annoyed, are you?

Raphael: No. Thank you, Fermin. Later I'll have some hot chocolate in my room.

Fermin: You don't mind if it's cold, do you?
Raphael: No. It doesn't matter.
(*Fermin smiles, leaves and shuts the door*)
Dolores: Have you forgiven me?
Raphael (decisively): No. (*They look at each other intensely. Long silence*) Yes . . . (*Brightly smiling, Dolores runs toward him*)

Scene IV

Dolores and Mother in Dolores's room. A shawl on a chair. Mother holds a dress in her arms; Dolores, in a slip, hums. When Mother approaches with the dress and holds it out so Dolores can put her head through, Dolores bows to her and takes off in the other direction. She dances about humming.

Mother: Dolores, come on. Get dressed. (*Looks at her*) You're happy.
Dolores: Why not?
Mother: I'm glad you're happy.
Dolores: Papa's idea is wonderful. (*Sweetly*) He makes the plans for people and they agree.
Mother: That person is his daughter.
Dolores: Or his wife. Or his servants . . . No one can say no to the master of the house. He moves his little finger and that's that.
Mother: That gentleman is your father.
Dolores: And the other gentleman, mama? The one who chops off heads?
Mother: Oh! Whoever hears you would think he cuts heads off all day long. He's good-natured. He doesn't like to do it.
Dolores (smiles): No.
Mother: They go against him and give him no choice.
Dolores (sweetly suspicious): I don't go against him, mama. I let him choose. Did he make a good choice?
Mother: Yes. (*Draws near with the dress*)
Dolores (runs off): What's he like?
Mother: A fine young man.
Dolores: Rich.
Mother: Good-looking and rich. Let's go. Your father gets impatient.
Dolores: What do I care? Handsome and rich. But fifty years old, right?

Mother: No. He's young. You must have seen him already!

Dolores: I swear I haven't! Where?

Mother: At mass. He's so in love . . .

Dolores (mocks): How exciting! (*Whirls around, hums*) I'm so in love, too!

Mother: Don't make fun of me. Let's go.

Dolores: It's better for him to wait, mama. He'll become more . . . ! (*finishes with a suggestive gesture*)

Mother: But your father! He gets mad at the drop of a hat and then takes it out on me.

Dolores: He's never *with* you, always *against* you. And you like it. (*She looks at Mother's arm*) What happened here? He really pinches when he's mad!

Mother: I bumped into a door.

Dolores: Yes. Because you're dumb and blind.

Mother: Get dressed.

Dolores (dresses): What's his name?

Mother: John Peter.

Dolores: John Peter what?

Mother (hesitates): Goldenfields.

Dolores: What?

Mother: Goldenfields.

Dolores (smiles in disbelief): It can't be . . .

Mother: Why not? What's the matter?

Dolores: Oh, mama! (*Enticed*) is that his real name . . . since childhood?

Mother: Yes. His name is . . . Goldenfields!

Dolores: Mama, it can't be true! (*Laughs*) Is that what's in store for me? What have I done to deserve it? Goldenfields! (*Laughs*)

Mother: So what? (*Smiles*) It's a good name!

Dolores: Yes! Goldenfields! Brilliant! Silverfields would have been worse! (*Laughs*) How . . . how can I marry him? Oh! You shouldn't have . . . you shouldn't have told me! . . .

Mother (smiles): What's wrong? His name isn't . . .

Dolores: Floodedfields . . . ? (*She has a laughing fit, embraces Mother, who breaks out laughing uncontrollably. The two laugh, embracing each other. Stopping little by little*)

Mother: Let's go . . .

Dolores (with her head resting on Mother's shoulder): Mama . . .

Mother: What?

Dolores (draws away a little and looks at her): How pretty you are like this.

Mother: How?

Dolores: Like this, laughing.

Mother (becomes serious): Let's go, your father is waiting . . . (*Tries to pull away*)

Dolores (holds her back): Why not say: let your father wait . . .

Mother: That's enough. (*Pulls free*) He has a bad temper. You'd better comb your hair.

Dolores: So do I.

Mother (tries to comb her hair): You ought to tie your hair back . . .

Dolores (pushes her away, shakes her head): There's no need to.

Mother: Then let's go.

Dolores: Dolores Goldenfields! (*Laughs unhappily. Mother doesn't join in. Dolores tickles her under the chin*) Laugh.

Mother: That's enough now.

Dolores: It's a good name. You're right. At least it made you forget.

Mother: Forget what?

Dolores: That you can't laugh.

(Father enters)

Father: So? I'm fed up entertaining that idiot! What are you waiting for?

Mother: We're coming, Benigno. We're ready.

Dolores: Oh, this one has a great name, too! (*Laughs*) Benigno is *so-o-o* kind!

Father (looks at her, gloomily): Just what's going on here?

Dolores: I'm happy.

Father (softens): Really? (*Caresses her cheek*) Did I make a good choice this time?

Dolores: You couldn't have left it up to me, could you, papa?

Father: What are you saying, Dolores? You're just a child, my girl. (*Kisses her on the forehead*) I want the best for you.

Dolores (for a second she leans against him): I know you're telling the truth. And the terrible thing is that it's touching. (*Draws away. Alters tone of voice*) Let's go, papa. Is he an idiot?

Father (tender): No. I would never marry you off to an idiot. (*He smiles affectionately. Looks at Mother and his face becomes gloomy*) Dear, you should be more tactful. You're not a nobody.

Mother (insecure, touches her hair): What's wrong? What did I do wrong?

Father: Change your dress.

Mother: Why? You used to like this one a lot.

Father: Long sleeves are more discreet . . . for a married woman.

Mother: I have a shawl (*Puts it on*)

Father: It can slide off. (*He makes it slide off. Looks at her arm*) What would he think?

Dolores: That a door banged into her, papa.

Father: Yes.

Dolores: And she's blind and dumb.

Father: Yes. (*Pause*) I'm not honored to have made such a bad choice. (*Leaves. Mother and Dolores look at each other*)

Dolores: I'm ready now. Let's go.

Mother: No.

Dolores: They're waiting for us.

Mother: I'll change my dress. (*They look at each other*)

Scene V

Drawing room. Father and John Peter Goldenfields, a good-looking young man, too well dressed. They are seated, Father's fingers drumming on his knees. Silence. Raphael enters.

Raphael: You called me, sir?

Father (without looking at him): Yes, stay here. (*John Peter glances at him. Raphael remains standing near the door. Father drums on his knees. Prolonged, uncomfortable silence. John Peter smiles at no one in particular. He realizes it and stops. Father, in an annoyed voice, mumbles*) Women always keep you waiting.

John: Yes.

Father: She was ready. But had to change her red dress . . . (*smiles slyly*) for another red one.

John: Yes.

Father: They always want to look better.

John: Dolores is very young.

Father: Dolores . . . ? (*In a vulgar tone*) I meant the old lady. My wife. (*Laughs convulsively*) Excuse my familiarity. She's my wife, right? (*He looks at John awaiting an answer*) I can take a few liberties.

John (uncomfortable): Yes.

Father (gets up, barely controlling himself. John does the same. Father smiles at him hypocritically): She's got me under her thumb.

John: Some prisons are sweet, sir.

Father (looks at him, bursts out laughing amused, pats him on the shoulder. Dolores and Mother enter. He greets them, laughing): Finally! (*Courteously, kisses their hands*)

Dolores (feigning sweetness): Mama had to change her dress. Remember you told her to?

Father: Me? Your mother's vain. And indecisive. (*Introduces*) John Peter. My wife, my daughter Dolores.

(John Peter kisses their hands. Dolores smiles and looks at him mockingly. Mother and Dolores sit down on the sofa)

Father: Raphael, serve us a drink.

Dolores: Fermin is here, papa.

Father (pays no attention, to John Peter): Do you prefer a liqueur, we have a cherry liqueur, tea or . . . perhaps some *mate**?

John: Not *mate*. It disagrees with me. I'll have . . . some liqueur.

Father: Liqueur, Raphael. (*Raphael goes to the sideboard, takes out a bottle and glasses. John Peter watches him with curiosity. Father discovers his glance*) He's Dolores's teacher. Her tutor here at home. One of the family. But it's always wise to be cautious . . . when choosing. (*Laughs convulsively*)

John (takes a moment to understand): Oh! (*Laughs discreetly*) Very wise, sir! My father chose a stupid teacher for me because he couldn't stand having anyone smarter than me around.

Dolores (sweetly): How difficult that must have been!

John: Why? Am I so stupid?

Dolores (Sweetly): No. I was just kidding. (*Silly laughter*)

Father: Dolores studies French. And Latin, which no one studies.

Dolores: And drawing, papa.

Father: And drawing. You can show him your sketches, Dolores.

Mother (timidly): There's one I like . . .

Dolores (interrupts her without listening): Of course! I can recite a poem too! Would you like to hear a poem?

John: It would be a pleasure.

*A hot beverage with stimulant properties made from the dry leaves of the South American holly.

Dolores (without getting up from the sofa, with a vacant stare):
   I am surrounded by imbeciles
   and pretend I am stupid
   the imbeciles believe me
   so I keep on acting dumb.
(Looks at John Peter) What do you think?
John (perplexed, tries to laugh): . . . It's nice . . .
Dolores (with a syrupy smile): Really?
John: Nice, but very obvious.
Dolores: How so?
Father (puts his hand on her shoulder and squeezes): Dolores is spoiled. She's an only child, and needs a firm hand.
Dolores (abruptly): You're hurting me, papa.
Father (hypocritically): Sorry. *(Removes his hand)* Strong hand, soft touch. That's what the ladies need. *(Sound of a cart going by)* And not only the ladies.
John: I agree. That's not a high price to pay for peace.
Dolores (malicious smile): If *others* pay.
John: Or for wealth.
Dolores: If *you're* the one to enjoy it . . . and father.
Father (as if playing, sweetly and quietly, with pent-up anger, he strikes her on the mouth with the tips of his fingers): Dolores, silence is golden. So be quiet! Raphael? That drink?
Raphael (picks up the tray he had left on the table and serves): Right away, sir.
Father (toward John Peter): To your health! *(Drinks)*
John: To yours. And to the ladies'! *(Drinks)*
Dolores: Raphael, why didn't you help yourself? Don't you like liqueur?
Raphael: Thank you, miss. I don't . . . drink.
Father: Help yourself, Raphael! You're one of the family! *(To John Peter)* He eats with us.
John: And . . . it doesn't bother you?
Dolores (curtly): Why?
John: I . . . I'm particularly sensitive when it comes to cripples . . . Any physical defect makes me cringe.
Mother (smiles kindly): But Raphael is . . .
Father (doesn't pay attention to her): I'll tell him to go! Raphael, leave! After all there's no reason for you to put up with us.

Raphael: As you wish, sir. (*Bows*)

Dolores: No! (*Smiles at John Peter*) As proof of your affection for me let him stay. You couldn't be so weak, could you?

John: I'm sensitive. But of course, let him stay if you like. (*Villainous little laugh*) I'll look at him sideways!

Raphael (gets ready to leave): Good day.

John: The young lady wants you to stay. And her wish is my command.

Father (since Raphael hesitates): Stay.

Raphael: Yes, sir.

(*Fermin enters holding a tray. On the tray, a silver plate with a cup*)

Father: What is it, Fermin?

Fermin: I know the professor doesn't drink so I brought him some tea.

Father: And since when . . . ? (*Catching on*) Oh, all right!

Fermin (to Raphael): Help yourself.

Raphael: Thank you. (*Takes the plate, which is red hot and burns his fingers. Screams and drops everything*)

Dolores (gets up, furious): Father, how can you allow . . . ?

Father (laughing convulsively): Fermin, you beast! Raphael, did you burn yourself?

Raphael (face contorted): No, sir. (*Bends down to get the cup. Mother, who stood up alarmed, sits down again. Shakes her head, meekly disapproving*)

Fermin: Leave it, I'm the servant.

Dolores: Papa, how can you tolerate . . . ?

Father: It's only a joke. Fermin, if you do that again I'll kick you out.

Fermin (pleased): Yes, sir. (*Leaves*)

Father: Sit down, Dolores. Nothing happened. Calm her, Raphael.

Raphael: I didn't burn myself, miss.

John: How curious . . . (*looks aside*)

Father (confidentially): You saw it! (*Laughs, chokes*)

Dolores (abruptly): Mother plays the piano.

Mother (shy): No, Dolores! What are you saying?

Dolores (to John Peter): Would you like to dance?

John (gets up): Delighted. If your parents will allow me. But madam was not sure . . .

Father: Madam has no doubts. It's a good opportunity to show she exists! (*Laughs, chokes*)

Mother: It's been so long since . . .

Dolores (quietly): Papa prefers to think in silence. And mama was always playing some kind of music. (*Stretches her fingers out*) The keyboard cover fell on top of her fingers! (*Laughs bitterly*)

Mother (hurriedly): It was an accident! Because of that . . . I probably play very poorly. I don't even remember how. It's been so long since . . .

Father: Come now, don't be vain. (*Sincerely*) I have a bad temper. Music irritated me. You ought to know me by now.

Mother (disarmed and almost tender): I know you, Benigno.

Father: Then you know I'm asking you sincerely.

Dolores: Raphael, will you dance? Won't you join us?

Rapahel: Pardon me, miss. I'll excuse myself.

John (laughing): Oh how funny it would be! (*Covers his eyes*) I'll peek out between my fingers so it won't affect me!

Dolores (with a look that kills): Affect you how?

John: Sometimes I'm clumsy.

Dolores (smiles hatefully): No! Everyone's tactless nowadays. Shall we dance? Raphael?

Raphael: No thank you, miss.

Father: Dance, Raphael. I didn't ask you if you were a dance teacher. But a man of your talents knows everything. (*Mother has already seated herself at the piano and tries the keyboard. Father draws near*) Do you remember?

Mother (raises her happy face toward him): Yes, Benigno, I remember! (*She begins to play a minuet very poorly, then catches on*) John (approaches Dolores with an outstretched hand, quickly glances towards the parents and when he sees they're not watching, in a vulgar gesture grabs at her breast. Dolores pulls away and looks at him stupefied. As if the gesture had nothing to do with him, John Peter listens to the music for a minute and at a given moment offers Dolores his hand. After hesitating briefly, Dolores accepts. They dance)

Dolores: Please, Raphael, join us. (*She stares at him*) You're not going to be afraid to dance.

Raphael: Excuse me, miss.

Dolores (irritated): Don't ask for my pardon! (*Moves away from John Peter, who finishes a dance step ending up where Dolores should be. But she is dancing alone on the other side of the room*) I want you to dance . . . with me. (*Without drawing near, she holds out her hand to Raphael*)

Raphael: I'll make a . . . fool of myself.

Dolores (defiant): Yes.

Raphael: Pathetic.

Dolores: Yes!

Father (laughs convulsively, misinterpreting the scene): Dolores . . . (*Timidly, Raphael comes forward. The three of them dance, but it's obvious that Dolores is paying no attention to John Peter. She and Raphael stare at each other. Father watches them amused, but gradually he stops smiling, watching gloomily. Rings the bell. Then hits the piano with the palm of his hand*) A waltz! (*Mother stops playing, the dancing stops*) Do you like waltzes, Dolores?

Dolores: Yes, papa.

Father (to Mother): A waltz then.

Mother (content): Benigno, you're asking for a lot!

Father: No, it's easy. (*Hums*) You used to play it when we were engaged. (*He takes her hand and kisses it*) Try. For me.

Mother (smiles timidly at that sign of affection and tries to remember the waltz: begins, makes mistakes, catches on): I thought I didn't like music anymore, but . . . (*Lifts her head, smiles at father, who returns the smile. Surprised*) I like it! If it doesn't bore you! (*Plays. Fermin enters*)

Fermin: Sir?

Father: The young people are dancing.

Fermin: I'm glad, sir.

Father: Raphael has no partner.

Fermin (understands the hint and so the entire dialogue occurs with both knowing exactly where it is leading): What should I do? Look for a maid?

Father: No! That's not good enough. Besides, since when do maids dance the waltz? They dance "candombe"* to African drums, Fermin.

Fermin: And what about me?

Father: You're more than a servant.

Fermin: Thank you, sir. (*Smiles*) Shall I dance with him?

Father: Be so kind . . .

---

*A dance of African origins still seen in Argentina and Uruguay during Carnival.

Dolores (becomes pale): That's not necessary, papa.

Fermin: Will he dance with me?

Father: He'll be delighted, isn't that so Raphael? Fermin's not very elegant, but . . . (*Laughs. Mother stops*) Don't stop! Keep playing.

Fermin: How should I dance?

Father: However you like.

Fermin: Slowly?

Father: Very slowly.

Fermin (ironically to Raphael): May I have this dance?

Raphael (confronts the humiliation, proudly): Yes! As many as you like . . . miss.

Fermin: No! You're the lady! (*He grabs him by the waist; they dance*)

John (smiling looks on, then at Dolores): Shall we dance? (*Without answering, Dolores runs toward the door. Quickly, her father stops her, and holds her against his chest*)

Father (feigning sweetness): Why are you leaving? Are you tired of our company?

Dolores: No, papa. I'm not tired.

Father: Then dance. (*Pause*) Or look at the happy couple. Aren't they delightful?

Dolores: Yes . . . papa. (*John Peter lets loose a snicker*) Why are you laughing?

John (smiling): Excuse me. Like your father says, they're delightful.

Dolores: Yes! Let go of me, papa. I won't leave. (*Father releases her. Dolores looks at him*) I like to see people make fools of themselves.

Father (points to Fermin and Raphael): You have to look at *them.* (*Draws near to the piano*) Faster! What a sleepy waltz! (*To Mother*) You used to be livelier. You loved me more. Faster! (*Pounds with his open hand on the piano. Mother quickens the beat, not so much because Father has asked her to but for her own pleasure. Raphael is exhausted but fights to keep up with Fermin*) Faster! (*Fermin picks up the pace even more*)

Dolores (looks, can't stand it): Enough! (*To Mother*) Stop playing!

Father: Faster!

Dolores: I don't want them to dance! (*Tries to separate Raphael and Fermin, but the two are whirling around so rapidly that she is pushed from one side to the other. Defeated*) Please, please . . . (*Jostled, she falls over John Peter*)

John: What beasts! (*Helps her get up. With a quick glance, sees no one is watching them and grabs Dolores vulgarly, taking advantage of the moment*)

Dolores (pushing him away. Looks at him as if she doesn't recognize him): Please, please . . .

Father (shouts, banging his open hand on the piano while Fermin and Raphael dance in a whirl, turning and spinning around): Faster! Faster! Faster!

Scene VI

The drawing room. Books and notebooks on the table. Dolores and Raphael. Dolores raises the top of the piano, plays a few notes.

Dolores: My mother always used to play the piano. She likes music. But my father hates to see anyone else have fun. Since he can't give pleasure, he's inspired by hate. And he calls it love. My mother no longer plays the piano; she thinks he doesn't like music. What's even more curious is that . . . she also calls my father's hate, love. And sometimes . . . I even think of it the same way.

Raphael (gently removes her hands from the keys, closes the top): Let's study.

Dolores: Don't you want me to tell you something?

Raphael: No, miss . . . Dolores. It's not my place to know anything. (*Sits down at the desk without looking at her*) Why did you want to separate us yesterday? In the end . . . you couldn't see me make a fool of myself.

Dolores: No, you weren't the fool. You *do* believe me?

Raphael (looks at her, doesn't answer. Gently): Sit down. (*She sits at his side. Raphael opens a book, reads*)

> Elle avait pris ce pli dans son âge enfantin
> De venir dans ma chambre un peu chaque matin
> Je l'attendais ainsi qu'un rayon qu'on espère . . .

(*Raises his eyes to her*) Et je lui disais: je t'aime.

Dolores (looks at him): And I said: I love you.

Raphael: In French, it's "je t'aime." (*Feigns reading*) Il lui disait: je t'aime.

Dolores: I love you.

Raphael (pauses): You shouldn't do this . . . to me. (*Looks at her, utters his own words*) Je t'aime.

Dolores (puts her hand on top of his): We'll go away together. His name is Goldenfields. And he's set the wedding date for three months from now.

Raphael: In Latin they say destiny lies in a name.

Dolores (apprehensive): My name is Dolores. Is that my destiny? Suffering?

Raphael: Your real name is Beauty or Happiness. Dolores my happiness.

Dolores: We'll go away together.

Raphael: Where?

Dolores: Far away. (*The door opens. Dolores pulls her hand away quickly. Fermin enters with a tray, pitcher, and one cup. He puts it all down on the table, looks at them with curiosity and leaves*)

Dolores: Where they'll serve us two cups of hot chocolate and we can drink them together. Where they don't shout about melons and leave heads behind. Where my father doesn't exist. Where at least hate will be called by its real name.

Raphael: It's impossible.

Dolores: You're afraid.

Raphael: I'm not afraid. But I know it's impossible. We won't be able to hide. My hunchback will give us away.

Dolores: You mean it's not worth it?

Raphael: Yes it is. (*His hand reaches out and squeezes Dolores's. Fermin enters and Raphael quickly withdraws his hand*)

Dolores: What do you want, Fermin? Who called for you?

Fermin: The master has to give some instructions to the hunchback. He wants to see him.

Dolores (furious): Don't call him that!

Raphael: It doesn't matter. That's what I am. (*Smiles meekly. Mocking*) I'm "made in such a way that a poor painter couldn't have drawn me worse in the dark." I'll be right back. (*Leaves. Fermin remains in the drawing room, shuffles around, indecisively*)

Dolores: What do you want?

Fermin (shyly): I brought you something.

Dolores: What?

Fermin (puts his hand in his pocket, takes out a dark-colored little bird and offers it to Dolores): It's dead.

144

Dolores: Yes.

Fermin: I like dead things, don't you?

Dolores: No, Fermin.

Fermin: They don't move. They don't scold.

Dolores: I'm scolding you. You're mean to Raphael.

Fermin: He doesn't care.

Dolores: I do.

Fermin: Does your father know that?

Dolores: What?

Fermin: That you care about him?

Dolores: I only care that you don't call him . . .

Fermin (pleased): Hunch-back. All right. I won't call him that anymore. (*Insists on showing her the dead bird*) Do you want it?

Dolores: No.

Fermin (not understanding. Smiles): You're kidding! Take it! (*He puts it in her hand*) When you were a child you used to like the presents I brought you.

Dolores (softly): They terrified me.

Fermin (hurt): During one whole summer I brought you spiders!

Dolores: They terrified me.

Fermin: Give it back! (*He takes the bird. Furious*) His hump is covered with scars! From me!

Dolores: Shut up!

Fermin: From my hand! Because of you! If you want . . .

Dolores: What?

Fermin: I can grab him one night and . . .

Dolores (frightened): No, that's not necessary.

Fermin: I'm good to you. I know you from birth.

Dolores: Yes. Give it to me. (*Holds her hand out toward the little bird*)

Fermin: (willful): No! (*Hides it behind his back*) I broke its neck for you, and you despise me for it.

Dolores: I was wrong. Give it to me. (*Like a willful child, Fermin shakes his head no*) Yes. I'll take care of it. (*Fermin gives her the little bird. Dolores takes it, smoothes its feathers with the tip of her finger*) It's pretty.

Fermin (smiles): So still. It doesn't sing.

Dolores: Thank you, Fermin. I'll keep it. Now . . . run along.

Fermin: Aren't you going to give me a reward for my gift?

Dolores: Yes. (*Fermin draws near, kneels and kisses her foot. Dolores separates him from her immediately*)

Fermin: Before you used to let me do more. I don't like you to be with him so much. I told the master.

Dolores: What did you tell him?

Fermin (wickedly): Are you interested? What'll you give me if I tell you?

Dolores: Nothing! Gossips make me sick!

Fermin: Give me the little bird!

Dolores (laughs with difficulty): No, Fermin! Why are you getting mad? It's a pretty bird . . . only it's dead. (*Caresses it*) Thank you, Fermin.

Fermin: If you like it . . . let me. (*Dolores puts her foot out, Fermin kisses her shoe, stretches his hand timidly toward her ankle*)

Dolores: Enough! (*Softens her tone of voice*) That's enough, Fermin. My dear Fermin. My father is probably looking for you. You're his right hand.

Fermin (gets up): You bet I'm his right hand! (*Goes toward the door. Turns around*) It's been a while since you've called me dear Fermin. I won't tell the master anything! And I'll look for more presents for you, like before! (*About to leave*) And don't you talk so much with the hunchback! I left my mark on his hump! (*Laughs, leaves*)

Dolores: It was my fault. Hunchback. Why don't I say it, why does it offend me when others say it? (*With determination*) Hunch-back. My Raphael is a hunchback. No! He doesn't have a hunchback or any other defect. I would love him without legs. Blind. (*Carefully, without looking, puts the bird on the table. Without looking, wipes her hands*) Hunch-back. Why did I fall in love with a hunchback if there are so many, straight normal men who walk around without any weight on their backs! (*With determination*) The hunchback Raphael. Hunch-back! (*Covers her mouth*) I can't!

(*Raphael enters*)

Raphael: I don't know why he called me! Some nonsense! Something he cooked up with Fermin and . . . (*looks at her*) What's wrong?

Dolores: Nothing. (*Gets up*) I'm looking at you.

Raphael (sadly): And what do you see?

Dolores (runs to him, embraces him, repeats with certainty): You're beautiful, beautiful, beautiful!

Scene VII

Dolores and Mother in the drawing room. Mother straightens out Dolores's dress. Looks at her.

Mother: You look pretty. But pale.

Dolores: It's the emotion, mama.

Mother: John Peter is wonderful, so courteous. Did you notice? He always asks my permission.

Dolores (mocking): And he's won you over.

Mother: And what about you? Your father's very pleased.

Dolores: Did they already make a deal?

Mother: What an idea!

Dolores (feigns innocence): Why? Papa had some land to sell, John Peter some land to buy. Papa is well connected and John Peter more so. Papa approves and John Peter applauds him. And the two of them say that the filthy, disgusting barbarians should die. And that includes a lot of people. Who isn't a barbarian? Who isn't disgusting? Who isn't filthy? Only power confers untouchable purity.

Mother: Dolores, when you talk this way I don't recognize you. Could it be Raphael who . . . ?

Dolores: Him? He doesn't know anything but French and Latin, mama. If he thinks, he thinks in a language no one understands.

Mother: You're pale. (*Pinches her cheeks*) There, that'll give you more color.

Dolores: More happiness.

(Fermin opens the door for John Peter)

John: Ladies. (*Greets Mother, then Dolores, whose hand he holds for a moment in his*) I feel very happy.

Dolores: Me, too.

John: I just bought a house. I'm anxious for you to see it. We could go tomorrow. With your permission, madam.

Mother (content): You have it.

John (to Dolores): I want you to like it.

Dolores: I like everything.

John: And I want you to choose the furniture. I already have my eye on some, but I'd like your approval.

Dolores (imitating Mother): You have it!

John (to Mother): Would you like to join us, madam?

Mother: Yes, I'd be delighted. About noon? (*To Dolores, insecure*) Do you think it will be all right with your father? When it comes to lunchtime, he's . . .

Dolores (interrupts her): Of course. But why go? Everything must be perfect. Even if there are only two chairs, a table, a bed.

John (smiling): There'll be more than that.

Dolores: I know. We'll buy plants. It will be our only luxury. Plants and flowers. And I'd like some ivy.

John: Our luxury will be curtains made of garnet red satin, imported furniture and rugs. We'll have lots of servants so you'll never get tired.

Dolores: I like to take care of plants.

John: Of course, you'll care for them. As a hobby.

Dolores: You're very kind. And we'll have children.

John (embarrassed, smiles toward Mother): That too.

Mother: Sit down and chat a while. I'll bring my sewing and keep you company. (*Leaves*)

Dolores: She leaves me alone with the professor.

John: He's a hunchback. And . . . (*smiles*) and I have more rights with you. (*Without further ado, he jumps on her. Touches her brutally and tries to kiss her. Dolores resists. The scene is violent and tense and occurs in silence. Hearing a noise from the doorway, John Peter separates from Dolores and quickly composes himself. Mother enters*)

Mother (smiling): Here I am. (*She notices Dolores is agitated, but doesn't allow herself to show she knows what has happened. Caresses Dolores's cheek as she passes by*) What rosy cheeks! Sit down! I'll finish this. (*Sits down with her needlework, apart from them*)

John: I was telling Dolores how happy I am. (*To Dolores*) I didn't know . . .

Dolores: Neither did I. I thought all men were stupid and groveling. Now I understand.

John: What?

Dolores: That nothing is as simple as one thinks. And nothing is so complicated either. That what is straight can be twisted and what is hunched over can be as straight as a golden field. (*Laughs bitterly*)

John: I don't understand. Why don't you talk plain? I'm not an intellectual type.

Dolores: That must be because your father chose a stupid teacher for you. I meant it's enough to find the one destiny chooses for us.

John: Is that me?

Dolores: It's who it should be.

John: Thank you. (*Looks toward Mother to see if she's watching them. Mother raises her head at that moment and smiles. Then, John Peter gently brushes Dolores's hand, with his*) I asked your father to dismiss the hunchback.

Dolores: Why?

John: He's a sight to see. (*Lets loose with a giggle*) Beauty should be surrounded by beauty, and besides, we'll be married soon, in barely three months . . . He's superfluous. You already know what any woman should know and the rest . . . I'll teach you.

Dolores: All right. But let him stay until we marry. Afterward I won't learn anything more.

John: Except how to be my wife.

Dolores: I'll learn that well. Will you ask my father to let him stay until then?

John: Yes. If you wish.

Dolores: It's my "silly" wish. I'll tell him to hide when you visit me. I don't look at him. I don't need to look at him.

John: You're beautiful. (*Looks toward Mother who is bent over her needlework. Then takes Dolores's hand and presses it against his penis. Dolores pulls away outraged*)

Dolores: Mama, John Peter is leaving.

Mother: So soon?

John: Yes. (*Stands up*) I'll come by for you tomorrow so we can look at the house.

Mother: It's our pleasure.

Dolores: I can picture it now. Whitewashed walls . . .

John (smiling): Red ones . . .

Dolores: And a pine table.

John: Oak.

Dolores: And caned chairs. (*John Peter laughs*) And a medium-sized bed . . .

Mother: Dolores . . .

Dolores: Excuse me, mama.

John: Until tomorrow. I'll be here at noon. (*Kisses Dolores's hand. Mother accompanies him. They leave*)

Dolores: That will be *our* home, not yours, idiot. (*Raphael appears*) Raphael!

Raphael: Dolores! Did you see him?

Dolores: He just left.

Raphael: What did you talk about?

Dolores: It's not important.

Raphael: Yes it is.

Dolores: Are you jealous?

Raphael: Yes.

Dolores: How jealous?

Raphael (feigns ferocity): Grrrr! I could kill him! (*Alters the tone of his voice*) I hate him . . . with his straight back.

Dolores: Straight? It's in a lascivious knot.

Raphael: What? Why?

Dolores: Nothing! Did you arrange everything?

Raphael: Yes. On the other side of the river there are no carts to pass by the houses, no imposed silence.

Dolores: They say it's a small, peaceful city. When, Raphael?

Raphael: Today. We'll cross the river at ten tonight. (*He notices she's scared and jokes around*) You ate up my life's savings, glutton! Your father doesn't pay much, but with room and board . . .

Dolores: Oh, Raphael, I'm so scared!

Raphael: Me, too. To take a chance with a rich girl is serious business!

Dolores: We're in it together.

Raphael: It's not as serious for you as for me.

Dolores: Am I putting you in danger?

Raphael: No. What's at risk is infamy. Fermin or . . .

Dolores: My father.

Raphael: Yes. And the whole city behind him. But everything'll be all right.

Dolores: We'll have a house with violets and bougainvilleas. And a small bed.

Raphael: A big one.

Dolores: Why big?

Raphael (it's hard for him, but he cracks a joke): So you don't bump into my hump! (*Strained laughter, but Dolores laughs openly, happily. He's happy, too*) And we won't have anything red. Nothing that smells like blood.

Dolores: Everything white.

Raphael: Everything white even in the dark.

Dolores: Show me your eyes. (*She kisses them*) I love you with your eyes open or closed. And we'll have children.

Raphael: Not mine.

Dolores (angry): Whose then if not yours? What are you thinking?

Raphael (smiles, sadly): Don't show your claws, lioness.

Dolores: I only show them to dummies. The children will be beautiful. I'm sure. Like you, so straight inside, so well built.

Raphael: This is too much!

Dolores: What's too much?

Raphael: This love . . .

Dolores (laughs, in a sing-song):
 Raphael got scared! She's a pretty young girl
 And he's afraid of love!

Raphael: Who's afraid? (*Embraces her*)

Dolores (answers): Raphael!

Raphael: I'm afraid? Really? (*Squeezes her tight*)

Dolores (for a second doesn't understand. Suddenly): Oh, Raphael! (Raphael laughs) Let go of me! I'm engaged!

Raphael (lets her go): To Mr. Goldenfields! (*Mimics John Peter*) May I have this dance?

Dolores (mimics with her hands over her eyes): I won't look at him so as not to become frightened!

Raphael: Yes, you *will* look at me! (*He chases her around the table*)

Dolores: No, I'm so impressionable!

Raphael (manages to grab her by the hand): You'll be saved from a good name, Mrs. Goldenfields!

Dolores (laughs): Oh what a name! Silverfields!

Raphael: Golden!

Dolores: Flooded! (*Mimics*) It's superfluous for you to study. You already know what every woman should know and the rest . . . I will teach you.

Raphael (tenderly and suggestively): I will teach you! (*Laughs*) Come here.

Dolores: No! (*Laughs, escapes. Makes a lot of noise protecting herself with a chair. Sound of a cart going by. The two listen, stop laughing*)

Raphael: Sh! Let's be quiet.

Dolores: No! That damn cart doesn't scare me! I'm not just choosing you, I'm choosing heads on shoulders!

Raphael: Yes, but let's be quiet. Don't be foolish!

Dolores: I'm not! I, Dolores, am sane and leave madness to sad people. Come here. Do you want to marry me?

Raphael: Yes.

Dolores: When?

Raphael: Tomorrow.

Dolores: Tomorrow at this time we'll be far away. Do you want some wine?

Raphael: I don't drink.

Dolores (embraces him): Then I'll drink to you.

Raphael (tenderly suggestive): But to all of me, huh? (*Dolores laughs, closes her eyes with her head on Raphael's shoulder. Sound of a cart passing by*)

Dolores (becomes tense, moves away): The cart is passing by again.

Raphael: Yes. Let's not forget it, Dolores. Even if we're happy, we shouldn't forget that the cart rolls on. Me too: I don't just choose you, I choose heads on shoulders . . . (*Sound of the cart passing by. They look at each other motionless. After a moment, Dolores reaches her hand out toward Raphael's face, but holds her hand motionless in the air. Raphael leans forward and rests his face in her hand*)

Scene VIII

The drawing room in semidarkness. Dolores waits in a corner, a coat over her shoulders, holding a small bundle in her hands. There's a muffled sound outside, like a door that bangs or opens and closes.

Dolores (startled, whispers): Raphael? (*Silence. Sighs and leaves the bundle on the floor. Sings like a child who's afraid of the dark, but her voice cracks. Silently someone enters*) Raphael? (*She draws near and touches. In a choked exclamation*) Mother!

Mother: What are you doing here, Dolores? At this hour.

Dolores: I couldn't sleep. I . . . was hungry.

Mother (serious and reticent): Of course. You didn't eat dinner.

Dolores: That's why.

Mother: You should have gone to the kitchen. Called a servant.

Dolores: It didn't . . . occur to me.

Mother: You can go to sleep. (*Pause*) He won't come.

Dolores: Who?

Mother: Raphael. (*She takes the coat from Dolores's shoulders*) Dressed to go out. (*Points to the bundle on the floor*) You were going to leave together. You robbed the house.

Dolores (laughs trembling): What an idea! It was cold. I'm cold. (*She makes a gesture to put on the coat, but doesn't*)

Mother: You never used to lie.

Dolores (silence): That's true. (*The following dialogue unfolds in an almost confidential tone, Dolores's voice is too calm*)

Mother: Your father found out.

Dolores: He found out? How? (*Mother remains silent*) How? Did you know?

Mother: I realized.

Dolores: You realized, and what about him? Did Fermin tell him? (*Mother remains silent*) Was it Fermin?

Mother: No.

Dolores: You don't lie either. (*Caresses her cheek*) I'm grateful for that. You told him? When?

Mother: Before dinner, this afternoon.

Dolores: But we ate together then and . . . Papa said to me: little one, eat. And he joked around. He was happy and he knew . . . Why was he happy?

Mother: He knew.

Dolores: Where's Raphael?

Mother (tries to leave): Let's go to sleep.

Dolores (holds her back): Where is he?

Mother: It doesn't matter any more.

Dolores (very softly, but very tense): Any more? To me it matters now, later, and always. (*Raises her voice*) Any more?

Mother: Don't shout.

Dolores: Is everyone sleeping?

Mother: No. No one's sleeping.

Dolores: And Raphael?

Mother: He's sleeping.

Dolores: He's . . . ?

Mother: Asleep!

Dolores (in disbelief): You . . . told on us. You were spying and . . . told on us.

Mother: No. I thought that . . .

Dolores: You never thought anything. When did you start to think? Why?

Mother: I thought it would be best.

Dolores: Oh how yellow-bellied you are. How damned yellow . . .

Mother: Dolores.

Dolores: Dolores my happiness.

Mother: Where were you going? My little girl who robs her own home and . . . and a hunchback . . .

Dolores (coldly and intensely hateful): Jealous. You accepted everything from the beginning, jealous of others who live. Not out of affection but fear. Shy about everything. You did this to me. Afraid of living even through me. A humiliated person who loves her humiliation.

Mother: I don't want to listen to you, I don't understand, no . . . You were always obstinate. Let's go to sleep! (*Anguished*) Get into bed and . . .

Dolores: I'm waiting for Raphael.

Mother: Cover yourself . . . and close your eyes and . . . the door to your room so no one can come in . . .

Dolores: I'm waiting for Raphael.

Mother: He won't come.

Dolores: Why are you so sure? You said he was sleeping. How can he be sleeping?

Mother: He won't come.

Dolores: Why? What have they done to him? What has he done, that man who hates everything except his own power?

Mother: I know . . .

Dolores (wildly): Don't say "he won't come"! I'm going to look for him!

Mother: No! (*Holds her back*)

Dolores: Let go of me! No one's asleep? Then let them show themselves! (*Pulls free*) I'm going to look for him!

Mother: Don't go!

Dolores (stops): Why?

Mother: They'll bring him here. I didn't want them to!

Dolores: To what?

Mother (defeated): To bring him . . .

Dolores: Have they . . . beaten him? To teach him a lesson? Do they think people learn lessons? What do they think we are? What kind of beasts are they?

Mother: Be quiet. (*Bursts into tears*)

Dolores: Tears. (*Slowly*) Now I understand.

Mother (cries): Dolores!

Dolores: Your tears frighten me so. You gave me the right name. A name is destiny. (*Raises her voice*) I won't cry! Arid in my hatred. Why are we in the dark? It's nighttime. (*Smiles nervously*) I was going to run away. But there's no reason for the dark. I'll light the candles. (*Frantically lights the candles, one by one, but talks in a tensely tranquil state*) So we can see each other's faces, mama. Otherwise we could be deceived, I hear you crying, but I can hardly see you. Did papa hit you? Is that why you're crying? Let's see your face? (*Brutally she takes hold of Mother's face as Mother tries to hide it*) It's the same. Uglier. Touch yourself. (*Makes Mother touch her own face*) A tumor on your mouth and cobwebs over your eyes. Encrusted pus, too. Touch yourself! You're going to feel your own ugliness. (*Lets go*) And what does *my* face look like now? (*Touches herself*) I don't recognize myself. But my face isn't important. Neither is yours!

Mother: Don't shout, Dolores, don't be mad at me. It got out of hand! Your father asked me and . . .

Dolores (containing her exasperation, as if uttering a commonplace explanation): That's what happens, mama. When one person decides for another, that's what happens, it gets out of hand and no one's at fault. Then you make believe that nothing's happened and everyone's asleep in the dark, and since the sun doesn't fall from the sky, the next day you say: nothing happened. And deny your own ugliness! Touch yourself! (*Smiling nervously*) And to top it off, I lit the candles. (*Mother reaches out to put out a candle*) Don't you dare! I need to see the punishment! Don't take the punished body away from me.

(*Goes toward the door, shouting furiously and painfully*) Fermin! Fermin! (*Fermin appears at once*) Nobody's asleep in this house today. What did my father tell you to do?

Fermin: To bring him here.

Dolores: What are you waiting for, lackey? To see me cry?

Fermin: I know you, miss, since childhood. I don't like you to suffer.

Dolores (laughs): Good answer! (*Curtly. Angrily*) Bring him in!

Fermin: Your father told me to. (*His cruelty takes hold of him. Smiles*) He didn't want the hunchback to miss his date.

Dolores (softly): Don't let him miss it. (*Fermin leaves. Dolores lights another candle with difficulty*): This one went out. Can you see me, mama?

Mother: Dolores, why didn't you go?

Dolores (coldly contemptuous): And lock myself up in my room? There's no door for pain, mama. Stupid! (*The door opens. Fermin is carrying Raphael's dead body. He throws it like a sack on the floor. Motionless, Dolores stares at him*)

Fermin (as if making excuses): I would have only hit him. (*Lets loose a laugh*) On his hump!

Mother: All right, Fermin. Run along.

(*Fermin leaves*)

Dolores (keeps staring at Raphael): Thank you, mama. (*Stiffly she draws near, kneels next to him. Serenely and silently. She doesn't touch him. Looks at him for a long time*) It wasn't enough to beat you, dear hunchback. But it wasn't because of your hump. Dear hunchback. We must all live the same way. And whoever tries to escape, dies. (*Mother sighs. Dolores gets up*) Get out!

Mother (tries to draw near): Don't throw me out! It's your father who's so strict!

Dolores (wild): Out! I want to be alone! Tell him thank you! I thank him for letting me see my dead man! But I don't want tears around me! Hypocritical tears! Get out!

(*Father enters with Fermin, who is carrying a tray with a pitcher and three cups*)

Father (very calm): Who's shouting? Dolores, I don't like shouting. It doesn't let me think. Let's all go to sleep, all right? We won't even talk about this. Let's have a cup of hot chocolate and . . .

Dolores: Go to sleep . . . (*Looks at the three of them, mutters, containing a violent anger*) Bastards! You bastards! I hope hatred eats you alive. And your memory never lets you live in peace! You and your power and you, henchman, and you, puny hypocrite!

Father: What have we raised? A viper? We'll take the venom from your lips!

Dolores: You can't! My venom is sweet, I chew it and swallow!

Father: Worse for you. Now go to sleep, and that's an order!

Dolores (laughs): What? How come you don't realize, dear papa? Who's so wise. (*Furious*) No one gives me orders anymore! Now there's nothing to be afraid of! I'm not scared any more! *I'm free!*

Father (furious): Silence! No one is free without my consent! In this house, I'm still the boss! I said to bed!

Dolores: I'll never close my eyes! If you let me live, I will never close my eyes! I'm going to watch you all the time, wide awake, angry, disgusted!

Father: Silence!

Dolores: I'll give you silence! I don't know what I'll do, but it's enough not to be afraid any more! (*Laughs out loud wildly*) You didn't expect this! Your little girl, your tender creature . . . !

Mother: Dolores!

Dolores: Dolores what? (*Defiantly to Father*) The hunchback used to say to me Dolores my happiness! Behind your back!

Father: I'll break every bone in your body! (*Goes to hit her, but Mother intercedes and receives the blow*)

Dolores: Thank you, mama! Just in time! The filthy yellow-belly's good for something! I said I'm no longer afraid! And least of all of you!

Father: Shut up! Fermin, take her away! Get her out of my sight!

Dolores (struggles while Fermin drags her away; she is shouting furiously): I hate you! I hate you!

Father: Silence.

Dolores (in a strange and broken voice): Silence cries out! I'll be quiet, but silence cries out!

(*Fermin, along with Mother, drags her off, and the last sentence is prolonged in an angry cry. Long pause*)

Father (looks at Raphael's body out of the corner of his eye. Straightens up immobile, staring off into space. Sighs): What silence . . .

After a moment

Curtain

> *Translated by Evelyn Picon Garfield*

Elvira Orphée

Argentina

Elvira Orphée. (Photo courtesy of José Eduardo Lamarca.)

Born in San Miguel, Tucumán, Argentina, in 1930, Elvira Orphée has studied and lived abroad, primarily in France, Italy, and Spain. The early years of this author of four novels and three collections of short stories were marked by physical illness and were spent in the northern province of Tucumán, where she says you can hear the voices of the Incas emanating from the rocks of the high plateaus nearby, now inhabited by their descendants, the Coyas. This primordial presence infuses her fiction with primeval forces of good and evil embodied in her characters.

Outcasts and orphans, they are characterized as victims of destiny who often try to vindicate their impotence by cruel acts. Such is the case with the protagonist of *Angel's Last Conquest* (*La última conquista de El Angel*), a torturer in the Argentinean Secret Police who searches for the unattainable splendor of Carrara marble and emeralds in the mucous membranes of his victims. Although this novel has been published in a translation by Magda Bogin entitled *El Angel's Last Conquest* (New York, 1985), we offer the reader our own translation of the last chapter of this novel, which forms part of a Latin American tradition, especially among Argentinean authors concerned with the horrors of political persecution. Julio Cortázar, Luisa Valenzuela, Marta Traba, and Manuel Puig are but a few who have written prose concerning political torture and disappearances. Orphée's novel, however, touches a hypersensitive nerve by equating torture with a "mystical" experience, a need to seek access to the unknown through the suffering of others.

Orphée prefers the first person narrative to the omniscient point of view, elliptical dialogue and lyrical introspection to external detail and descriptions. This is evident in the short story "The Silken Whale" ("La ballena de seda"), a horror tale based on the innocent savagery of a demented adolescent. "The Silken Whale" takes its rightful place alongside the works of two other masters of this type of Latin American short story: the Uruguayan Horacio Quiroga in stories like "La gallina degollada" ("The Decapitated Chicken") and the Mexican Juan Rulfo in stories like "Macario." In "The Silken Whale," the demented adolescent is depicted as hypersensitive to the unspoken thoughts of others. Sometimes Paco expresses himself in wordplay that is difficult to capture in translation and for which we have provided some explanatory footnotes. We find it important to maintain the sense of this wordplay as much as possible. In the novel *Aire tan dulce* (How Sweet the Air), another one of Orphée's characters offers a rationalization for our choice: "You don't need a dirty shawl for life to become radiant. The rain's enough. But you don't even need that if you're permeated with words. That's what stories are for when life's not enough."

Angel's Last Conquest
[Selection from the novel]

AT THE POLICE STATION I met a guy with eyebrows like bird's wings. He mouthed off all the time with his big fat lips.

"As far as I know when a gal pulls out a gun she must be threatening someone."

The clerk was taking a deposition. They hadn't taught him how to keep people from running off at the mouth, so he was bouncing from one litigant to another and just then was listening to the girl's protests as she argued with the big-mouth.

"You're not important enough, Horace, not important enough for me to threaten you at gunpoint. In any case I'm flattering you, because if I told you the truth, your self-esteem would curdle."

"Nevertheless, Miss, you were shouting when the policeman approached you," the employee said.

"You'd shout, too, and so would the commissioner, and the whole damned secret police, if you'd gotten the same beating. Besides, I didn't shout. I simply answered Horace in kind. But Horace would like you to write down: 'As proof of the passions I arouse, I declare that Miss So-

and-so threatened me with a weapon.' It was a playful weapon, in any case."

The big-mouth's eyes appeared to envision people who subverted the human race, up to now ordered according to his taste and in keeping with his fastidious nature.

"The gun" he shouted, "had that damn witch's initials carved in it with a penknife."

The girl interrupted him.

"Sometimes you have to use flattery to win someone over. Anyway, what difference does it make? It only ends up making a difference because man's vanity is boundless and whatever little you tell him puffs him up until he's as big as a cathedral . . . Where he's God."

It turned out that she was right and that the guy was wrong. Because the gun was nowhere to be found, not in the car or nearby or in the girl's purse or in his pockets. The weapon was nowhere to be found, so we threw the two of them out, even though we felt like keeping them around, to teach him not to bother the police with stories, and to show her our male superiority so she'd stop flaunting her liberated airs.

But it was clear to me that a girl like that wasn't going to let herself be caught in the cradle by a fat slob like him. It's a good thing Croveri wasn't here to see her. For so many years now his stories about how the Mrs. doesn't want to and how the daughter's going to end up bad left him with off-key strings in place of nerves. Mostly because all of us had our own problems at home for not being homebodies. That poor guy's intrigues were so pathetic. His old lady's rejections turned his brain into mush—even if it never was too solid from the start—so the sight of any female muddled it even more. That's why he only perked up when women were arrested; he regained hope and even showed off the confessor in him. I bet he asked them: how often do you get it, honey?

But the girl with the gun could have handled him.

In those days I just kept on crowding in with the others on the winter buses, with doors wide open as if they were driving around Miami; and on the springtime ones as drafty as the others and the summer ones with red-hot metal sides. And that's when it happened. Once again, I entered the ranks of specialists, thanks to my knack for getting recruits. I returned home to the Special Section, only its name had changed.

Then I boarded the autumn buses, the year's best. But only for a little while. Soon I'd be driving my own VW. But at that time I boarded the bus going to the four hundred block on Emerald Street. I rapped on the door, and that girl from a year ago opened up. I scolded her: "Why don't you ask who it is? It's dangerous to open that way."

"I'm ashamed to ask . . . But don't I know you?"

"Yes, you know me. I see you remember faces. Do you remember the face of a young cop with kind of thick blond curls and a long nose?"

"All cops are the same."

"This one's on duty on Independence Street alongside the College of Letters. And he's not like the others."

"Ah, wait. I know. Now I remember."

"Why did he have your gun?"

"What gun? I don't own one."

"The one you used last year to threaten that ugly guy with the fish face."

"If you think everyone you see is guilty, you're mistaken. The cops are always wrong."

"But you had a very small gun with initials scratched out like with a pin."

"I never had my own gun."

"We'll see about that."

"Why don't you ask the cop why he has that kind of gun."

"You know we can't ask him, don't you?"

"Why not? Throw him in a cell, hit him, torture him, and you'll see you can."

"You'll have to come with me."

"Why?"

"I've always been courteous with the ladies, so I'll ask you politely. But it's the last time. From now on you're not a lady, just a prisoner. We can't ask him because he's dead. It was a bullet from a very small gun like a toy, with some initials on it. Yours."

"No!"

"Yes! Why are you so pale? He was killed in the back room of your brother-in-law's house where he lived with a friend."

"Why are you giving me all those details if I'm a prisoner?"

"Because you remind me of a very young girl I was attracted to when I was also very young."

"You *are* young."

"You're flattering me now. But what difference does it make? Like you said to the big-mouth at the police station."

"What a memory!"

"I always remember what interests me. I remember a damp alley a while back where a girl who looked like you used to go walking . . . Look, let's make a deal. I won't take you in if you'll tell me everything you know about Angel."

She looked at me surprised. I went on, "I promise not to bother you afterward."

"You must be kidding, a cop's word's no word at all."

"You had some contact with Angel, right?"

"I used to see him on the corner near the university; he was always in a bad mood."

"Didn't you talk to him?"

"Some girls approached him. He treated them bad. It was his way of conquering them."

"You hated him."

"I disliked him a little, that's all. He treated the girls bad for the hell of it. There are guys who can only seduce by hiding things. If they expose themselves, they wear out right away. They're poor slobs with idiotic maneuvers for making it with other idiots."

"Why did you deny knowing him?"

"I don't spend my time thinking about cops. When you asked me I didn't remember. Now it's all coming back."

"He wasn't called Angel. You were surprised when I said it, but you didn't correct me."

"I called him the Angel of Sodom."

"What? Do you want me to think he was a pervert? You should know that isn't possible. The police are choosy. Get that crazy idea out of your mind. Anyway as far as I can see, there was more between you two than meets the eye. I'll have to take you in after all."

"I expected you would. That's what you get from friendly cops."

"Next to the dead man's bed was a book and on the first page someone had written: For the Angel of Sodom. Do you want to write something here so I can see it?"

"What choice do I have?"

"You don't know how well I'm treating you."

"Yes I do, because I know how you treated some friends of mine who didn't do anything wrong."

"If you know that then either you're a witch or you despise us. Why do you hate the police?"

"Some day maybe I'll tell you how you're cursed around here. Some people even bless anyone who stands up to you. In a province up north, they sanctify those who are killed by the police. Those are their real saints, they know their needs, suffer their misery and are just like them. Not those painted saints who are strangers removed from their problems."

"Look, even though I shouldn't stand for your lip, I'll leave you alone if you talk. You get under my skin just by talking. And next time before opening the door, ask who's there. Do you live alone?"

"No. This belongs to an old lady who rents rooms. A reporter and I are the tenants. But neither of us is ever here."

"Will you go see him before they bury him?"

"No. Why?"

"Aren't you interested in an angel's transformations?"

"Why? Was he shot in the head?"

"You don't seem very surprised. You were sure it wasn't in the head."

"Who'd dare ruin a pretty boy's face? A bloody body hidden by clothes isn't so repugnant."

"That's a woman's opinion, anyway."

"That tendency of dead bodies to give off moisture is pretty unbearable. They end up like water caught in its own current. Then their moisture dissipates and they become one of those incredible creatures of death."

I'd never heard anyone talk so delicately about the stench of dead bodies with their loosed sphincters. This girl had to be a poet.

"Have you seen many dead bodies?"

"My family's."

I put my coat on and said, "We'll meet again."

"Hope the cops calm down. I didn't call him the Angel of Sodom for his tendencies, only for his beauty."

I was just over forty. She was nineteen. And it seemed true that a forty year old turns soft, like putty. Imagine, I'd never been interested in what a woman said before. Imagine, no woman ever turned my head away from my duty before. And so many other things were happening. This part of the work was distracting me from my *real* job.

I went off to see Angel in his coffin, with a bullet hidden in his body and his face intact, except for his sleepy expression and the blue of his open eyes that had turned dark gray like a frozen pond.

I was forty years old. My age was enough to keep me from insisting on the writing sample. Anyway, what difference did it make whose handwriting it was? You can't pin the rap on someone for a dedication. It was just that in the old days I would have demanded that sample to show who we were and that we were in charge. Even though we knew she wasn't guilty.

At the wake there were some old women, a mother, a friend, a brother-in-law, and a dog. I approached the mother to give my heartfelt condolences. She was staring at the face in the casket and from time to time she trembled.

"You don't shudder for the usual reasons, only for the unnatural ones," I heard her say to an old lady.

The mother didn't look at me or listen when I spoke to her. The brother-in-law approached like the master of the house. I got suspicious stares.

"The poor old lady's not rude," he said, "but she never understood her own unhappiness so she's beside herself from not being able to see why her son wasn't happy either."

From the room where the wake took place, you could see the patio. A few women with sagging breasts were hurriedly cleaning up here and there.

"Of course, when I say her son was unhappy, I don't mean it the way she does. I'm saying it because he was a bastard. I'm not the type who thinks that just because someone's dead he deserves praise. I don't care if he's dead or alive. He even bugged his roommate. Of course you know that the poor guy slept there for a while, oblivious to the corpse in the other bed. A table in between blocked his view. But when he went over to wake him up for work, he went wild. We had to put him in another room. He's still shaking . . . Forgive the mother. She's riddled with guilt. She must feel guilty that her son inherited her unhappiness."

With that, a pretty good-looking girl arrived. I asked who she was.

"One of his girlfriends. Angel was a wholesaler at that."

"You call him Angel?"

167

"Well, not exactly," he became upset, "but we knew one of his conquests called him that."

"You mean there were others?"

"Sure. Didn't I tell you? Knowing him like I did, I'm sure he wanted to make them all suffer just to prove his power. I don't know if he succeeded with the last one."

"Do you know who that last one was?"

"The one who called him Angel. You see that other girl over there? She turned twenty-two again after he died. Before that she was sort of faded, desperate."

I returned to the four hundred block on Emerald Street. I rapped on the door. No one asked who I was this time either.

"Now I'm not leaving until you tell me the truth. Or I'll drag you down to the police station."

"Are you going to torture me?"

"Don't use that word again or you'll be sorry. So it was true that you threatened the bigmouthed Spaniard with a gun."

"What do you take me for? Do you think I'm stupid? That guy only believes what he wants to, he doesn't care about the evidence. If a woman doesn't threaten him with homicide, she threatens him with suicide."

"Then why'd you go out with him?"

"Because he fed me. I think they call that 'selling your firstborn for a plate of beans.' Even if this platter had lobster on it."

"How did you manage to hide the gun when the cop took you to the precinct?"

"If I'd done that, I wouldn't tell you. Every magician has his own tricks and doesn't show them to competitors."

"So we're your competitors. How's that?"

"They only teach you cops one thing: anything goes to compromise someone, promises, blows, favors, threats, insults, anything. To make him confess anything, even though he doesn't know what it's all about. To me a cop and a traffic light are the same; you have to step on the gas before the light changes."

And there I was listening to her insult us, without beating her up. I stayed to talk instead of dragging her off to headquarters to show her she was right, that's exactly what we do to the prisoners. Oh, those forty years!

"Shut up. You're coming with me to explain why you lied about the gun. We'll search the house."

In spite of her insolence, she became pale.

"Can I take a coat?"

"Hurry up."

She left and returned almost at once.

"So you called a lawyer."

She looked at the telephone. She thought I was too dumb to lift the receiver while she was inside talking.

"Yes, so they know where you're taking me. I'm a prisoner, right?"

"No. We only want some explanations."

"A cop turns up dead. They find a gun but don't know whose it is. All the same, they arrest me. I already know about your interrogations."

I hated her. She was living proof that I was turning into a spineless mollusk. Limp limbs, lusterless skin, dark rings under my eyes. How they change us men!

We questioned her for two hours. She still denied handing over that gun. We didn't allow the lawyer to show his face. Finally we let her go off with him. For a while I was soured by life, then suddenly took off like a flash for her house. She was suspicious when she saw me.

"No one thinks you killed him," I said to begin with. "We know it wasn't you. No one thinks you supplied him with the gun, except me because I have a good memory and know he was involved with a girl who dedicated a book 'to the Angel of Sodom.' Something you didn't care to hide."

"So then, if no one believes anything, why are you persecuting me?"

"Because curiosity's got me and I want to know about Angel so I can get to know you. Do you want proof? I'll tell you something confidential. No one killed Angel. He committed suicide. Why did you give him the gun? Why did you have a gun?"

"A foreigner who took off lent it to me. I etched my initials on it. But I didn't threaten Horace, the big-mouth, with it. He saw the gun at home once and his vanity imagined the rest. It didn't work, didn't even have bullets."

"But it *did* work. Why did he kill himself?"

"There's a wave of suicides among the cops. Maybe they've become desperate over how little they're paid for all the work they have to do. Not all of them can make ends meet like that police chief at the motor vehicle section in Córdoba, who robbed cars under his own jurisdiction and sold them."

"Hasn't anyone told you that for every dishonest crook, there's a heroic cop?"

"Don't be so hard on him. The guy had to earn better wages. How else could he buy his wife shoes, send the kids to school, and still have something left over to fool around?"

"One case in a thousand. Someday we'll manage to get rid of them all . . . So, what was your relationship with Angel?"

"I used to see him on the corner. He acted bad with me like with all the girls. It occurred to me to act suspicious. I approached him and put a useless gun in his hand. I said to him: look what they've given me, I'm giving it to you. He still acted bad, asked where I got it, my address, why I had it. He just wanted to scare me."

"He fixed it so it worked. Did he kill himself because of you?"

"You're nuts. A pretty boy doesn't commit suicide for a woman. I pity the women who fall for pretty boys."

"Did you fall in love to prove it?"

"God forbid. Do you take me for one of those women who thinks a pretty boy is going to invite you to share his good looks? Or contaminate them? Men who only have good looks don't have anything else to give. They only trust their looks and stand around waiting for the world to kiss their feet. But from lack of thought and action, their senses and intelligence atrophy. They become allergic to people. They don't smell people. One or the other, it's all the same to them. No, there's nothing about beauty that can persuade you to forgive. And you can be sure the police's good name isn't damaged because I baptized him the Angel of Sodom. If you think he was a homosexual, you're wrong. He was worse. A masturbator with pimp's aspirations."

Lightning struck. That insolence could only be theirs, those knights of the round table. That presumptuousness with me from the start. The attraction disappeared in a flash. I was so fiercely disgusted, I felt a burning desire to maim her. She was an excuse for a woman. I would even have thrown her into the cell right then and there if I could have stood being near her.

It took a while for the wave of nausea to subside. By then I was already in the street. Really, women are good for very little. Which one of them would be able to offer us life's pure essence, the way work does? And this story was full of women: the individual, Angel's adventures, his girlfriend, the shocked roommate's girlfriend. The guy who left the room with his heart aching so that it affected his stomach. Like a robot he answered his own girlfriend's telephone call; she sighed from the other end of the line: "Angel, haven't you left yet?"

He dropped the telephone. Who knows how long it took him to realize that they were talking to him in endearing terms and it was not a matter of an idyll from beyond the grave.

But, why did his friends call him Angel if his name was William? Someone called him that or they knew about the girl more than they let on. I was cold. I had missed out on something in this whole affair. From sheer routine I was taking too many things for granted. Does being forty years old make you blind? Do forty years make you dumb? Do you forget who you are? "Divine spittoons." A long time ago a man said we were God's spittoons. And maybe he even said chamber pots because in a crazy house words transform people, their faces and souls.

I now had the same job that Winkel, my illuminated boss, had when I first worked with him. The profession was the same, but vaguely different. These were rookie cops who had it easy. They took the initiative and the boss carried out the routine stuff. That's what they thought. But what great initiatives did they take with Angel? Proving by guesswork that he had committed suicide, finding the dedicated book, reading the letter where he talked of death. And afterward, did they search, investigate, interrogate? Maybe they despised me. Maybe they said I preferred they send the report in to me without involving me personally. But they were wrong to despise me. The profession is in my flesh; for them it is in the grease, and the carrion. Paperwork, procedures. Did they know that my indifference toward them, those street dwarfs of power and their bureaucratic tasks, stems from my deep-seated, all-out attack on routine? How were they to know! (They didn't stay awake at night over that.)

I'd show them how to do it. I arrived at headquarters and began shouting. They had to be ready right away to leave on assignment for William Romero's house. Someone mentioned that his friends were mourning him. I hope they're not as incompetent as the ones who discovered his body, I shouted.

The wake was in full swing when we got there. A working-class house, neighborhood women, some young people, a few of the deceased's friends. I approached the brother-in-law: "Do you want to make up a list of the tenants in this house?"

"But, officer, you're interrupting a wake. Look how agitated the mother's getting."

"I'm sorry. My people didn't do their job well. Maybe because they were friends of the deceased. Aren't you married to his sister? Which one is she?"

"There's been a mistake. I'm not married to anyone. I used to live in this house with my sister. My sister met him and brought him home. You know, we're young and don't believe in those stories about marriage and morality. Instead we're straightening out what's been screwing people up for a while now."

"And where's your sister?"

"We don't know. She left about a month ago. She couldn't stand all of his girlfriends. She doesn't even know he's dead. We couldn't find her. She didn't tell anyone where she was going."

"And he always lived in the small room at the back with that friend?"

"No. He used to live here with her. But by chance when she left, that friend who was on the outs with his family dropped by."

"And you live here, too?"

"Well, sort of."

"What does that mean?"

"Well, from time to time I stay with the old folks. But you know how it is, they live in another world. You're more comfortable with guys from your own generation. I spend time here when I want to be free to do as I please."

"Does agent Romero's last conquest live here, too?"

"No. She has her own place."

"Give me her address."

"I don't know it."

"You know that girl, tell me her name."

"I don't know it."

"Where does Romero's mother live?"

"In Liniers."

Two of my men came over to tell me the deceased's room was locked.

"Please open it, Mr. In-law."

172

"But I don't even know where they've put the key. With all the confusion . . . Didn't the police take it?"

"No."

"Then I don't know what to do."

"Try other keys, call a locksmith, knock the door down, as you please."

"Well, if the police want to make people suffer even more, no one can stop them."

The key turned up. There was very little in the room, not even a trace of the recent death. The autopsy had already been done, the suicide diagnosis given, the permission for burial granted. Everything happened very quickly since the dead man belonged to the police force.

"Now Mr. In-law, kindly find me your sister and let's search the other rooms."

"But this is abusive, officer. A house is never searched when someone's committed suicide."

For once he left off the *well* at the beginning of the sentence.

"Then this search establishes a precedent. And don't you or anyone else move from this spot. Do you hear?"

They heard all right, and my cohorts were surprised. The order was for the dead man's friends standing around the coffin in their street clothes.

"You, start by showing us the room the friend moved into, the one who was on the outs with his family . . . And you, get identification from everyone."

The brother-in-law tried to refuse, made all kinds of excuses, but we searched the room anyway. And by God, there we found all the loose ends to this affair. Had the world become invulnerable to me? No sir, just as vulnerable as ever, thanks to my gut feeling. I cracked the case open on a pure hunch. Yes, I cracked it open on an amazing hunch.

In the room, behind an old piece of furniture that used to be a wardrobe but was now full of books, we found a hollow in the wall stuffed with two machine guns, several revolvers, maps of key sites, lists of planned maneuvers. Whose idea was it to move the wardrobe? My subordinates' in their bureaucratic guise? My subordinates' who gave up on inventiveness? No. It was me, the old man lying in ambush. It didn't even occur to them to ask why the wood behind the wardrobe was painted, made to look as much as possible like the wall. A touch for undercurrents is what *I* have. Not them. Or maybe it's just that I haven't lost the knack for sensing what others feel, caught up by strong emotions. But what kind of emotions could the person with the small gun have had when she let loose her foul words and felt the ridicule, the drunken superiority at having deceived me? Her current of ridicule penetrated my brain and there her thoughts entered mine.

I had in my hands the list of people: Michael (surely the archangel), Judith (the individual?), Simon (why, just seeing the friend's face you'd think of Bolívar), Lia (Angel's woman). What a relief there was no Marcos. It was enough to see the names that turn up in all the guerrilla novels.

The brother-in-law was duly handcuffed, along with the friend. Now we would find out if the brother-in-law was the Henry on the list. They never suspected we'd nab them this way; they were so sure of Judith's seduction and the dead man's state. They were so brazen as to fill the house with police without getting rid of any evidence. Or did they do away with some of it? Or couldn't they, precisely because Angel's friends were always around. My bureaucrats had already left to look for Angel's disappeared woman; others went off with the little twenty-two-year-old girlfriend; I left to cut off unsuccessful Judith's retreat.

The bureaucratic cops took charge of the others, pretending of course to be tough and wise. I announced to the assistants: "The burial permission is canceled."

The traitorous angel's mother fainted into someone's arms. I had the corpse carried off. I ordered the brother-in-law pressured right away on the spot. Lean on him till his craters burst. The bureaucrat cop looked at me like a dummy.

"Yes," I advised him, "wring his neck, stand on his gut, hit him in the balls—you do know what they are?—until he explodes from every opening."

I set out in the direction of Judith's place, my unsuccessful, predestined Judith.

What intuition, pregnant with omens, made me rap at her door each time I looked for her? What made me hit upon their signal? There was no need for Judith to ask me who it was, she thought she knew.

This time my rapping didn't fail either. She appeared at the door and quickly acted pleasantly surprised. This nickel-plated woman would give me another chance. I was changing the course of time, boomeranging toward youth. Exactly when had I lost my way? It didn't matter. I would find it again.

I summoned up all the sweetness of a child to my eyes, the rotten sweetness of molasses spilled on dirt roads. "I want your clothes."

"What?"

"Take off everything. I want all the clothing that touches you."

Astonishment and false contentment disappeared. She tried to complain, get mad. My voice flowed like honey. The light of her body, I needed to see it or I would die of darkness, asphyxiated. There would be nothing dirty or impure, she could relax; I would look at her like a precious gem in a showcase, I wouldn't come near her. It was a great speech. Her thoughts, her words ran through my mind, and I found myself thinking about the rising temperature of her vanity, her triumphant superiority over me; me, the one trapped and deceived by her, Judith the great one who had wounded my soul.

She decides, undresses as if accustomed to doing it in front of any stranger, all at once without a fuss. I beg her to hand over the clothes, I smell them and sweetly say: "With a stench like that you managed to get an angel up your hole?"

In the middle of the room atop the chair where I made her stand, statue, martyr and nude queen, the way she felt a moment ago, I watched her falter. Yes, there she began to tremble with fear. She didn't know what was happening to her. Her nickel-plate began to peel off.

"Those spindly legs squeezed an angel."

She tries to get down. I take out the gun and place it on the table in front of me.

"That fat ass seduced an angel."

Pointing the gun at her I move away toward the door, open it. There were my bureaucrats. I ordered:

"Take her away at once. She stinks too much to interest you. She must have the clap."

It wouldn't be long before our more intimate conversation took place. I'd grab her with the left hand, I'd stand to her left, her whole left side would end up destroyed by needle jabs. I'd annoint every opening she had with the needles' holy oils, and if she didn't have enough, I'd make more.

Few prisoners had the right to such preparations. Black all over, black papers hanging, hoods for everyone. My bureaucrats, their tranquil membranes rent, watching my every move; at last, they were going to be delivered into paroxysm. Judith was already on the stretcher, open like a steer's carcass. Her broken nerve waves were making me dizzy; I was vulnerable to her stream of terror.

The fear was prolonged. We waited, she waited. Finally the stretcher arrived with the other prisoner, his head beneath a hood, a thick shirt on his torso. From the waist down, nothing. She couldn't see everything that was going on, nor did she suspect that for once we were going to act like priests in a marriage consecrated by terror. She was perfectly bathed and perfumed for the wedding. And so I could draw near without getting sick to my stomach.

The newly arrived body was thrown atop hers. She shuddered wildly. The ceremony had hardly begun and she already wanted to sabotage it by passing out. The nickel-plated broad, hard and shiny, who had pulled my leg a few hours before and held the world at her feet, remained unexpectedly paralyzed. Of course everyone is well prepared for the expected. I gave it to her left and right. First with the body atop hers, tied to her. Then charges in her vagina and on the man's penis, synchronized. The consummation of coitus by electric shock. And just when she was about to guess who that husband was, jumping about from the shocks without uttering caressing words or squeals of pleasure, just when she was probably suspecting who that very cold husband was that I had provided for her, we took off his hood, and he fell on her mouth with rigor mortis on his angel's face. Mouth to mouth. Let her drink in the lost blue of his eyes, the two ponds of winter. Frost on top, something gray, brown, rotten underneath.

Confessions? Everything. I had decided not to destroy her left side. There was hardly any preparation. I wanted her to arrive at the wedding with all her faculties intact. So it was. But she was three-fourths gone, reality in retreat and unreality stuck to her brain like a leech, ready for the snapshot: *Incurable insanity.*

But we had time to find out that Angel tried to get out when he saw how far things had gone. They suspected him. In part because of the sad girlfriend who was a cop's daughter and who wanted him to be a real financé. She was leading him down the straight and narrow path. But he knew too much. Judith put the gun in his hand, that small object that he once helped her hide during the argument with the big-mouth. Not because she threatened the guy, but because the big-mouth surprised her during a kind of mini-maneuver he didn't understand, and Angel had to intervene putting on an act.

When he wanted out, they put the gun in his hand and cocked the trigger. While the others held him, Judith fired the shot.

And all because his comrades refused to believe that for him they were no longer the most important thing in the world.

Translated by Evelyn Picon Garfield

The Silken Whale

—There's never been a day like this. Nor kids so dumb. Staying out in the blowtorch heat of the sun instead of under the patch of shade from the trees.

—When it comes to shade, it's better to be indoors all together, in the cool bedrooms. We're stupid, too, putting up with this glare.

—No one can talk to you about your kids. How come you never defended them from their bully father?

—I told you before. I don't want to talk about it now.

—Kids, if Uncle Coco were fifteen years old now instead of fifty-four, what difference would it make? He's so stupid.

—Poor mom, she has to put up with his chatter. What if we called her to take a dip with us in the pool?

—She won't do it. She's vain and doesn't like us to see her legs.

—What's wrong with her legs, huh, why can't we see them? Are they made of gold?

—No, Paco, you dummy, they're just made of old skin. They must already be kind of old and ugly.

—Sheep's skin. A wolf in sheep's skin. I want to see mama's legs. I want to see them. Why doesn't she show me them if she's my mother? A mother's good for everything. Why is she stingy about her legs? She's stingy with her really unusual sheepskin legs.

—Shut up, you idiot, it's old skin not sheepskin.* And she's not stingy with you; she's ashamed to show them . . . Drink this, you must be thirsty and overheated.

—What a beautiful color in that glass. How lucky to lose so much blood. To be able to die.

—Don't be an idiot. It's *sangría* not blood.**

—Aren't they the same? . . . If you'd seen what I saw. They came in a truck without back doors down the road from Mar del Plata before the Boca bridge. They were hanging headless, and dancing about. The truck drove along slowly where they're fixing the road. You should've seen how they danced. They shook and beat about. The stumps danced around delicately. They must be common cattle, you know, what they call *res publica*.*** Exactly what is *res publica*?

—Didn't they teach you in school, Paquito you blockhead?

—I don't go to school like you, Santiago-of-my-very-own-guts. I read anything I want to, but I don't go to school.

—Filthy dunce.

—Don't talk so loud, Santiago. He'll tear you to shreds if he hears you called him a filthy dunce.

—I dare him.

—I already heard you. María Beanhead told Santiago to speak softly, and Santiago answered quietly, acting brave like a little cock.

—I'll make you swallow that María Beanhead. Either call me José María or don't talk to me at all.

—Little precious ears can't hear what he really is, a María Beanhead.

—Mom, mom, Paco is calling me María Beanhead.

---

*Wordplay between *piel de oveja* (sheepskin) and *piel vieja* (old skin).
**Wordplay between *sangría* (a wine and fruit drink) and *sangre* (blood).
***Wordplay between the Latin *res publica* (in the public domain or republic) and the Spanish *res* (cattle).

—Don't fight, boys, it's too hot. And don't make me yell at you from here.

—You big fools-of-my-very-own-guts, talk, cackle, screech. My dear brothers can't you defend yourselves? And on top of it all that poor woman has to put up with Uncle Coco's chatter. There's never been such a bright, golden day, Uncle Coco must be saying. There've never been such dumb kids, look how they prefer that torturous sun. There've never been such dumb kids, just like all kids. Mama listens very sadly to what Uncle Coco would say if his seven senses, I mean his cerebellum, weren't so shriveled up, but not because of old age. Who isn't cursed? Some have fried brains and others have swollen heads. Venomous little kids, Uncle Coco's saying, poisoned by lingering summers, by exuberance, by intentional physical exhaustion. With the venom of those who are still young. Oh to be twenty-seven years old, unfortunate Uncle Coco wishes.

—Shut up already. No one's listening to you.

—What would Uncle Coco do if he were twenty-seven years old? He's so stupid . . . So many *reses* are born in the spring!

—*Roses* come out in the spring, dummy, not *reses*.*

—*Reses*. I'm saying *reses*. Their carcasses came in a truck, by night down the road from Mar del Plata before the Boca bridge. I felt like being one of the *reses*, those steers born in the spring. Like the ones in the truck.

—But stupid, to be the carcass of a *res* you'd have to be dead. You'd be inside the steer. Or do you think that the steers separate themselves from the animals they used to be?

—Yes. The steers no longer keep anything inside. They let everything loose, blood, people. People slip away from them, outside of them. I want to be a brilliant steer.

—How stupid! Boy are you dumb.

—I want to be a private steer, a *res privada*.

—Be careful, Santi, look at how his eyes are changing.

—Better take Carlitos away on the sly. He's too young to defend himself.

—He won't want to go, the filthy kid . . . Look, look how our very own

*Wordplay between *rosas* (roses) and *reses* (cattle).

Paco scratches himself. No one scratches so desperately. This is getting good. Take Carlitos away. He listens to you.

—Why don't you take him? You're not in the pool. Or that bum Vincent, lying around with a piece of straw in his mouth like some broad on a billboard.

—Mama, mama, they're biting me all over. Come here, mama, get rid of the itch.

—*But child, if you lie down in the grass, of course, they'll bite you. They must be ticks.*

—Look at the dummy run to the veranda. "Mama, mama." He sure can call her, that big oaf, even though he's sixteen years old. We don't do that.

—*Mama, they're biting me all over. The sun! The dizzying sun.*
—*What do you mean, son?*
—*It's dazzling me.*
—*Your eyes are very red. Why don't you stay inside for a while?*
—*The bees are dying from indigestion among the flowers. The grass and sun want to die from indigestion biting me.*
—*I'll pull out the straws so they won't prick you anymore. But why don't you jump into the water if the sun's stinging you?*

—Take advantage now that Paco's gone and take Carlitos through the back door.

—Take him, take him away. Why don't you take him, you two lying around like sultans? Come on, Carlitos, you've bathed enough. Get out of the water, your lips are purple. Let's go home.

—Why do I have to go?

—Because Paco's going to have an attack, stupid, and you're only twelve years old; you're a sissy and won't even be able to stand his sight.

—All right, stop hitting me on the head. I'm going. I'll go because I feel like it. Quit it.

—This is going to get hot, Vincent. When Paco stops complaining to mom on the veranda and María Beanhead comes back, the game'll really begin.

—And what if Paco stays on the veranda?
—He won't. He likes us too much.

—*See? No more straws. No more itching. I took them all out.*
—*I'm going inside. It makes me mad to see you be a servant to your sons. They're old enough to do things for themselves.*
—*Uncle Coco doesn't love us because we're fifteen years old.*
—*That's not so, of course he loves you, but he doesn't like me to spoil you so much. Don't you feel better now, Paco?*
—*The garden's drunk with heat and gold.*
—*What beautiful things you say, Adam.*
—*Adam? I'm Paco.*
—*This is paradise. All gardens have animals from paradise, serpents and others.*
—*I don't want to be Adam. I'm guilty enough already. Just as I am.*
—*You said a garden drunk with heat and gold. Shimmering gold shifting about among the trees, merciless gold, a dart far from the protected shade . . . Where did the founders, the makers of paradise go? Don't look so strange, child. What pretty mouths my sons have. Your lips turn up more than the others. Curved lips, the edges almost trembling. Your father's mouth wasn't like that. All my sons owe that mouth to my yearning. Silken sons. You're like moist ferns, velvety milkweed.*
—*Who was the mentally retarded one, mama, you or papa? You can't be saying what I'm hearing. Why does it sound like that to me? You said what a garden full of nettles, my son, full of hemlock. I think you said where did the founders of paradise go. You can't be calling me Adam. I'm leaving, mama, I'm going out on the lawn, because you can't be saying that I owe my mouth to your yearning. When did I start to hear what others were thinking as if they were saying it out loud? When did I begin to hear what the others must be thinking?*
—*I don't know what you're talking about, dear. I said the extravagant vegetation is very orderly in this paradise. Violet clusters, jasmine arches, perfume and color forming cathedrals.*
—*I'm going out on the grass, mama. I'm afraid of you. Why are you saying things you don't know how to say? You said "I don't know what you're talking about, dear." Nothing else, right?*

—Guys, here comes Paco running.
—And what if we tell them to watch from the house?

182

—Whoever tells is a sissy. Whoever runs away has a yellow streak.

—What do you think? That mom's an idiot because she favors that idiot?

—Maybe she loves him because the old man beat him more.

—He's already lying down again on the grass. And he's scratching to beat the band. He's really getting mad.

—Does the dry straw bother you, Strawboy?

—What's he doing? He's cutting the straw and putting it between his legs . . . No! You gave him that idea. The kid doesn't know how it's done so he's walking with a handful between his legs.

—He scared you.

—Me? Do you want to see how I'm scared? Who dares take the straw away from him?

—Whoever does is the boss . . . Watch out he doesn't turn around and grab you! Now it's my turn.

—I got them! See, you big dummy? The very same María Beanhead got them away from you.

—Watch out, José María! Jump into the pool. Watch out, he'll grab you!

—Boy, the idiot jumped in, too. María Beanhead can't defend himself alone. Let's go. Let's throw Paco around.

—Give it to him. Hit him under the water.

—Get away, José María. Get away, I say, now that you can. I'm holding his legs.

—He can't. Paco's holding on to him tight like a madman.

—He got away!

—Here he comes.

—I'm coming. Help, José María, don't just stand there . . . Yeah! I dunked him. Hold his head under . . . Someone grab his arms.

—Okay, that's enough. Let go or he's going to drown.

—Besides you can't imagine the beating mom'll give us later. Can't you hear her? She's already shouting what's going on out there.

—But he's not moving . . . Man, he's floating. Did he drown?

—Come on! He's only floating cause he's full of air.

—Should we pass him around like a ball?

—Let's knock the air out of him.

—Look at him. He's a killer whale. Everyone get the whale.

—No, dear little brothers. No, dear little brothers playing with me who suddenly look at one another and say to themselves: let's explore terror.

You see how I can jump out of the water before you can, even though I'm a whale? Terror's very amusing. You think I don't know? I'm a diver who explores terror. I'll kill the first one who leaves the pool. Because I'm not just a diver, I'm a destroyer whale, too. And you're not going to catch me off guard just because mama came out on the veranda again and is watching us.

—Are his eyes red from the water or from anger?

—I don't know. He seems to be calming down a little. The crisis cooled him off. If he puts straw between his legs again, he'll tear us to shreds . . . Hey, Paco, look at the straws you left there. Grab them or the breeze'll blow them into the pool.

—Mama, there's a mosquito buzzing in my ear.

—The big oaf's running to mom.

—*Did the water help the itch?*

—*Yes, mama. Poor mama.*

—*Your eyes are like sequins. Like minerals, mica.*

—*Did you say my eyes are golden or red? Why do you love me? Are you really thinking: how does he know how to imitate the mentally retarded so well? Am I retarded?*

—*What are you saying?*

—*What do you call the guy who studies fossils buried in the earth? . . . A paleontologist.*

—*Your eyes, dear, your eyes are so red . . . Don't hug me you're sopping wet. You'll drown me.*

—*I'll make your waist real tiny some day, squeezing it like this.*

—*Ay!*

—*It's clouding over. You shouldn't leave the windows open. The hot air comes in. It's because of those mindless boys.*

—Come out from behind the metal blinds, Uncle Coco. Come out and stop complaining. Come get wet. Look at those clouds.

—*Yes, it's going to rain any minute . . . I'd like to feel the sensuous grass beneath my feet. But my feet refuse to do anything that's not practical. They don't want to sin anymore. And those kids over there, their bodies crushing the grass like frogs, playing around with stupid dares. Children's*

*games have to be played out on some silly turf to be enjoyed. Yes, these
hot clouds are already over us.*
—*Uncle Coco, why don't your feet want to sin?*
—*What's that? What are you talking about?*
—*About what you said.*
—*I only said it's clouding over and it's going to rain any minute now.*
—*Go take a dip, dear. It's suffocating out.*
—*Yes, mama.*

—Here comes the idiot again. Everyone into the pool.
—The dummy's not coming in. He's staying out in the heat. The itch-
ing's starting up. He's getting crazier.
—He's getting up. Who's he talking to? He's moving his arms like a
windmill. Like he's talking to the sky.
—Perverse brothers. I'm not an idiot; I gush forth from terror. From the
source. What do you know about fear? You explore it from the outside.
I'm in the center of terror and I create it at the same time. So it's not
funny, you unhappy dunces, children of a madman, a drunkard.
—He's worse than ever. Wild. Why doesn't mom come out?
—Don't be chicken. We can handle this by ourselves.
—I'm a doctor who takes the pulse of fear. And I'm a paleontologist
who extracts the fossilized plesiosaurus from within. Fear goes way back
to the time of the plesiosaurus. You're happy, you wretches who don't
flow from the heart of terror. Anything distracts you from it. I'm panic,
I'm shrouded in panic. I create it and bear it. Why can't fear come to me
from outside like with you?
—Shut up, you idiot, or your mouth'll fill up with rain.
—It's already raining. Now's when the storm lets loose. Let's play shipwreck in the pool.
—For many days now the shipwrecked men have been adrift; the storm
attacks them; the downpour punishes them. They have to eat each
other. Let's form two sides. And let the idiot be the whale. If we hunt
him down, we won't be hungry anymore.
—Come, sickly whale, if you're really a man, jump in.
—To mama I'm a silken whale.
—Hey whale, you're making waves. Spit the water out, whale.
—Hey, he's coming at us.

—What a tremendous storm! The drops are striking like hammers. The world's disappeared.

—*Children, children! Get out of the water. If lightning strikes you'll be electrocuted. Come inside the house now. I'm going in.*

—Do you suppose mom is good-natured or dumb? Why do you think she loves the idiot so much?
—You have to run risks, mom. That's what life's all about.
—Look at Santiago, the things he's saying. Did the idiot teach you?
—Our water is covered with friends and enemies. With the living and the dead, with fleeting fish slipping by. You are friends. I am everyone's enemy. Boys aglow from lightning slither by me like wet scales.
—Where are the dead men, whale?
—In my hands, damned perverts. The dead are inside the bodies of the first and second and third one of you that I grab . . . come to me my springtime steer. Come, so I can hit your heads against the drainpipe. See? Just like this.
—Help!

Translated by Evelyn Picon Garfield

Carmen Naranjo

Costa Rica

Carmen Naranjo.

Carmen Naranjo, born in Costa Rica in 1930, has been the most visible woman in public office in her country during this century, holding positions as general manager of the Social Security Agency, minister of culture, youth, and sports, ambassador to Israel, and director of the Museum of Costa Rican Art. She is presently the director of EDUCA, the publishing company of Central American universities.

She has won literary prizes for several of her six books of poetry, six novels, three collections of short stories, and two books of essays. For our anthology we turn to her prose, in which she breaks with Costa Rica's traditional interest in rural scenes and self-identity based on the land to focus instead on the routine life of her country's vast urban middle class in novels such as *Camino al mediodía* (Noontime Walk), *Los perros no ladraron* (The Dogs Didn't Bark), and *Memorias de un hombre de palabra* (Memoirs of a Man of Words). Naranjo herself establishes a certain stratification—lower, middle, and upper-middle class—when she speaks of that "trilogy." In her prose she depicts office workers and bosses through whom she criticizes modern, industrialized society where consumerism and bureaucracy alienate and dehumanize people at work and at home.

Although mediocrity and triviality abound in the lives of her characters, there is nothing humdrum about her prose style. For example, Naranjo experiments with narrative perspective: one novel is based entirely on dialogues between several identifiable first-person narrators, as in a film; another, entirely on a myriad of anonymous voices that create a collective stream of consciousness, representative of the masses of individuals that make up society; and yet another is written with a pointillist technique borrowed from painting. Her interest in mass media influences the use of a reporter with a tape recorder in one of the short stories presented here, "Why Kill the Countess?" ("¿Para qué matar a la Condesa?"). In fact, her short stories often have female protagonists like the Countess, in contrast to her novels (with the exception of the last one, *Sobrepunto*).

She has published thirty-seven richly varied stories: realistic and fantastic, set in the country and the city, about psychological, aesthetic, and socioeconomic themes. In them she explores the human condition, denounces social vices, and above all sympathizes with her characters, an attitude that does not prevent her from using humor and irony in stories such as the two we have translated here.

Ondina

When they invited me to have a cup of coffee that Monday at five o'clock in the afternoon—who knew what that meant, maybe black coffee with lemon pastry or homemade bread or coffee laced with rich cognac—I thought of everything, everything but the surprise of being introduced to someone in bits and snatches: Ondina.

Ondina always came to me intuitively like a puzzle with a hundred thousand pieces. Even in inflationary times such high figures are truly exhausting. I didn't know her name or what she was like but I sensed her presence in every gesture, in every sentence.

My relationship with the Brenes family was always quite traditional, courteous, cordial, the usual formalities for birthdays, Christmas Eve and New Year's. I never forgot to send the appropriate card for each occasion and even flowers on the grandmother's saint's day.* The Brenes politely made me wait in the hallway. That was after making it through the entry gate and along the road lined with pine trees and

*In Hispanic cultures a person celebrates the birthday of the saint for whom (s)he was named.

190

fragrant solandra that lent a churchlike aura to the foliage-covered lime-stone house you imagined full of nooks and crannies beyond the gardens of daisies and chrysanthemums buzzing with bees and hummingbirds. Then as now I suppose they assumed I was courting Merceditas, sensual and pretty, with her air of a rabbit about to go into heat. But she promptly slipped out of my hands, perhaps because I saw her touch the keyboard of the IBM electric typewriter too much. There she lost her personality among the keys and seemed to take pleasure in dear sir, colon, thank you for your letter of the fourth of whatever month in which you intelligently offer such positive, concrete ideas, comma, but . . .

Perhaps she was too bubbly for my taste that delighted in Picasso's deformities; she only let me enjoy silence when she was busily typing or when her eyes filled with unexpected sensations expressing oh, how I hate these foggy, drizzly days that make me want to stay in bed under the sensuous sheets; and that makes me sick.

Maybe in a moment of boredom I thought of going to bed with her and kissed the back of her neck and close to her ear, while hearing her wise advice, what can Mr. Boss be thinking about, give up such thoughts, remember the rules and act like the gentleman you are, that's the limit. I always responded by giving her a raise and devoutly asking her how are your dear grandparents and parents. What incredible longevity there is in underdevelopment! Very well, and your family. Mine, full of melancholy cancers, had left me alone in this world: what happiness, what tranquility . . . what sadness.

On long days at work, now the budget, now the annual plan, now the rebuttal to the critics of institutionalized work, I would accompany Merceditas to the gate of her house. Good night, thank you for everything, I don't deserve so much goodness and loyalty. A waltzlike kiss on the hand and may God bless you. Sir, you're a good man and deserve a happy home.

That would leave me thinking for some six blocks from Merceditas's home with her grandparents and parents, alive and kicking, and mine under dated gravestones in the rich man's cemetery, very securely settled in the dance of death.

I knew her gate, her pine tree entranceway and her jasmine corridor. I saw her smiling grandparents, her parents as content as if they had won the grand prize in the last lottery drawing. So much happiness seemed strange to me, like a platter prepared so that the bachelor and the old maid would weave their nest with I love you and you love me and from then on every man for himself!

Nevertheless, beyond the doors I sensed an orgy of hot ovens where bronze corrodes and silver glistens.

I couldn't put my finger on it. For example, in front of the camellias, I saw a very tiny bench unnecessary for cutting the flowers up above or those below.

Political intrigue cost me my job and I became Mr. Nobody by means of someone else's unwitting signature. I bid farewell to Merceditas promising to remember her, that she was my life; but she didn't listen to me because at that moment she was writing the goodbye memo to my loyal colleagues.

Afterward I heard about the Brenes family very little except for the death notices appearing shortly before burial that informed me of the grandparents' passing away. I quickly dressed in mourning and joined the funeral procession barely on time on its way to the cemetery. For each grandparent I embraced Merceditas in impassioned consolation and felt her full breasts buried against the buttons on my black jacket. Rather than excite me, her breasts frightened me. Too big for my small hands.

The invitation that Monday at five o'clock in the afternoon to have coffee (it was only black coffee with small cakes from a bakery) offered me the opportunity to see that house, neither poor nor rich, nor in good or bad taste, but rather the dwelling one inherits and leaves "as is" due to a certain inertia about maintaining order, adding some incidental gifts along with the modern appliances one acquires because life marches on: to deny it is stupid. The house established by the great-grandparents, lived in by the smiling grandparents who patched up the leaks, and now by the parents fighting with the humidity and termites. In a plush easy chair with a thick crocheted cover, Merceditas struggled all afternoon to accommodate her buttocks without damaging a throw pillow, surely knitted by her great-grandmother who smiled from a carnivalesque photo framed in tarnished silver. Flanked by her parents on the bright green sofa, there I sat with a cushion between my open legs, verging on bad manners. I was puzzled by a very low chair with a miniature throw pillow; I thought it was a childhood keepsake.

Painted in a modern style, the main portrait in the room was of a very beautiful young lady with piercing, light green eyes. The strength of that portrait eclipsed the vase, the china, the angel sculpture, the marble column, the photographs of great-grandparents and grandparents, the altarpiece to the Virgin's miracles, the intertwined pattern of the tapestry, and even the picture of Merceditas, who seemed to lull her newborn bunnies to sleep.

And when the conversation revealed to me that the reason for the invitation to have coffee was that rumors were going around, that I would again be named to the high position of councillor, and was that true, I made up my mind to ask who she was. They answered, curtly and simply: Ondina. At that moment her eyes, Ondina's eyes followed me, responded and caressed me. I discovered her boldness and audacity, her overt excitement.

I could barely follow the gist of the conversation. Me, name me? But my life had become so simple that I barely read the newspapers and only worried about personal trivia like collecting my income, walking to the big fig tree every day to do five kilometers or deceiving myself a little by thinking that life has meaning and is transcendental.

Ondina caught my eye and I think she even winked at me. Nobody can be so beautiful, it's a trick, I said to myself unconvincingly. Who is Ondina? Just Ondina, they answered almost in unison. Merceditas's younger sister, added the good, smiling father, Jacinto. I calculated it. Despite firm, erect breasts, mahogany-colored hair, no eyeglasses and a hip-swaying walk, Merceditas seemed to be gaining on her forties. Ondina, at the most, would be in her thirties, because mother Vicenta, close to her seventies with chronic asthma, rheumatism and diabetes, couldn't have conceived after her forties.

I didn't want to leave, I couldn't, transfixed as I was by the portrait and the eyes. That's why I didn't notice the silences and the questions they repeatedly asked me. It was mother Vicenta who obliged me to end that brazen contemplation. She touched my shoulder and said it was seven o'clock, they must remind me that they went to bed early after saying the rosary. I left immediately, excusing the imposition, but you know with them time flew by imperceptibly. Merceditas held my hand during the farewell and assured me that it meant more to her than I could imagine.

I dreamt about Ondina week after week. I remember her numerous visits to my room. Tall and thin, with her hair down to her waist, nude or

193

in a transparent negligee, she would open the door and jump onto my bed. She would always undress me and then play with my penis until I became wild. At breakfast time my gentlemanly spirit obliged me to feel ashamed of my dreams, but I began to daydream, conscious of my acts, and the orgies were more prolific and gratifying. She rode me like a horse, licked me, and with her legs wide open she let me penetrate her deeply, time and again, insatiably.

I sent flowers to her mother, chocolates to Merceditas, a history book to father Jacinto. I wasn't even notified of the delivery, no less thanked. I telephoned and asked for Ondina. Mother Vicenta's voice asked who's calling, cousin Emmanuel, then the line went dead.

I asked friends and neighbors about Ondina Brenes but no one knew her. They spoke to me of father Jacinto, mother Vicenta and the too chaste, good Merceditas, whom they had been trying to marry off in vain since she was fifteen years old; she was still there, still there with them, much too clean and tidy, never had a fling, as far as we know.

In the grocery store I asked what they bought, in the pharmacy, in the fish store . . . nothing. Someone informed me that they were very much in debt and barely made ends meet.

I began to read the newspapers, up to the very last line. Ondina's beauty couldn't go unnoticed. I listened to the radio, watched television, went to the registry office: Ondina Brenes Cedeño. After a tip, she appeared: born June 18, 1935. I studied her horoscope. Complicated double personality.

I knocked at the gate. Father Jacinto answered. I confessed: I'm in love with Ondina, want to get to know her and have the opportunity to see her with good intentions, to marry her if necessary and if she accepted me. He listened to me, smiled and answered that I should forget it; it was impossible. Ondina wouldn't accept me, she had rejected many better than I. When I asked him why, why, he closed the gate gently and disappeared among the pine trees.

I wrote her a passionate letter, sent it certified mail, but got no response. At the post office they told me that Merceditas took it in.

I had no idea of how the whole family was mocking me, but Ondina told me about it one night when she came to my room not feeling much like pawing my body, panting and shaking.

The next morning I found out about the tragedy: after mass at six thirty in the morning, the Brenes, the old couple Brenes was run over by a drunk driver. Instantly killed, practically destroyed. Merceditas went wild. And from the entire touching story, all I saw was a door opening to Ondina.

I presented myself immediately at the house, just as I was, dressed informally.

Family, friends and acquaintances from work had already arrived. I asked for Ondina and nobody knew her, they only said that Merceditas was locked up in her room, hysterical.

Seated in a corner, I saw how a bossy aunt, skillful in such tragedies, organized the mourning. She put the two bodies in closed caskets in the living room, put out candles and flowers, lined up funeral wreaths, distributed coffee and empanadas, denied entrance to strangers, disabused spectacle seekers and after four o'clock had the intimate family ready for the wake. She accepted me because when asked who I was, I answered in a deathly serious tone that I was Merceditas's formal fiance, Mr. Vega. Fortunately she's not alone, welcome sir, we're going to be relatives.

Then I slipped in among those who were praying to see Ondina close up. She was waiting for me. It seemed to me she had changed her dress, for I didn't remember that violet gauze blowing in the wind. I saw her face to face, anxious to memorize each detail: her hands, neck, trembling lips, half-closed eyes and that straight, keen gaze.

The aunt interrupted me to say: go to Merceditas, she needs you. And she almost dragged me to a door in a corridor where many doors looked alike. Thank you, madam, and she left me alone in the privacy of the house. I heard sobs and cries. Perhaps Ondina was there, too, but I didn't dare enter.

I opened another door. In a small room adjoining the dining room, seated in the middle of a table, was a dwarf, barely grazing the floor, mouth open and eyes bulging, letting a mangy cat wedged between her legs grotesquely lick her vagina. I was horrified by the scene, even though it attracted me for some moments, for I saw the drops of sweaty pleasure stream down the cheeks of that womanlike creature with the face of an old lady and the body of a little girl, while the insatiable cat sucked and sucked, suckling, absorbing, grunting. They didn't even realize I was there, or perhaps I didn't bother them.

I returned to my place in the living room, in front of Ondina's portrait. The scene in that other room adjoining the dining area almost slipped

195

from sight when Ondina's sensual energy filled me with strange caresses. She began to play with my ears, blew in them like seashells, rested her tongue in the opening to my left ear and with sealike sensations left me exhausted with excitement that paid no mind to strengths or weaknesses. Then she kissed my eyes very gently and afterward fiercely, but when she tried to suck at them I had to free myself from her lips that were wounding me with blind pain. When someone said I needed a tranquilizer, the aunt told him they were almost my relatives, then gave me some pills that must have made me drop off to sleep all contorted up in an uncomfortable chair, with more uncomfortable cushions.

When I awoke at nighttime, the rosary was being organized. The priest, Father Jovel in person, beads in hand, incense on the sides and between the coffins. He waited impatiently for the main characters, who in these cases are not the deceased but the closest relatives. Then Merceditas appeared, pale and weak, dressed entirely in black with her well-supported, erect full breasts; she was holding the hand of the tiniest and most beautiful dwarf I had ever seen, also dressed entirely in black, except for a white crocheted collar, and with Ondina's eyes, Ondina's rebellious hair, Ondina's fleshly trembling lips. The rosary began. I couldn't follow, because the waist, the hips, the back were Ondina's, my Ondina.

After midnight only six of us remained in the living room: the dwarf, Merceditas, the aunt, the uncle, the cousin and I. Merceditas's sighs were so deep and rhythmic that her fainting spells came on with the rapidity of sea swells. The aunt brought her two pills and Merceditas was shortly sleeping like a baby, snoring intermittently. In her backless chair the dwarf cried calmly, without a sob. She came toward me and asked to sit on my lap. Almost everyone was nodding sleepily. It occurred to me to sing her a baby's lullaby. Sleep, sleep, my little girl. Then she curled up near my penis. It was really uncomfortable, but what could I do. I rocked her as best I could and she, active and generous, opened up my fly and began to rock what was inside. After enduring the best I could, I lifted her in my arms and carried her into the room adjoining the dining area. Gentle, sweet, barely a little girl. Then she said to me: let Ondina teach you everything she's learned in her solitude. She opened my shirt and began to pull the hairs from my chest with her funnel-like hollow kisses. I searched for her vagina and opened it like orange wedges. The cat jumped at that moment and scratched my penis causing it to bleed pain and fear. Ondina waited for me but I couldn't come until I finally found the key to coexistence.

I walked in the procession, tired and sleepless, and thought of Ondina, the cat and Merceditas. With every step I thought. And I made up my mind decisively and unequivocally.

The betrothal was set for a month after the mourning period. Ondina attended the wedding; the cat stayed home.

Translated by Evelyn Picon Garfield

Why Kill the Countess?

"I CAME TO THIS CITY of routine order and 'don't you
dare be different,' with something else in mind. I thought I'd find adventure, heroism. Instead I'm faced with a trivial tale of petty intrigue. The
people are weak and simple, the poor countess, a silly, old, presumptu-
ous woman. The scenery isn't even worth such a long trip. The trees are
very big and the narrow, cold streets make you ache with rheumatism."

I was already used to those comments. Nobody was interested in the
story, neither the educated people nor those who shut themselves up in
their houses as if suddenly expecting to find bloody footprints.

They hadn't been summoned. First a reporter arrived, then he attracted the rest. The portrait he painted of the countess was extraordinary: a sweet, poetic girl who planted geraniums while she dreamt of
building a white church with towers and spires on that very hill, like a
balcony overlooking the precipice to remind you of the Fall and enrich
the heavenly prayer for that was the essence of a temple. And the church
could not stand alone, for around it were streets and houses in meander-
ing spirals. Almost playfully the girl ordered pines, cedars and cypress to

be planted from the valley along the hillside just up to the edge of the upper plain where the church and houses stood. She wanted a forest and when the little countess wanted something there was no alternative but to give in to her. Whatever happened afterward, the truth is that she founded the town.

"I remember her younger years." The tape recorder captures the slow voice of an old man. "I don't know if she was pretty, maybe that never crossed my mind. I never dared look at her the way you look straight ahead at what's in front of you. I remember she was stubborn; three times the church fell because of her, she wanted it to stand at the very edge of the cliff, didn't understand that the waters wash away the earth and the wind howls up above. She didn't learn from mistakes, that's why it's twisted, the tower's ended up like a quivering arrow and any day now it'll fall on us."

Filled with emotion, the janitor's voice is being taped. He can't conceive of the countess as ever having been a little girl and then a young woman, he has the notion that she was always old, shrunk into wrinkles and an old lady's impatient gestures, in her white lace bonnet and her black silk cloak. "Because she was a moody, unpredictable demon, an old witch, more spiteful than most, always dealing with the devil and tempting us to kill her like a wild animal."

Someone thought of some hidden drama in all this and began questioning the neighbors. You, what opinion do you have of the countess? The question is directed toward a middle-aged woman on the patio who's just frightened off the chickens with a broom; it's a place where the tower's shadow falls like a twisted hand on an old clock. "Don't come to me with such nonsense. Let others judge the countess; it's certainly time to take her title away. Nobody has one of those anymore, everyone's equal now, and anyway, she never had one either. I'm not from this town, I came here when I married the fool who's the church sexton, a poor slob who hasn't changed much, not even since the revolution. I know he's praying on the sly and that irks me. There are mules everywhere and my husband's part of the herd. When it thunders, he names the saints and afterward, feeling ashamed of himself, assures me it's only a trick. A fool's trick I know all too well. My family knew her all right. She was rich, you bet, rich from exploitation and rich from her parents and grandparents. Her husband contributed nothing, only lost whatever he could; but luck was on his side, he died soon and left the widow alone, never tired of counting her money. A woman without a conscience, exploiting those poor idiots, greedily increasing her wealth every day. When the revolution came, those dunces warned her, even asked her permission to raise the new flag, and she hid everything in her house: money, jewelry, they only found a broken set of china and some damned portraits of ugly men. She was called the countess but didn't have a title, just a name and some slaves to show off. I don't want to talk anymore about her or my husband or this disgusting town."

You, what kind of a relationship did you have with the countess? A thin boy with irritated eyes who was learning to be cheeky and to smoke without choking: "Talking about the countess is getting boring. How can it be so hard to get rid of her? Before at home and in the streets we used to talk about other things, the cold weather, food, women. Of course if she passed by or the bells rang, together we'd all say 'God bless the countess with good health,' like we needed to serve her or act stupid. But we all said it. I think if the bells rang or she passed by again, we would repeat the same words. Some things stick like glue. Now we talk about her all day long and they tell stories that'd make your hair stand on end: that she whipped a kid to death because he crossed in front of her path, that she poisoned a maid for entering the room when the countess was calling on the devil, that night and day she roamed around town deciding each person's fate. They talk of her lovers, her sins, her abuses. They talk so much that you don't know what's true and what's a lie. I'm fed up with the stories and the countess. She spoke to me only once before the revolution and called me by name: Peter, stop bothering the García family's daughter, you're both too young to get married, don't miss mass and work harder in the fields. I was very impressed, stood there like a statue. I don't know if it was her voice that echoed far away as if torn loose from the very heavens, or the honor of being called by my name. Maybe it was her green eyes that kept on penetrating you only just so far, no further. Later I saw her in jail, I went with the others to insult her, to shout old lady, wicked witch, whore. She looked at us so calm and proud that she frightened me. She didn't say anything to me, like she didn't hear. At night I couldn't sleep, afterward I was glad they locked her up. It's better that way, I don't like to mistreat old people, even though they may be as miserable as her."

You, who arrested the countess, tell me how it happened. As the afternoon comes to a close without the clanging of bells, this tall husky guy, chief-of-police inside and out, moves his moustache with an agile gesture of his lips: "I've never known a bigger bunch of cowards than the people around these parts. When I arrived, I realized right away that they were ignorant about revolutionary goals and the new popular government. The countess was everything: the government, the law, the authority and the absolute landlord. The land belonged to her, houses, shops, trees, even the whorehouse. They told me a group talked to her about the changes taking place in the country, the implied sacrifices, the blood, the dead, the execution of those who opposed the revolution and the measures that had to be taken. Of course to tell her all of that, they looked for a student from a nearby town; it could be no other way, they cowered before her, an old woman already in complete decay, physically weak like a wingless bird, but powerful and strong in her resolve. She received them and heard their speech, smiling and passing the rosary beads between her fingers. When the student finished, she said the story was very sad, that on Sunday there would be a special mass in memory of the dead, that they should return to work and she would talk to God about it. They all left, except the student. He explained to her that there would be no mass, they had shot the priest in a nearby town, he saw him crying, pleading for clemency and offering to join the revolution. He said the soldiers would arrive soon and she, too, would be judged and perhaps . . . The Countess invited him into the kitchen and offered him some tea; she made it. The student continued talking, relating in detail what had happened to the rich people and the priests. She remained unmoved; when he finished the tea she accompanied him in silence to the door. When she said goodbye, she added, 'In my world I'm in charge, not even God intervenes. He's with us for more important things. In my world there is no government, no revolutions.' That testimony was revealed during the trial and she confirmed her words. Strange woman. When I arrived, I sensed she was waiting for me, I inspired neither fear nor lack of confidence in her, she welcomed me. I placed the handcuffs on the boniest wrists I've ever seen, cold and shriveled up like a dead person's. I read her the charges of exploiting the townspeople and of being a counterrevolutionary. She smiled remote from us all, to the point that I wanted to slap her to make her feel my authority. The poor old lady, perhaps she was senile, that's why I limited myself to helping her up in a friendly way; you know the revolution doesn't prevent good manners. This town doesn't have a jail so I locked her up in the house I took for a police station. After their indoctrination, the people came to insult her. Those who were after jobs and farms made too much noise. That made me move her back to her home, duly guarded, of course. These women are the devil himself; when you least expect it they escape and these idiots here are capable of believing that she produced a miracle and flew off to heaven."

You served for many years in the countess's house, tell us something about her life and habits. Before answering, the old woman, hands trembling and face like a map of long winter and summer days, looked to both sides, perhaps thinking of escaping somewhere or finding someone else to answer. "She was bad like the wicked, but even worse, she never felt at peace with her wickedness, she always wanted more. She despised us; what were we to her? Animals, beasts who only understood bad manners and vulgar remarks. She always looked down her nose at me, never tired of calling me stupid, or overworking me even when it was unnecessary and I couldn't . . . She took away my youth and my strength for free because she was stingy with pay. She didn't care if the rest of us died of starvation, she didn't know what that meant with her high-class airs and her sweets. When I couldn't make the tiles shine like mirrors any more or be on call day and night, she told me to go to live with my kind, just like that, without a show of gratitude. A vain monster puffed up with herself. She decided to stay in her mansion alone and wallow around in her greed. She was doing something strange behind closed doors, I never found out what, maybe some devilish ritual, because I guarantee she didn't believe in God or in anybody. It seems she was always praying, maybe they were curses and witchcraft. Poor woman . . . so alone and so quiet with her sad memories. Her mother committed suicide when the countess was barely seven years old. The old servants who died in that house from tuberculosis and hunger told me she found her mother hanging from a rafter tied by the neck with linen sheets, the ones that had the family crest between flowers and leaves. The woman was hanging with her tongue out, eyes bulging and feet dancing in the air. The little girl turned mute for a long time. Afterward she shouted at night like a madwoman. Her father took her off far away and then returned. They say that since then her green eyes turned to stone and she never sang or danced. The father was her inseparable companion, even after she married. In the afternoon they used to walk together arm in arm down the path between the pine trees up to the lilies, the ones that still grow at the far end of the stream. That's where he ended up one day when a sudden pain in his stomach took away his breath and strangled him while the breeze blew by full of butterflies and leaves. I didn't know him, they say he was very good looking, sad like his daughter, but nicer and sweeter, talked with the servants, pleasant and generous. She built the church for her parents, brought their bones there and placed them in the altar. That's sacrilegious because they weren't saints, the mother didn't even await God's will and he died without confessing. I'd say it isn't a temple, it's a cemetery, a cemetery for rich folk and the wicked. The poor penniless husband is buried in our cemetery with no tombstone or cross. The countess ordered his grave covered with rocks, maybe she was afraid he'd come out at night, although they say he was really dead when they buried him, swollen and half-rotten. He died in a nearby town from some high, rare fever that ate him alive as if he were full of worms. As far as I'm concerned they never loved each other. The countess never mentioned him while I lived with her, even though she talked about her parents with tears in her eyes. She was very sentimental, became weak and helpless when anyone remembered them, begging them over and over again to repeat her parents' words. The town folk who remembered them were her favorites, her guests of honor even if they didn't know the difference between a dessert spoon and a soup spoon. How they took advantage of her generosity . . . they were her weakness, the only weakness I knew of in that bad, unjust woman."

What impression did the countess leave you with? The student polishes his voice and prepares his speech, underneath his eyeglasses an opaque and melancholy look empties the words of their militant tone: "An old woman like any other, nothing extraordinary, as common as the dirty capitalists we see governing the world, shortsighted about the people's interests and with a marked tendency toward exploiting them without conscience, those poor people sacrificed by their ignorance and impotence. She doesn't deserve my respect, but I was surprised by her lack of sensitivity and incomprehension of man's immediate needs. I felt she wasn't a real, live person; she seemed more like someone dead for a long time now, but nevertheless dominating a group of fools by sheer conditioning to authority and religion. A worthless prototype traditionally recognized, devoid of any notion of minimal respect for human beings. She was one of those people who believes in the natural existence of privilege and receives the work and sacrifice of others without any idea of limitations. To talk to her was like talking to a wall. I don't think she understands the humanitarian principles of the revolution, nor our right to social justice. Those very same words seemed new to her, without any meaning in her tongue dominated by the verbs I want, I desire, I command.

It is the typical case of chains that have no idea of freedom, of prisons that ignore law and justice. Nevertheless I ought to mention that I was impressed by that old woman's energy, despite her appearance of a dried-up doll from the past who never matured in her ideals or consideration for others. A kind of queen or very old mummy that was still breathing and had sufficient physical vitality to keep on exploiting. In any case, we arrived in time to stop that corrupt accommodation to arbitrary rule. In the future the revolution will not allow that class of countesses, proprietors of lives and destinies. We're going to change the course of this town. No more countess idols; now ideas and human rights rule. The revolution is . . ."

The countess walked across the long hall without disturbing the silence of an abandoned museum adorned with a few solemn pieces of furniture, dark paintings with white faces and hands of saints, open empty boxes, lusterless objects, new and old designs made by one and many spiderwebs. Every hour she made the same journey, from the room to the garden where all kinds of herbs grew among roses left unpruned for so long, with tall, ugly stems bearing new blossoms, limbs, leaves and dried flowers. Perhaps down below, near the now invisible earth, there were violets, daisies, pansies, a nursery of aristocratic and wild plants. From the garden, after gathering some mint leaves, the countess went on to the kitchen where ceramic, copper and perhaps silver plates hung decorated with designs of fruit and birds, and scenes of lakes and snow. In the pantry, pots and machines remained where they had been placed the last time, on a broken chair, on a table with peeling varnish or broken tiles, or on the very floor with dark stains from the humidity. While the water came to a boil the countess looked up at the sky through the now darkened skylight, for the long and wide kitchen with its closed windows was a conundrum of shadows.

Papa, I want everyone to live near the church, up there on the hill, little by little we will move them, each one in his house, close to

God. We will make the most beautiful town on earth, our town of peace and love.

You see, mama, I didn't desire anything from life and everything is gone, but the town is more beautiful each day and perhaps its people will have the happiness that slipped through my fingers when you left. I have your dolls, your diary, your books of poetry and your bible. How the children grow in the streets! Yesterday I led them by the hand and today they already play alone, tomorrow I will see them holding their own children by the hand. Life is a miracle that never ends but at times I don't know if it has any meaning.

Daughter, my little countess, I want you to understand that I was never bad. I just don't like life. I think that at the very moment when I first opened my eyes I was horrified by life. I won't see you grow up, you're so pretty and small, you make my soul and bones ache, but I didn't want to bear you nor did I want you to come into this world of misery and suffering. You're what pains me most. Your father will find a woman he likes full of smiles. I'm his only sadness, you can't be happy with a woman who has no life in her arms, a woman who desires nothing, not food or jewels or houses in the city or the countryside, who doesn't like the air or the sea, who only wants to be in the dark, speechless in order to think about how and when. Don't inherit my sadness, fight for something, do something, love the people, those poor people who amuse their unknown sorrow by eating and making love. Be strong and live, be like your father, to him life is short and he never thinks about death.

"Mr. Chief-of-Police, I've found out some very strange things about the countess's life. First, for a long time now she's been the poorest person in this town. She even sold her jewelry and personal belongings to build the last house that the people asked for. A really miserable person, she didn't even have money for food. She hasn't hidden anything in her house, so there's no need to keep on digging and destroying furniture. She kept selling her possessions and for a while now there's been nothing left. I've found her things in neighboring villages. The merchants came here to buy from her and she gave away paintings, china, knickknacks, jewels, tablecloths, furniture for any price. The people didn't pay her at sowing time, or for their business or their houses. She never received a penny from those people. She asked them to work but didn't ask them to work for her. Each one owns land, a house and a business of his own. There are several rich people in the town, but no other as poor as the countess. But don't be disheartened, these will become charges against her, you'll see how we twist them around. Who does that old lady think she is? Surely she smelled the revolutionary process and wanted to save her hide by giving everything away. There's nothing more obvious than her deliberate sabotage. But that obvious gesture won't do her any good. Besides, the whole town is clamoring for an execution and if the town asks for it, there must be some reason. The people are always right."

Countess, we haven't been happy and I don't know why. As a gentleman I must recognize my blame first of all. I'm different, I'm not interested in the countryside or the people. These people make me sick, always asking for a handout. Couldn't we live somewhere else? There are happy places in the world, places where people talk and laugh. I feel sick, here I tire of doing nothing. Maybe it's the altitude, the cold, this wind that doesn't leave you in peace, or the aridity that's making me age. Let's go away! Tomorrow. Countess, somewhere else where there is life. Here death smells, stinks. I'm not the kind of person to share this atmosphere. I don't believe in God but God shows up everywhere to watch me. I think I'm about to die.

Countess, my son is sick. Can't you see his jaundiced skin and those dilated eyes no longer yearning for life? Give him some money so he can go away to the sea, to the city, somewhere where he can recover his strength. Give him his properties in the capital, if only in consideration of the years he's spent here. Don't let your conscience bear what's bound to happen soon. He's like a little boy, doesn't know how to work, doesn't think of order, he's defenseless. The only wealth he had was his good manners, his aristocratic appearance, his youth. All that's left is his graciousness, although he's so weak that it's difficult for him to open the door and offer his arm.

"Mr. Chief-of-Police, the countess has no land, nothing appears in the register. Years ago everything was transferred to the people, the fields, the streets, the squares, the church. A while ago she sold the property in the capital city and with the money she paid for new construction, improved drainage systems and services. What do we do now, Mr. Chief-of-Police? The countess isn't guilty, she isn't a landowner, she isn't rich, she isn't exploiting the people, perhaps she's the one who's been exploited by them."

These strange messages are windborne. Your husband had a son with the baker's daughter. Your husband doesn't sleep, he roams through the town, knocks at doors, asks for food, demands love. Your husband is in the valley vomiting up wine, vomiting up blood. Your husband brought along some strange women, with enormous shaking breasts; when they talk no one understands them. Your husband isn't your husband, nor does he know you, nor do you know him.

Whatever you say, father, whatever you say. Your wish is mine. I know no other. I only ask that you leave me here with mother's things. They don't harm me, I swear, don't you see how different I am, happy and very fond of life.

She was good and sweet, besides very beautiful. With your eyes, but deeper and sadder. Her silence was always so impressive; day after day she didn't utter a word. That silence created too great a distance for me. I ended up not speaking to her, ignoring her too, because I felt as lonely as she. I couldn't force her, she was too fragile. I couldn't even kiss her, it was impossible, she couldn't stand physical contact, she would cry and shout. With you, even with you, it was the same, she never kissed you or caressed you.

You're lying, father, you're lying because you didn't love her and she could only be reached by a great love. Mother kissed me all the time when we were alone, she combed my hair with her fingers. How I remember her embrace and that perfume all her own of roses and spring! You're lying, father, like I'm lying by loving and respecting you, but that isn't important because I love you lying, I truly love you. I don't want your strength, your gift for being in charge, for making others do things. I want your paucity of dreams and ideals, your absent eyes when it comes to beautiful things. You've never seen how the butterflies fly around my head because I have honeyed lights and am a big wingless butterfly. They know me and revere me.

"I'd like to substantiate your testimony again. You said that the countess was always the most negative example of capitalism because of her avaricious attitude, without taking into account the needs of others, or paying them justly for their work. I think your judgment is correct, but I want to know why when you saw her chained, when we led her through the town, when we hoped that you and the others would not only speak out but also take justice into your own hands, why you, yes you who accused her with such serious words, obeyed her pleas and ran to fetch water for her. Don't tell me you did it for charity's sake or because she was an old lady; you and the others know that she's more than that. She's perverse and contemptible, she's an institution, she represents a system of work that opposes the people. Why serve her water so promptly and with the pomp and circumstance of a high dignitary? Why did you do that? Why didn't you spit in her face? Why didn't you ignore the plea? Did you like her system of exploitation? Are you opposed to the new government?

My father was harsh, you can't imagine how harsh. I trembled when his eyes followed me, slow eyes, always wide open like your own father's eyes. I didn't know my mother. She died in childbirth. That's how you came into the world, killing. If they didn't say it, I know that they always thought it. My brothers remained buried in the mines with many of my father's other workers. He just said: this is a dog's life. He made up a list of my dowry and gave it to your father. We were wed without a big ceremony, I was in mourning. I went to the altar alone. My father had gone far away, I didn't even find out when he died, maybe he's still alive. Those who are mine, truly mine, have been waiting for me a long time.

"I'm afraid, Michael, I'm afraid of the countess. You'd better ask them to lock her up in another house where they'll treat her as they should. Here I can't, I can't even shout at her or act mean. I'm pleased when she likes my soup, when she smiles at me; I get pleasure out of arranging and cleaning her clothes. To me she's a saint, a good woman who hasn't done any harm. You should see her mended petticoats, how shabby her underclothes are, why even her silk cape has runs in it and her lace bonnet is riddled with holes. Here she's putting on some weight and getting some color back in her face. It's better if they take her somewhere else before they call us traitors."

The wind jumps in the night with the violence of fear, brings messages, old voices and new ones, sustained groans. The countess is sadly awaiting the sentence. The countess was good, forgive the lies. God give health to the countess, what good is that now. Our hour will come, too, it comes to us all. The countess will go to heaven, and us? What will become of us? You have to live in tune with the times. Now it's winter for everyone even though the sun is shining. If we were in charge, we could talk about conscience. Perhaps if they shoot her, we can make her a nice burial with flowers and mourning.

"We've got to get rid of the countess as soon as possible. She's a senile old woman who hardly talks, but she's causing tremendous damage. The people love her, you can't deny that. They admire her, know she's given them her all. Now they're ashamed, feel they're sinning by just talking about her. On the other hand, they haven't accepted the taxes, refuse to pay tribute, and there are no volunteers for the army. The countess is responsible for their not understanding the revolution. She gave and gave without exacting anything, she's a terrible example. In this state of affairs, as extravagant and crazy as she is, it's impossible to establish a new governmental system. The countess is a motto that can turn them against us."

Dawn broke that day earlier than ever. The signs were ready and so were the parade orders, the cameras, the tape recorders and the reporters. The mottos were written out beforehand, the real truth is that mottos have preceded the greatest events, even genesis was genesis before the creation of the world. TODAY FREEDOM WAS BORN IN THIS TOWN. THE REVOLUTION TRIUMPHS AND CREATES JUSTICE. HERE TYRANNY ENDS.

They say she was very peaceful and smiling, perhaps she didn't understand what was going on. A lady like her couldn't lose her composure. Nobody knew whom she cared for. It happened over there, at the opening to the woods where she used to walk with her father.

Father, my father, my dear papa, I want to be a vine that doesn't grow in the earth but is born of the air, without needing support, bearing flowers and fruit all year long.

Mother, my mother, my dear mama, your distant silence is music that brings us together to dance. I loved no one either, only myself, your dolls, father who never understood us, you who carried away my life when you left. I hated the others with love and they've loved me with hatred.

She didn't shout out, cry, or pray, perhaps she didn't realize. It was better that way. They say she didn't fall with the first command to fire; at the second, she slumped very slowly as if she were fainting. They say she confessed to all charges and thanked them for their generosity. They say for her last supper she asked only for tea made from the mint that grows in her own garden. They say she only asked if they had known her parents. They say that a halo of butterflies fluttered above her head. They say she accepted no handkerchief nor closed her eyes. She was already crazy, senile, an old woman with a sunken stomach and shriveled bones.

At nine o' clock the whole town is on parade and the cameras capture every detail. The signs read: "Slavery is dead." "Now vice and shame are buried." "We will never pardon her: wicked and perverse woman." "To hell with the countess."

The procession becomes disorderly, many want to push ahead so the chief-of-police will see them and read the signs. Today we are free, we hate her, she exploited hunger and misery, death to egoism, long live the revolution . . .

And the tears are invisible, you have to laugh and shout, your conscience isn't on display, it's something private, a hidden treasure.

The cameras tell the story of I was there and saw it. But the cameras don't focus on the sign held by a little boy, a boy who's crying like the others: "Why kill the countess?"

Translated by Evelyn Picon Garfield

Marta Traba

Argentina

Marta Traba. (Photo courtesy of Orlando García Valverde,
San José, Costa Rica.)

Marta Traba was born in Buenos Aires, Argentina, in 1930. She studied art in Rome and Paris, and became one of the most important art critics in Latin America. She lived most of her life outside of Argentina in Colombia, Uruguay, Puerto Rico, Venezuela, the United States, and France. In Colombia her influence on the arts was far-reaching, including the task of founding and directing the Museum of Modern Art in Bogotá. Recipient of a Guggenheim fellowship (1968) and the Casa de las Américas Prize from Cuba for her first novel, *Las ceremonias del verano* (Summer Rites), Traba lectured extensively in the United States at Harvard, the University of Massachusetts, Oberlin, the University of Maryland, Middlebury, and Princeton. She moved to Paris in 1982, after being denied permanent residence in the United States for unspecified reasons. In 1983, she died in a plane crash near Madrid, Spain.

Apart from more than a dozen volumes of art history and art criticism, Traba has published more than six novels and two collections of short stories. After her death her son, the Colombian artist Gustavo Zalamea, saw to it that several manuscripts were published posthumously. The selections presented here are representative of several important characteristics of her fiction. The two short stories, "All in a Lifetime" ("Pasó así") and "Conformity" ("La identificación") in our translation form part of the collection *Pasó así,* published early in her literary career. These stories are set in Bogotá's tenement neighborhoods and share recurrent characters whose dehumanized existence is as gray as the barren urban ghetto they inhabit. Most are resigned to their destinies; those who try to escape the crushing repetition of vacant lots and ashen buildings are frustrated by external forces such as commercial and political hypocrisy and by internal forces such as lack of motivation and the neighbors' petty intrigue and envy. Inventiveness, irony, and even humor enter into some of these stories, including "All in a Lifetime."

Traba's commitment is not merely social, however. With compatriots such as Luisa Valenzuela, Elvira Orphée, Griselda Gambaro, Julio Cortázar, Manuel Puig, and Jacobo Timerman, she writes about those who have been tortured, have disappeared, and have been forced into exile during the civil strife of the seventies in the Southern Cone countries of Argentina, Uruguay, and Chile. Her novel *Conversación al Sur,* translated by Jo Labanyi as *Mothers and Shadows* (London, 1986), is based on a series of conversations between two women, five years after their first meeting: Irene, an Argentinean actress in her forties who was accidentally drawn into contact with young revolutionaries through acquaintances and her son's involvement in Allende's Chile rather than through her own political convictions, and Dolores, a twenty-eight-year-old Uruguayan writer and political activist who has been tortured by the police. By means of their thoughts and conversations, first from Irene's perspective and then from Dolores's, and through flashbacks that introduce us to two other women—Irene's old college friend Elena and her daughter Victoria, whom Dolores knew—a tapestry of female voices weaves a story of the physical and psychological ravages caused by political turmoil in the Southern Cone. The sensitive development of a sympathetic and symbiotic relationship between two protagonists whose story does not depend on their relationships with men is a unique contribution to Latin American literature.

From Labanyi's translation of this novel, we have chosen a selection about the "Mothers of the Plaza de Mayo." Irene is explaining to Dolores an experience she had when she returned from Bogotá, Colombia, to Buenos Aires where she visited with her old friend Elena, whose daughter Victoria had disappeared. She explains to Dolores how Elena took her along for the first time to visit the square where once a week women gather in front of the presidential palace called the Casa Rosada to protest the disappearance of their loved ones.

Mothers and Shadows
[Selection from the novel]

FOUR O'CLOCK. Half an hour to go before the demonstration started. She briefly explained to me how she'd first met the 'Madwomen of the Plaza de Mayo.' On her interminable, harrowing visits to law courts, police stations, prison waiting rooms, she began to notice she was always coming across the same people. To start with she thought they were following her, but after a while, when she looked more carefully at various women she kept encountering again and again, she realised her suspicions were unfounded. Haggard, wan, those faces reflected her own despair. How could she fail to recognise the signs of that night-long pacing round and round a room on the verge of breakdown? On one occasion, a woman she'd bumped into three times that same day invited her to go for a coffee, and they got talking; when Elena learnt that for some women the search had gone on for years, and that in the case of the woman she was talking to it had been nearly a year and a half, she thought she was going out of her mind. She was feeling very weak; her head began to spin and she had to clutch at the edge of the table to stop herself fainting. The other woman felt sorry for her and

215

gave her her phone number, in case she wanted to join the protest. She heard, dimly, that they met every Thursday in the Plaza de Mayo carrying photographs and lists of names of those who had disappeared. That evening, she staggered back to the empty apartment in the Calle San Martín. She spent several days in bed, barely stirring; every now and then she would climb down to make some coffee and nibble a biscuit. Everything she ate, she vomited. But one morning she woke up to the realisation that, if she went on like that, she was never going to find Victoria, and to give up the search was tantamount to signing her death warrant. She got out the woman's phone number and dialled. The woman's voice sounded flat. No, she hadn't made any progress. She'd had a good-quality enlargement made of her son and took it with her every Thursday. He looked really smart in his school uniform; it had been taken the day he left school, just two weeks before.

Suddenly the voice at the end of the phone perked up; she was really pleased she'd decided to join them, she must let her have her daughter's name so she could add it to the stencilled lists, and her photo too for their records. Did she know how to knit?

'No,' Elena gulped. What a pity, because there was a big group of them that knitted all sorts of things; then they raffled them to raise money for those women whose husbands had disappeared, or for the grandparents who'd been left looking after the babies. Elena wanted to ask 'What babies?' but kept quiet. 'It's better to be on a list than to be nowhere,' the voice concluded. It was a Wednesday. The following day she went to the Plaza de Mayo for the first time, and since then had not missed a week.

'We've got time for one last cup of coffee. It's only a few blocks away.' She got up gracefully and went to light the stove again.

For some time she'd been waiting to ask her something but couldn't pluck up the courage. She didn't quite know how to put it either. She would have liked her to provide an explanation—any explanation—that made sense of Victoria's behaviour. But who was she thinking of: Victoria? Or her son whose letters from Chile were increasingly enthusiastic but increasingly vague about the one thing that mattered to her, that is, how he was getting on at university? She couldn't bring herself to accept that he might lose interest in his research and devote all his energies to politics. It wasn't that she objected to what he was doing, any more than she'd objected to what Victoria had done. It was just that she didn't understand them. She couldn't see the point of their relinquishing their hard-won positions in a society that had time only for winners. In Victoria's case, she was clearly going all-out to lose. And how could a loser win the revolution? She was completely stuck for an answer, she always had been. A smell of coagulated blood, of incinerated bones would haunt her; she would have terrible nightmares in which ghoulish crematoria loomed in the fog. And she would recognise the traces of the intense hatred she'd felt as a child, whenever her father had explained over the dinner table, moving round the plates and forks, how that madman, that criminal had advanced, how he'd entered Russia, how he'd got as far as Stalingrad.

I watched her coming towards me with the cup of coffee in one hand and the sugar bowl in the other. Were we not both kidding each other in our heart of hearts? She must think I'd come all the way from Bogotá to accompany her in her futile ritual. But what I wanted was relief from the tension I could feel mounting inside me, choking me. Yet neither of us could do anything to help the other. She must know perfectly well the ritual was going to get her nowhere; I knew no one could free me from the sensation of failure, of having made a mistake, which always seemed to mar my major stage triumphs. Someone ought to be able to explain why unhappiness homes in on you precisely at those moments when everything seems to be in perfect order; anyway, my son could look after himself, good for him if he's found his ideal place to live, even if it means being a loser.

So, it was time to go. She went over to the dining table littered with papers and put something in her handbag; then she disappeared behind the flowery curtain and brought out an impeccably cut jacket, matching her tartan skirt. (So that was where she hung her clothes . . .) She took out a white scarf and tied it round her neck. She glanced at me and produced an identical scarf for me.

'I've got a scarf, thanks.'

She stood looking at me.

'That's not the point. It's in case you want to go dressed like the rest of us. We all wear a white scarf as a token.'

I clutched the white scarf and felt close to tears.

'The last time I saw a big demonstration waving white scarves was in Chile, a few months ago, outside La Moneda Palace. It's a wonderful sight to see thousands of white scarves waving in the air.'

'We've got thousands of white scarves too,' she replied as she locked the door. 'But it's not a wonderful sight.'

As we went down the stairs I said it was a sign of hope, anyway. We were met by a disgusting smell of cabbage soup.

'So we believe,' she murmured out on the pavement, pressing my hand. She was smiling ruefully, as if apologising for being less than honest with me.

The two women walk one behind the other because of the narrow pavement and the odd person sitting out on the doorstep with legs protruding, in time-honoured indifference to the passers-by. She would rather have gone down another street, Florida for example, but Elena presumably wanted to avoid the risk of bumping into someone she knew. She looked down the first side-street towards the port, and with a twinge of nostalgia recognised the distant outlines of the ships at anchor. It was as if she'd flashed back to the childhood days when ships and ports dizzied her with an attraction nothing else could equal, rescuing her from the urban greyness of Buenos Aires. They went on walking in silence till they came out into the square.

She stopped short, dazzled by the whiteness of that vast, bleak, open space, with its ludicrous obelisk sticking up in the middle. 'It must be the light reflecting on the paving stones,' she thought, confronted by a stream of images in which she crossed the square again and again, first as a child and then as a girl. She began to make her way falteringly across the horrid square, squinting at the blinding light. When finally she opened her eyes wide, she saw the sun was still high overhead, in an unblemished sky without a hint of cloud. She felt irritated by that conjunction of blue and white, evoking the national colours and flag. Argentine nationalism was, it seemed, doomed to belong to the category of the kitsch. Give her the tropics any day, with their stormy skies perpetually rent by the play of warring elements. She noted that a handful of people, no more than that, were dotted around the middle of the square. But something felt wrong. She looked and looked again, trying to work out what was out of place in that provincial square whose every detail she knew so well. Her eyes went from the Cabildo to the Cathedral, and back again. The Casa Rosada, as unspeakably hideous as ever, was blocking the view of the river. When would they pull that pink monstrosity down? Everything was as it had always been, drab, bare and ugly.

And then it hit her; apart from the groups of women arriving for the demonstration, there was nobody in the square. No sightseers were standing around, no school children or men going about their daily business were hurrying across it, no old people were sunning themselves on the park benches. There were no street vendors anywhere to be seen. 'I'm going mad like the other women,' she thought, and looked round the square again, surveying it inch by inch. The gathering in the middle of the square was growing; women on their own or arm-in-arm were streaming out of the side-streets. 'I can't believe it,' she said to herself again. 'Why is there no one here?' She turned round and saw four women coming towards her, knotting their scarves under their chins. On the corner behind them, a little girl was tying her scarf round her neck. She looked up at the windows overlooking the square. No one was looking out. With a puzzled frown, she took her white scarf out of her bag and put it on. Elena was watching the demonstration grow from the pavement at the edge of the square. But her mind was completely taken up with the fact that, at half past four in the afternoon, there was not a single person there except for the women taking part in the demonstration. Elena took Victoria's photograph out of her handbag and started to study it; it looked somewhat the worse for wear, though she did her best to flatten it out and straighten the corners. She felt embarrassed to ask if she could have a look at it. From what she could make out, it seemed that Victoria was standing on a beach though wearing a polo-neck sweater and trousers. Did she have her hands in her pockets? But Elena lowered the photo and started to walk towards the centre of the square. In the fraction of a second that she was left stranded not knowing quite what to do, a woman dashed past with a bundle of duplicated lists and handed her one. It went on for twenty-three pages; she felt an urge to count the names and started to run her forefinger down the columns to work out how many names were on each page. She'd got to the forty-fifth line when someone stopped at her elbow and said: 'You needn't bother to count them, sister, there are about a thousand names down here, but the actual number who've disappeared is much higher than that. We've only just started compiling the lists. The job is complicated by the fact that a lot of people are unwilling to give the full names and ages, or the parents' names and phone numbers.' She shrugged her shoulders and walked on. She felt annoyed with the woman for calling her 'sister' and poking her nose into what was none of her business, but she took another glance at the list. Only now did she notice the ages; they mostly ranged from fifteen to twenty-five; she went on going through it page by page. A woman of sixty-eight, another of seventy-five. She shuddered. A four-month-old baby, a two-year-old girl, another of five, a brother and sister of three and four. The list in her hand began to quiver. How can a four-month-old baby disappear? The entry read: Anselmo Furco, four months, disappeared on . . . Parents: Juan Gustavo Furco, 23, Alicia, 20, also missing. It was followed by the name, address and telephone number of the grandparents. A violent lurch in the pit of her stomach made her grope for the nearest wall to lean against. Someone came up to her and said: 'Come on now, you mustn't give up.' They steered her back to the square. She felt better in the open air and looked around her. So these were the Madwomen of the Plaza de Mayo . . . The number of women was incredible and so was the silence; apart from the rapid footsteps and muffled greetings, there was not a sound. Not a single prison van, not a single policeman, not a single army jeep was in sight. The Casa Rosada looked like a stage set, with thick curtains drawn across its windows. There were no grenadier guards on sentry duty at the gates either. It was the realisation that the grenadier guards were not there that gave her a sudden, terrifying insight into the enemy's machinations: *every Thursday, for the two to three hours during which the demonstration took place, the Plaza de Mayo was wiped off the map.* They couldn't fire on the women or lock them all up. It would have undermined the concerted effort they'd made to project a carefree image of 'the Argentina I love'. Their ploy was simply to ignore them; to ignore the existence of the square and of the madwomen stamping their feet. Had they arrived at that degree of sophistication? And why not, if the same sophistication operated at the level of tortures and abductions? A developed nation does things properly.

She was beginning to give way to despair; more questions flooded into her head. What about the people who regularly passed through the square at that time of day? What about the bank clerks? What about the crowds permanently gathered on the corner by the Cabildo? Where the devil were they? What about the priests and parishioners who every afternoon without fail went to pray in the Cathedral? Did they sneak out of the back door or stay waiting inside in the dark? What about the people who at that precise moment had to get an important document signed at the solicitor's offices bordering the square? How had they managed to get such a motley collection of people, who couldn't possibly have come to a joint agreement, to melt into thin air? What had provoked this reaction of blind terror in each and every one of them? Or were they unanimously shunning this vast array of desperate women because it brought them face to face with a grief that words could not convey? And the same cowards who would not risk setting an immaculately shod foot in the square would loudly proclaim, contented citizens all, that they were avid football fans, that they ate meat every day, that they holidayed at Mar del Plata whenever the fancy took them, that they wouldn't dream of missing a Sunday on the beach despite all those dreadful rumours—put around by the enemies of the fatherland—of bodies floating in the River Plate. Or did they sleep uneasily at night?

Meanwhile more and more women kept on arriving; by now the square was so packed they were spilling out into the roadway. She lost sight of Elena and knew there was no point trying to look for her in such a crowd, but she plunged into it all the same, edging her way forward as best she could.

'Did I tell you I've got some terrible photos a friend took there one Thursday? If I'd known we were going to talk about it I'd have brought them with me. To be honest, I never really understood why you went back to Buenos Aires. Anyway, you wouldn't want to look at my pictures if you saw it for yourself. There's another group here that's printing copies of all the photographs in their records. That's an even more gruesome sight. But the photos of the missing children are important, because they've been known to turn up in other countries. It's a kind of hell we're living in.'

And what a hell, Dolores! A new man-made version, such as no one ever imagined. Without a word or command being uttered, the women raised the photographs above their heads. Why, when there was no one there to see them? I expected that, with so much handling and fondling, those childlike faces would soon be disfigured past the point of recognition. Near me, an old woman was holding up a cheap studio portrait with both hands. The girl was smiling stiffly, her head tilted to one side, no doubt obeying the photographer's instructions. She was sitting with her legs crossed, an organdie dress covering her knees. Another woman was holding a passport photograph in the palm of her hand, shielding it as if it were an egg she'd just that minute hatched; she raised it gingerly and started to wave it from side to side; she couldn't stop shaking and the tears were streaming down her face, but she kept her lips tightly pressed together. A woman right next to me took out of her handbag a tiny picture in an oval frame. She looked at me and smiled apologetically. The only photos she had of him were taken when he was a child, if only she'd known . . . I asked her how old he was now. 'He'll be twenty next month. We were so proud of him. We were going to hold a party to celebrate.' She could barely finish the sentence, but she pulled herself together, sighed and raised the tiny frame as high as she could, along with all the other photographs. I started to feel uncomfortable just standing there with nothing to hold up. I raised the list with both hands and waited expectantly. Was that it? Just this coming together to share one's silent grief with the silent grief of others?

And that was when it started, Dolores, I can't explain to you what it was that happened. How can I find the words? I could say that suddenly someone started to shout and everyone started shouting and in a matter of minutes the whole square was one single shout. But that wouldn't begin to tell you what it was like. There are so many people shouting all over the place . . . And you'll probably smile if I tell you I started to shout as well, though it had nothing to do with me, and I've no idea what I shouted, I couldn't understand a word of what the other women were shouting either, because it was as if the words were severed from one another by the sobbing and howling. Every now and then I thought I heard the words 'Where are they?', 'Where are they?' but it may have been my imagination. And yet they must have been voicing some demand that served as a focus for the general mood of anger, because the crowd of women surged forward like a tide. They continued to advance, we knocked into one another, stumbling over each other's feet. The chaos was indescribable as hundreds of sheets of paper were tossed into the air. I did exactly the same as the madwomen, and I couldn't begin to tell you what I felt; it was as if someone was trying to rip my insides out and I was clinging on to them for all I was worth. But that's not it, either. I can't be sure it was really like that. I keep groping for the words but it's useless. I heard an alarming whirring sound overhead and ducked instinctively; it soon dawned on me it was the pigeons flapping their wings in terror as they flew round and round, not knowing where to settle. They went on wheeling frantically, feathers flurrying, beaks snapping furiously. I collided head-on with a girl who was groaning, she can't have been more than twenty. Who had she lost? Her baby, her husband, her parents? I couldn't see the crumpled photo she was clutching with both hands. I thought I glimpsed a snatch of Elena's jacket in the middle of a circle of women and I elbowed my way towards her. She was part of a chorus chanting in unison, and this time I could clearly hear the words 'Where are they?', 'Where are they?' She had her back to me, but she didn't turn round even when I put my hand on her shoulder and shook her. Then I shouted her name. You say you knew her well, Dolores, but at that moment you'd never have recognised her. I'd grown up with her but she was a complete stranger to me. I wish I could forget that twisted face, that gaping, howling mouth and, even worse, her skin, that delicate skin of hers, discoloured with purple blotches. She wasn't holding Victoria's photo up in the air but was clasping it to her chest with both hands, huddling over it; an old woman cowering in the face of death. I put my arm round her and started to chant with her. Until everything began to quieten down. The madwomen began to drift away. Three women of indeterminate age were trying to calm another woman who was shaking her clenched fist at the Casa Rosada. They started to straighten their jackets, smooth their blouses, resettle their handbags on their arms; they tidied their hair and looked around for the best way out of the square. The crowd thinned out, revealing the paving stones strewn with stencilled sheets. I felt completely stunned, I needed more time to recover. I lost sight of Elena again. It was only a matter of minutes before the square had emptied itself. A woman took a packet out of her bag and started to throw bits of bread to the pigeons, but they were still chary; they kept skidding on the bits of paper and taking off again in panic, leaving the food. I felt like kicking the pigeons, but I took pity on the woman; how many times had she come to feed them with her missing son or daughter?

I crossed over to the opposite pavement and, looking up at the sky, saw that the pigeons were reassembling in flying formation and winging their way back to their usual perch on the obelisk. My friend was waiting for me on the corner of the Calle San Martín; her pale pointed face was calm and serene.

She must have noticed something alarming in my expression, because she gaped at me as if about to say something. Then she shook her head.

'Don't let it upset you like that, don't let it upset you like that,' she murmured and now it was her turn to put her arm around me. But I did something awful, really awful, I'll never forgive myself for it.

'What did you do?' the girl asked, putting down the blazer she was about to put on.

'I broke away from her and ran out into the middle of the road shouting how was I supposed to feel, for Christ's sake, how was I supposed to feel, and why didn't those bastards hiding behind the curtains come out into the open; I was ranting and raving like a maniac, while she stood there going red as if I'd slapped her in the face.'

Dolores sat watching her cigarette go out in the ashtray.

'I created a real scandal. And do you think anyone came out to see what was going on, do you think anyone looked out of the window? Not a soul.'

'I'm sorry,' Elena said. 'I'm really sorry.'

But I wasn't sorry; what I was feeling was completely different, horribly different. I told Elena I was going back to the square. She glanced at me briefly without a word, then turned on her heels and went back home, presumably. The square was still empty, or almost empty, I don't remember exactly. I sat down on a bench, muttering 'How am I supposed to feel, for Christ's sake, how am I supposed to feel?' over and over again, till I'd said it so many times it started to lose its force. I was distracted by the sight of an old man doing his utmost to get a little boy he was holding by the hand to touch a pigeon. I looked around me and realised why I'd returned to the square, I'd returned to watch the rats slinking back once they'd sensed that danger was over. Now the whole square was full of rats loitering or scurrying around. More and more rats kept pouring in and out of the side-streets. I looked over at the Cathedral and saw the steps lined with rats. But were they really rats? Disgusting, stinking, cowardly rats? Ought they to be exterminated like vermin? I looked at the little boy chasing the pigeons. I looked at the Casa Rosada, two grenadier guards were on sentry duty. At that point I leant my head against the back of the iron bench and began to weep, silently, so no one would notice.

The girl put her blazer on and went to look out of the window.

'It's got dark,' she said. 'The last thing I wanted was to go home in the dark.'

But something else was obviously on her mind. As they turned to face each other at the front door, she clutched her by the arm.

'I don't know how one's supposed to feel about it either. All I know is that you have to find some kind of breathing space. Because if you don't have room to breathe, you'll be dead as well. And the worst of it isn't that you'll be dead but that you'll have added another corpse to their collection.'

Translated by Jo Labanyi

Conformity

IT WAS A WHILE before she realized what was going on. All movements were perfectly coordinated. She started to pay attention and clearly heard him lower the bolt on the door at the same time she rested her hand on the handle and pushed it down. The other door squeaked a little less, but it was easy to picture, like hers, ajar at first, then opening more and more, giving way to whomever entered the house. It occurred to her to slip through the barely opened door, calculating that the fat man would be unable to manage the same maneuver so that his door would open more than hers and the hinges would creak in a different way and longer. Besides, that would allow her to gain time, enter quickly (which he couldn't do because of his obesity), and stand immediately against the vestibule wall, letting the other person move on into his house, thus annulling the similarity between each of their movements. When she heard the second door open at the end of the tiny corridor together with hers, she understood defeat. She paused a moment, beaten, her heart pounding. Slowly climbing the run-down stairway, she heard the stairs creak in unison. She could no longer resist.

226

She went into her room, slammed the door and clearly heard the blow echo. She threw herself into bed and began to sob, urgent, smothered sobs, biting the pillow. From the other side of the wall you could distinctly hear the mattress springs collapsing under the fat man's weight.

Then she stopped crying and rested her head on the pillow, looking up at the ceiling, absolutely motionless.

, She was weaving the events together one by one; a bitter sensation of being cornered welled up inside her. Maybe the first thing she remembered was the morning she planted the tree in the patch of earth on the sidewalk. The shovel was small and the dirt was as dried up as old, dead skin. At one point she ceased digging the hole for the tree and sat down on the curb without looking at the empty street. The row of identical houses seemed deserted so early in the morning. The day before in a very moving ceremony the mayor had distributed more than a thousand trees to the neighbors so that they could landscape the tenement block in the hope that its arid, dismal appearance might disappear. Distracted, she reviewed the facades of the houses, and her gaze moved up along the walls of the apartment blocks. Everything looked neglected, on the verge of destruction. Windows were broken, some covered up with cardboard and wads of newspapers and magazine covers. Gloomy clothes hung in disarray from improvised strings because when the tenement complex was built no one had thought about an appropriate place to hang the wash. It hung drooping there like faded, threadbare banners. "At least if there were a breeze," she thought, "they would wave gently." The walls were peeling, exposing large eroded patches. She remembered that the mayor had praised the cheerful appearance of the tenement neighborhood and predicted a promising future. She couldn't forget the term "promising," whose meaning escaped her but toward which she had felt an insuperable aversion from the start. Until the instant the mayor said "promising," she had listened to him in astonishment; but when he pronounced that word she had the unmistakable intuition that something was wrong about his speech and that he was beginning to get caught up in lies. Unfortunately he repeated the fatal word at least three times, as if he couldn't shake it off; it was no longer possible to believe in him. She saw him as stiff and ridiculous, and when his cohorts began to unload from the trucks thousands of leafless and sickly saplings that were supposed to metamorphose into "promising trees" and transform that fraternal community into a garden, she walked away slowly, full of sudden shame, toward the house.

Despite her inexplicable reaction, she began to think about the trees and at night returned to the square to retrieve one. Dozens of children had taken over the pile of trees in the middle of the empty lot and were stomping on them mercilessly. Some had made arrows, swords and clubs out of the fragile trunks and were attacking each other. Several women were rummaging around in the piles, dragging the trees away with the obvious intention of using them for firewood. Suddenly someone arrived, surely the caretaker or person designated to distribute the trees among the neighbors, and began to shout, cursing the children and the women. Nobody paid any attention to him because he reeled about, drunk, this way and that, unable to stop the destruction of the abandoned saplings. Then she began to examine them, stick by stick, until she discovered one that seemed slightly bigger, with a tiny crushed branch that had not yet broken off. She grasped it carefully, took it home and carried it into the hallway, wrapping the roots in a wet rag. She realized then that she had not seen the fat man anywhere that night. But that next morning when she went back to the task of digging a hole and took a sudden break to rest, she casually glanced next door and saw him. He was digging a hole just like hers and on the ground lay a sapling similar to hers, miserably rigid. This was logical because the mayor had asked everyone to participate and not just her, but something seemed to threaten her. Unable to think rationally, she kept on digging the hole with her back to the neighbor. She finished, put the tree in, tamped down the hard clay earth around it, and with her back to the neighbor returned to the door of her house. When she opened it, she heard the other door open. She stopped on the threshold to look at the tree. It was a ridiculously sad little stick, sure to die under the sun's first punishing rays. She observed the other tree on the sly, as if in a mirror image. She realized why she detested the neighbor with such painful intensity. She would have liked her tree to be the only one on the block so her house would be special, different. But it remained inexorably identical to the one next to it, and she experienced such great bitterness it was as if, one step away from achieving her own identity, they had seized it from her forever. Who had? A neighbor whom she had never noticed, except to register the fact that he was a fat man with whom she had not exchanged a single word, not even a conventional greeting.

She thinks she hears a muffled sound and is distracted from attempting to reconstruct the process. Was he getting out of bed? No. Total silence from the other side of the thin wall. Was he lying in bed, looking at the ceiling, thinking her very same thoughts? And how about his face? She'd never seen it; it was impossible to imagine.

What happened after the incident with the tree? Well, it was some days later. She went outside and the tree lay on the ground trampled and destroyed. Before drawing near, she instinctively looked at the one next door and saw it had been torn out by the roots, with its poor leaves crushed and scattered. She gathered up the pieces of her tree and threw them angrily into the middle of the street. The street was full of holes and trash. They never cleaned it. She imagined the tree would remain there for a long time like a person who'd been killed. She heard the sound of the other tree falling, like hers, into the ruts in the middle of the street. She began to walk in the opposite direction from the neighbor, but the desire to turn around was so keen that she finally stopped and could no longer control herself. She spun around. There was nobody in sight along the whole block. Now without the trees, the houses looked exactly alike. A neighbor came out of her house and threw a burned-out saucepan into the street; then ran after a kid who'd escaped through the crack of the door; and shoved him back in. A scream was heard and immediately after that, silence reigned.

The second time, almost without thinking about it, she bought a can of paint. Intent upon saving her room from such ugly anonymity, she decided to paint the window blue. She stood in front of her house and counted the identical windows. There were fourteen of them. Fourteen bedrooms like hers with the same window and the same faded, shabby window frame. All morning she painted, taking extreme care not to smear the glass or the walls, until the iron window frames were limpid blue, a dazzling sky blue. She finished and crossed to the other sidewalk, feeling irrational joy. It was no longer window number six counting from right to left. It was *her* window. She felt that something of her own had finally been salvaged from the uniform gray swamp and that she would laboriously make her way toward something uncertain, perhaps, but astonishing. She would succeed in possessing her room, her window, her hall, her kitchen and therefore would one day possess her own hands, her skin, her face. It felt as if she had just been born. All day that sensation persisted: a small, unexpected victory over the neighborhood and the gray mass of its inhabitants. Upon her return she couldn't resist the joy of crossing the street again to see her blue window. She looked once and then again; something began to chill her blood. At first she thought she was mistaken but then verified her impression, bit by bit, until there was no doubt. The window next door was painted the same blue color; the window sills were meticulously trimmed in the same dazzling sky blue. Defeated, she went inside and sat down on the edge of the bed. Perhaps it was at that precise moment that she perceived, for the first time, the corresponding movements on the other side of the wall; she heard the sound of the springs as someone sat down on the edge of the bed. She slowly approached the wall, spying on the sounds. The other steps also approached the wall. She leaned her head against it and felt another head brush the wall as it leaned against it on the other side. In a flash, she understood that she was condemned by some dark force, irrevocably condemned.

A long, horrifying struggle ensued. She painted the door in blue stripes and the next day the door alongside hers looked exactly the same. She got hold of four sickly geranium plants and feverishly planted them in the hole where the tree had died. She already knew, when she awoke chilled with fever and looked through the window, that in the other hole next door would be some weak geraniums doubled over for lack of earth and water. When she came to the conclusion that the fat man would never let her be herself, to somehow establish her identity, she realized that her only recourse lay in destruction.

At daybreak, after a night of insomnia and nightmares, she grabbed a bottle of Coca Cola and, barely able to sit up in bed, smashed it against the window. The glass fell noisily into pieces. She waited for a moment in the livid light and almost experienced relief upon hearing the noise of the glass next door falling onto the sidewalk. She didn't get up until very late, attentive to all sounds. Naturally she heard no steps until she finally stepped on the floor and the boards on the other side of the wall creaked. She went to the bathroom, motionless for a second, arms hanging at her sides, and flushed the toilet. The tank emptied in a commotion of repressed water. The dual gurgle of both tanks filling up again grew in the morning's silence like an indecent waterfall.

It was there, while the water rose noisily in the toilet bowl's tank, that she understood she could stand no more. Without getting dressed, barefoot, she went downstairs, opened the front door, went outside and only when she heard the blatant laughter of the children, realized that it was almost noon; the street was full of people, women who were sweeping and cursing, children who were throwing orange peels at each other's heads, and an ominous, morbid sun filtering between stubborn gusts of drizzle. Nothing could stop her now. She went toward the other door, looked for a second at the blue stripes, glanced down and saw the glass shards all over the ground. She noticed that her naked foot was bleeding. Bending over, she picked up a piece of glass without caring that the edge was cutting into her hand. Then she rang. The door opened at once as if awaiting her, her temples were beating so much as the door closed behind her that she could hardly discern, definitely not discern the face of the fat man standing in front of her.

Translated by Evelyn Picon Garfield

All in a Lifetime

THE WOMEN in my family live long, exasperatingly long. They never die and their eternal existence meddles endlessly in the lives of the young. That's why we value material things so little, become so irate when no one dies, and reach certain extremes of cruelty inconceivable to ordinary people who normally lose their dear ones.

I've tried unsuccessfully to explain this to some of the neighbors. But I finally had to resign myself to the fact that everyone turns their back on us and only Feliza, with her inquisitor's eyes, focuses on us with a look we can't quite place, between admiration, disdain and pity.

Even though they don't greet us anymore and we walk these repugnant streets like the neighborhood lepers, I know my grandmother's not suffering; on the contrary, she's happy during the usually tranquil daytime, nodding sleepily in her rocking chair, and at night the laughter, bustle and strange murmurs fill her insomniac's hours much more than spying on the leaden silence of a normal, sleepy house. I'm sure of this because sometimes when I've gone to see her, always during the day of course, she laboriously takes my hand in her boney, gnarled claws, throws her head back as if motioning upstairs to the perpetual nocturnal festivities, and tries to wink at me. It's her way of confirming that she's made peace with me.

It was useless, impossible to keep her at home any longer.

And especially after the last years when she became obsessed with Herbert, whom she watched with a fervor worthy of a better cause. She'd approach the window with her rocking chair and position herself sideways so as to see him come around the corner; then hit the wall with her stick so that Meche would prepare the sweet rice just right and serve it to him in the appropriate fashion. She was really creating such a hierarchical difference between Herbert and the rest of her children and grandchildren that we felt the humiliation grow and fester with rancor, day by day, hour by hour, in the rooms crammed with beds.

We've always been very poor so everything was shared among us, even complicity. When they awarded us the house, it was specified that we were a family consisting of a father, a mother and three living children, two married (a man and a woman) and one bachelor (me). A total of five people. We never let on that the married individuals each had their respective spouses and on top of that four children between the two couples, which brought us to twelve. Grandmother made thirteen. Perhaps it was that ominous number that brought us bad luck. The thirteen of us entered the house at different times and the four rooms were converted into bedrooms so that the kitchen functioned not only as a kitchen but also as a dining room and Meche's bedroom where she arranged a straw mattress on the floor at night. On the other hand we had neither dogs nor cats like the rest of the neighbors, and that should have been to our advantage. But since the neighborhood seethes with hatred and intrigue, no one noticed that circumstance but instead devoted themselves to counting us—one, two, three—six, seven—eleven, etc.—despite the fact that we used to leave the house at very different times, some only at night like prowlers. But finally they located all twelve.

I'm sure someone denounced us (it was a question of ousting us from the house), but happily, since you never know where to bring a suit and can't get beyond the intermediaries of the intermediaries, the subject gradually died out and they left us in peace. Nevertheless, the hostility was blatant. When we went out on the sidewalk on Sundays (there is no patio or miserable garden to sit out in the sun), they threw disapproving glances our way and made us feel like rabbits.

The last straw came when grandmother began to go crazy over Herbert. Forgetting the rules of the house, she made her way among the beds in the back, reached the room that overlooks the street, moved the cots aside with unsuspected strength and stood at the window. Surely someone saw her and sounded the alarm! Several of us were nowhere nearby and so when Meche finished shopping and came out of the store, we couldn't prevent the neighbors from slyly asking after grandmother's health. Meche swallowed the bait, assuring them that grandmother was the liveliest one in the whole family. And so we inevitably became thirteen then, victims of our neighbors' unbridled scorn.

I'd like to know which of those miserable wretches lives better than my grandmother today. More than that, which one of *us* lives better than her. She has the rocking chair, meals, entertainment. The girls are good to her, better than most, precisely because of the hard work that's their lot in life. They call her grandmother and tell her their gloomy stories; she listens with a maliciously wise grimace. They seem to understand everything although grandmother talks very little and those few words are incomprehensible because she's toothless. The sounds she emits are firmer and much more defined than the faltering babble of the girls she converses with. It's understandable, they must feel relieved that someone stronger is protecting them.

One day when grandmother still lived with us, Herbert turned the corner and she began her system of stick-banging signals on the walls. Throughout the month she'd been communicating her vital powers to Herbert, she was signaling him with her powerful energy. While Herbert was being nurtured on that dark strength, decidedly in his favor, we were being extinguished. I couldn't really say if it was that very process that made him run away; for he was actually more the victim than the chosen one. It's certainly possible, because when it comes to dingy people like us, no one resists being transformed into an exception. Herbert, always docile, would be summoned by the old lady and obliged to eat his rice pudding with bread in front of her. Rocking to and fro, she firmly urged him to open up. And Herbert talked, something he never did during his sixteen years at home with his mother and father. Once burning with curiosity we sneaked up to the room where Herbert was eating and talking with grandmother; but the creak from the awful boards on the staircase gave us away and Herbert suddenly fell silent.

Our lives were becoming gloomy. I don't know why. Like I said, maybe it's impossible for one of us to stand out. We have no other recourse than conformity, the least common denominator; better yet, nonexistence. We were all nothing, and now Herbert was turning out to be something just because the damned old lady had decreed it. During meals in the kitchen when we were all gathered together, he would throw distrustful glances our way as if he were no longer one of us. We were so disconcerted, we couldn't even make fun of him. His two younger brothers were the ones who paid for it; because my sister martyred them mercilessly when she felt herself losing ground day by day with Herbert. We began to throw things up to each other, insult one another with isolated words and mortify each other as never before. One night a crisis arose based on a stupid conversation about the return to Colombia. The verbal battle was between my brother and my father, but even though it was absolutely irrelevant, my sister turned around to reprimand Herbert, and when he lowered his head without answering, she slapped him soundly on the face. Herbert paled, stood up, looked at her for a fraction of a second and started up the stairs. It seemed as if the old lady was going to destroy the wall and never let up. We remained motionless in the kitchen for who knows how long, until the blows became less frequent and then stopped completely. No one went upstairs, not even Meche. I think those of us who lived up there waited until midnight to go to bed. All of this happened the night before Herbert disappeared.

Anyway no one's to blame for Feliza's winning the raffle. The drawing was strictly on the up-and-up, and Meche stirred up the little pieces of paper in the kitchen, in front of several neighbors who were filled with morbid curiosity, in spite of their disgust for us. Besides, almost the entire neighborhood participated in the drawing; some families had already kept grandmother for a while and others sought her. That's the truth. As far as we're concerned, you can't accuse us of greed or cruelty because we weren't the ones to throw her out, on the contrary, she was the one who left. Anyway, she went off without a word, heartily and desperately banging on the walls with her stick as two of us carried her downstairs in her rocker and put her in the street, following her orders to a tee. I remember very well that she scarcely made it to the middle of the street when several women approached her making a great fuss, and it was no use trying to explain that we weren't throwing her out of the house. We still didn't know then that Herbert would never return, but she seemed to know. She seemed to know everything, including about the neighbor who would charitably take her home in her rocker and settle her down in the dining room.

My sister took the shock of Herbert's running away in stride. To tell you the truth, after he and grandmother left, we recovered our tranquility and mutual trust. The three remaining children, freed of their fears, emerged from under their cots where they had been living those last days. My sister became pregnant, and everything returned to normal.

Only some weeks later did we begin to hear the first rumors about that incident. Grandmother had already moved through three different houses; perhaps that stupid rumor was fanned by her passivity, her enigmatic grimace, her hasty gestures and that imperious way of continuing to live on wherever she went. It seemed a senseless rumor to us but not to the others. One morning a neighbor threw it up to Meche in the store and she came home utterly terrified, incoherently relating the event. We started to understand why they fought over her in different homes and why the rocking chair always moved each time with more of a flurry and ceremony from one house to the next. Whatever grandmother had done, said or shown to achieve that result completely escaped us. She refused to ever see us again.

Now I sometimes think of Herbert and get a strange pain in my back. I began thinking about my nephew after he'd left, and maybe even idealizing him little by little. I realized that he had average features and an almost handsome face, very different from our gray and ordinary ones. If he'd stayed, this absurd story would never have taken place.

A story that segregated us forever from the rest of the neighborhood, as if we were the plague.

The idea sprang from a conversation in the shadows of the kitchen when year's end was near and our funds, as always, were exhausted. I couldn't say for sure who spoke of the raffle first, but someone did and it seemed like a brilliant idea. If grandmother was in such demand it didn't seem fair for her to move around so frequently with her rocking chair from one place to another, but instead for her to be raffled off and remain forever in the winner's home. "After all, saints rest in peace in church," my mother said, "and don't move around like market baskets." My mother suddenly took on a dignified air by saying this, and persuaded us all. We discussed the details of the raffle for a long time and the next day we dared to propose it to some neighbors. At first they seemed shocked, but then greed dazzled them. Raffling off the saint spread like wildfire through the neighborhood, and before Sunday, which we wanted to avoid because of possible curses from the priest, all the tickets were sold.

I repeat, that since they participated, it was unfair of them to heap all their trashy words and gestures on us.

Besides, anyone other than Feliza would never have been so happy to win her. She looked right through my grandmother with her shameless eyes and the old lady returned her glance with a lively, malicious twinkle, so they told us.

From the next day on grandmother settled into the whorehouse's corridor and true sainthood overcame her.

Among the black velvet throw pillows and the cat that a client gave her as a gift, she continued to live on with her indomitable will.

Translated by Evelyn Picon Garfield

Julieta Campos

Cuba/Mexico

Julieta Campos. (Photo courtesy of Paulina Lavista.)

Julieta Campos was born in Havana, Cuba, in 1932, and after studying in Paris moved to Mexico City in 1955. She has translated books about the social sciences, history, and psychoanalysis from English and French into Spanish, and has collaborated in Mexico's most prestigious literary magazines, *Plural, Vuelta,* and *Revista de la Universidad de México.* She was the editor of the latter during the early 1980s. In addition to fiction, Campos has published several books of literary theory and criticism of literature from Latin America, France, the United States, and most recently from the indigenous communities of Mecayapan in Veracruz, Mexico, in which she studied the oral tradition of the Nahuas. A world traveler, she has been president of the P.E.N. Club of Mexico and recipient of Mexico's important Xavier Villaurrutia Prize for her novel *Tiene los cabellos rojizos y se llama Sabina* (A Redhead Named Sabina).

In that second novel of three and in a collection of short stories, the themes of love, death, and writing are intertwined. Her fiction is very much concerned with the passage of time and how it affects and corrodes events and perceptions of them. It is prose that turns in on itself, over and over again, in spirals that seem to defy forward plotting of the action. This self-reflexive narrative is one of the best examples in Latin American literature today of what Umberto Eco defined as an "open work," replete with ambiguities, contradictions, plural meanings, and disjointed and fragmented structuring of characters and scenes in constant metamorphosis. This kind of narrative in which characters appear and disappear or multiply, in which the setting is in one place but also in others, in which the person who narrates is one and then many, confounds readers and forces them to participate in the plot in order to try to unravel it.

In much of her fiction, writing rescues the characters and sometimes even love from death, for as in her last novel *El miedo de perder a Eurídice* (Fear of Losing Eurydice), the novel itself represents desire, the eternal search for utopia, transformed into writing about writing, and by extension, intertextually about many aspects of Western cultures: art, drama, opera, film, music, geography, philosophy, and literature.

In "All the Roses" ("Todas las rosas"), the short story presented here, the sisters Alda and Aurelia live locked up in a house where their identities remain mysterious to the reader up to the very end of the story. And in the novel *A Redhead Named Sabina,* the narrator begins by circumscribing a space and a moment during which the entire novel takes place—while Sabina looks out to sea at four o'clock in the afternoon on the last day of her vacation in Acapulco. As you will see in these first pages—very typical of the novel's entire style and structure—a flood of implacable and mutable memories, hopes, and fantasies are set loose to prolong that moment of departure, whirling about in volutes of incessant reiterations and recollections that attempt to keep both novel and protagonist alive up to the last pages, which we have also translated here.

A Redhead Named Sabina
[Selections from the novel]

I will rest then on the shores of the sea I have loved so well.

—*Chateaubriand*

＼

"I AM NOT HERE. I am on another beach twenty-two years ago. There is a long pier and at this hour the waves are already gray, the color of melted lead. The sea is rough for night approaches." If this were the beginning of a novel it ought to have begun like this: *I have been going to bed early for a long time. Sometimes I had barely snuffed out the candle . . .* but I do not know how it would have ended, because the narrator would be someone else and there would be no waterlilies nor bellfries nor Normandy beaches nor, above all, that inconceivable confidence in the power of the word. This is, would be, my novel and Proust's sentence would have been of no use after all. The truth is that I have never known where to begin. There are so many words and so little to say. And if it is a question of telling something it is because it is assumed that things happen that are inexplicable by themselves and they seek words to surface as someone about to drown looks for a piece of wood to seize and hold him up. I am a character who looks out on the sea at four o'clock in the afternoon. But I am also someone who imagines I myself am that character. And I am the words that imagine the character that I am. And I am the words that I imagine and that being imagined oblige me to look out on the sea from a balcony in Acapulco. Every word is at once a beginning and an end. Nothing has happened here. No one knows how long ago silence was broken forever by the sound of the sea. There are many voices that cry out asking for help and they are heard closer and closer every time. Soon they will arrive and will be the ones that look at me. Why aren't we going to swim in the Blue Grotto? The cave looks out on the Fort. Moving is difficult when your feet are made of lead. Or you are in a leaden sea. I do not know where the music is coming from. This silence frightens me. They say that farther down the color of the water is very beautiful. I have dreamed about the sea many times. Remember that halfway down the road there is a dark forest. You have already dreamed what is happening. Remember. Try to remember. The sea is the sea. The light is the sunlight. It is the music that confuses you. The image of Venice pursues and besieges me like a lover. They are playing tropical music. At five fifteen the sun will set. Let yourself be fascinated by your own words. I have been here looking out on the sea for seven days. A scenographic sea, a sea ready for something, a sea that knows how to play its role. I also play a part but it is much more modest, almost minimal, I would say virtually nonexistent: I play a part that no one would care to steal from me because everyone dreams of great roles, transcendent and grandiose, and they do not stop, they never stop a single instant, never stop to contemplate the scenography. They are calling me. If I take the photograph I will remain excluded definitively. Vacation is over. I must go. We must go. I ought to have written a novel but novels, they say, are written with things that happen and nothing has ever happened to me. I have done nothing more than sit here, on this parapet that is a balcony that is a terrace, seeing that illuminated promontory like a magisterial scenography, this place that has been here since the beginning, ready for something that has not happened and that has always been about to happen. A place imagined by a congenial director for playing out the greatest fiction invented by man. Someone would be able, could, would have been able to draw it and put these words below: HAMLET by William Shakespeare. During each of these days, these seven days, I have been waiting to see him emerge on those stairs, to meet his father's angry ghost. I have been waiting as if something exceptional were to occur. It is a shame to leave now in broad daylight, when it could still be that, could be, could. And to this could there is, there ought to, ought to have been a period. Truncated sentences are constantly occurring to me, canceled out, nevertheless, by a period. Four o'clock in the afternoon and the entire hotel atop the cliff is shimmering suspended in the air, in the light that would seem unrepeatable but that infallibly repeats itself. I do not know, you do not know what to do with words and you let them escape, like the air that is lost through fingers when one says goodbye. Not to know what to do with words. Hardly anyone is left now in the swimming pool. Only that very slender girl in the yellow bikini. And the boyfriend she plays with every day at this hour, at cards or one of those fast games that can be interrupted at any time. And of course the solitary woman, who in a Fellini movie, accompanied by a tenuous Wagnerian tune, would listlessly cross the naturally symbolic and somewhat melodramatic vestibule of a luxury hotel in an Austrian spa. What could you do with them? Or with that other slightly chubby and almost ordinary woman who comes down to the swimming pool every day with pens and notebooks and a posthumous Hemingway novel and does not write anything but rather talks incessantly, perhaps desperately, with her companion, a young Japanese man whom she does not leave alone for a single moment as if she had to endlessly remind him of something? They are worthless to me. It would be useless to tell those stories as perhaps someone would tell them who was not I and would be, ought to be seated on that terrace, up above, on one of the hotel terraces higher up, among those palm trees where on some evenings I have seen the scenographic moon come out, disquieting and ruddy. The way he would tell them, that one whom I have trailed every day, knowing that he is here but without having ever succeeded in seeing him because I have not dared, I have preferred to avoid him, since a little more subtlety or perhaps simply the necessary boldness would have sufficed to stop a moment at the desk and ask a few questions as if it were the most natural thing in the world. I am absolutely sure that he keeps looking out from one of those terraces that correspond to the oldest hotel rooms, keeps looking at us with his opera glasses, because he is a puppet, a buffoon who would know how to play any role. Who would enjoy, for example, feigning a fortuitous encounter with the old German woman and her grandson, the ones who come down to the swimmng pool early, she never exposes herself to the sun, in any case showing that she only condescends to come at all for the sake of the child, to go back upstairs so deliberately once her husband shows up to replace her, the grandfather, the rigid, unapproachable old man, who in a swimsuit continues to be the same officer of modest rank who advances today, thirty years ago, on the Polish front; who would enjoy feigning that encounter just to have the pretext of asking "pardon" in the most correct high German. He, who knows how to imitate all accents, who could *impersonate*, pitiful sight such a succulent word, who could adopt the character of Francoise, the loyal and self-sacrificing Francoise, or Naphta's mask, exaggerating his intellectual posturings with suspicious refinement, or the Maga's French cadence to intone *"Alors mon p'tit voyou"* or would speak with secret complicity of one Larry Durrel, greatly stressing the accent on the *é*, "don't you know him: no, not the author of *The Quartet* but that dark jazzman of the forties?" I know that he is in one of those rooms, protected by the very dense vegetation up there, that does not prevent him from watching all the time, spying on us, witnessing every one of our movements in that shameful way. Do you remember Robbe-Grillet's Peeping Tom? Could he perhaps be any old harmless Peeping Tom, at the same time capable of committing a sordid, perfect crime? But no, you are wrong. You are taking him for something he is not, you are confusing him, attributing to him vices that belong to another character, to someone who is not a novelist, nor could ever write a novel, nor take advantage of the stories that parade by here offering themselves up to the highest bidder who could very well be him; he who is not prudish nor has any scruples but who is not that ridiculous failure of a buffoon either, whom you have viciously begun to imagine; he, who would invent ties and origins and endings without great consternation and who would be willing to wrench us all from this ambiguous anonymity, from this trembling latency that you have been perceiving without deciding to do anything about it. I must go now. It is the second time that they are calling me and I have said: "I am coming, one moment, just one moment because I want to take some last photos" and it is not the truth, although I may have taken the camera out to put it on the railing and may be almost caressing it with my right hand while I draw a sketch of the promontory in the air with my left one; it is not true because I will not take any photographs, knowing as I do that what I have seen in these seven days will not be reflected in them and that it would suffice for me to press this small button for my view, printed on a negative and later transferred to photographic paper, to disappear and for death alone to become fixed there, the atrocious coagulation of what I believe to have perceived in seven days of a vacation that is about to expire. I must go. Many have gone to dine but others arrive, some for the first time because they have just barely registered in the hotel and do not want to miss the day and have put on their bathing suits to go down to the swimming pool and take advantage of at least a half an hour before going upstairs to the dining room; others, because they have already dined and have felt too lonely in their rooms and have said they have not come for that and one is better off down below and it is preferable to take a siesta protected by the parasol, letting oneself doze from the chatter and the noise that the water makes when someone jumps into the pool. At this hour there are no longer any children. The children really do take a siesta in their rooms and then awake as if it were another day and come running down to the ocean lagoon, because crabs and snails are there, fish and even small starfish stuck to the stones covered with slippery greenness that is a little scary to touch. Yesterday or the day before, when it had already gotten dark and they had turned on the spotlights that illuminate the promontory between seven and ten o'clock, and I sat down here as I did every night to contemplate the scenography usually deserted at that hour, I realized that there was a girl down below, almost an adolescent, slipping in between the ropes that separate the cement floor constructed over the stones and around the lagoon from the rocks outside and the sea that constantly leaps over the cord and invades the platform and sometimes succeeds in reaching a few of the steps that lead to the promontory. The girl is completely alone and in her game there is a kind of defiance of the surf's violence, an ingenuous and spontaneous, perhaps irreflexive, defiance. I am about to shout to her or descend to warn her of the danger, but I do not. It seems to me, I do not know why, that I have no right to interrupt her, that she is carrying out a ritual game that frees her from something in that voluntary and defiant solitude. It is a privilege to see her play her solitary game, like the repetition of an ancestral gesture that she was unknowingly reproducing. Upon seeing her, you, I, her gesture was salvaged and would not be lost. Why those screams? Why those voices? Why the obstinacy of implacably remembering that I must remember? I am the one seated on the pier twenty-two years ago. The light at four o'clock is merciless. It is not certain that there is a story to tell. They are already impatient. They have already closed the suitcases but have not decided to leave the air-conditioned room. They barely open the door halfway so as not to let the heat slip in and they shout to you without being able to explain why you remain there as if you did not hear them. The voices resound, muffled in the heat, as if someone were speaking inside one bottle inside another. The light is greenish and lunar like a strange nocturnal dawn. The light is too white and can split you in two like an arrow, an apple. The light is yellow like a picture filmed in sepia color and captures both of them, characters in a book that is not this one, like butterflies inside an oval frame. The light is amber in the room with leaded glass windows where two girls act as if they were playing, levitate as if they were playing, pose as if they were playing, act as if the air did not smell of rotten ferns. It suffices to put out those lights for the ghosts to disappear. There are no ghosts at four o'clock in the afternoon. Everything could happen. They were to open the door a moment ago. They would have forced me to accompany them. Everything would have ended at once. Just how long would that novel last? The time in which she looks out on the sea before returning. Returning where? Returning as everyone has to when the moment comes. The end of vacation. It would not be the first novel that described a pregnant fictitious instant without any relationship to the true passage of time. It would not be original then. A novel has already been written that attempts to represent a two-minute lapse in two hundred pages, and it is the story of a gentleman who reflects on how to write a novel that the author has already written, and in another novel that pretends to be the chronicle of an instant, time bites its own tail like the mythical serpent. So? Time in that novel should be hardly a moment and at once the condensation of all vacation time. Or put another way, a duration that would have to join everything. Everything? Integrate all of it: her time, the time of those that are waiting inside the room and at the same time, as it were, the blossoming, maturation of life that would be gathered up and concentrated in the novel's moment like a compact and perfectly beautiful sheaf. Do you expect the vacation to be the essence of life? Do you mean that in that lapse of time one can make into a whole the character's entire existence and that of the other characters that inhabit life, if you permit me such an imprecise and metaphoric expression? More or less. But above all I am interested in the final moment when the vacation comes to a close: I am interested in the last moment = a certain experience of dying a little, accentuated by that exultant (I would say insulting) sensation of freedom that one has only during vacation or when one is on a trip. Nothing more than that, without exaggerating too much, without abusing. *Tu aimes les grands mots, n'est-ce pas?* Now books that had never been written would have to be written. How many times have you heard that? Well (I take out a cigarette). Well (I mean): something that is neither a novel nor a short story, something completely new. Do you understand me? Do I make myself clear? Everything or almost everything has already been written. I understand you, you make yourself clear, but you do not impress me, frankly it does not mean a thing to me. It is just another game. Nevertheless you cannot help playing it. He, that one you have placed up there, perhaps does not use opera glasses but rather a modern and exceptionally precise telescope with which, if he wished, he could see very close up, a point on the beach, let's say, some five kilometers away where a falsely pregnant young woman would be pursued by a false father, who would be her seducer, who would be her mother's lover. A plot made to measure that would occur to him. Don't kid around. Someone has already made that movie. A movie by Joseph Losey with a plot from Tennessee Williams? He is in that room called *the labyrinth,* inaccessible to the other hotel guests because at the entrance to the narrow hallway that borders the cliff and leads to that room there is a warning: PRIVATE. He thinks that he has the right to that privilege and if someone discovers him, a reporter or a foreign admirer or both, that it would be ideal, he might appear several more times in the newspapers. But I am not thinking about him now that seven days have passed and I believe I know something about this place. I am thinking about him on the second day, when I am still only intuiting his existence and have barely begun to settle into the scenography and do not know that the hotel is two hotels, the one here below and the one there above; this level that opens up without reservations and secrets to the sea, and that other one full of sinuous bends hidden among the profuse greenery on the cliff's heights. Things are not seen the same from here as from there, of that I am sure.

● ● ● ●

Certain facts recorded in the capital's newspapers, in the morning edition on Monday, May 9, 1971, would seem to corroborate this last version. The news says this: A woman of uncertain age died yesterday upon falling into a ravine some fifteen meters from her room in an Acapulco hotel; the fall was due to the fact that the woman was completely drunk; some hotel employees discovered the body at the bottom of the ravine; as a result of the fall she suffered a fractured skull and thorax, the former was surely the cause of death; the agent from the Ministry of Public Welfare recorded the case, visited the place and decided that there was no crime to investigate; according to the testimony of some people who were at the swimming pool at that hour, the woman lost her balance upon approaching the terrace's railing and plummeted to the bottom of the precipice; hotel waiters and Red Cross workers descended with great difficulty to the bottom of the ravine and finally found the body which was carried up on a stretcher with the aid of some ropes; the suicide hypothesis has certain elements of probability if one takes into account that it was a question of a lone woman, as one might assume from the fact that the corpse had not been claimed yesterday even late at night despite the news having been broadcast by radio and television, and if one adds to the circumstance of her solitude that of their not having found cash, checkbook or credit cards in her room, which makes one think that the dead woman would have found it impossible to pay the hotel bill after a seven-day stay. Nevertheless, I, who know the character better than anyone because I invented her, independent of the facts and even of her will, suggest that the only data the reader can rely on without fear of being deceived, that which constitutes the key to this book and consequently to the identity of said character, appears on page 111* where one ought to have already discovered it if one possesses keen sight, the ill will attributable to any contemporary reader and an elemental knowledge of the French language: she, the woman who from a balcony in Acapulco looks out on the sea, has reddish hair and her name is Sabina. That is, would definitely be the only certainty and everything else a mirage or a dream. "I am not here. I am on another beach twenty-two years ago . . . ," etcetera, would come to be the only imaginatively formulated words in a novel that will never be written and that is not, of course, *this* novel, but certainly the only one that would have been worthwhile writing. The only imaginative words, that are the only real words, the words that pursue me and surround me, I, on this balcony, now about to leave, looking at the promontory for the last time and in the radiant light of four o'clock in the afternoon on this Sunday, May 8, 1971, allowing a noise to invade

*On page 111, this sentence appears in French: "*Elle a les cheveux roux et s'appelle Sabine.*" (She has red hair and is called Sabina.)

me that seems like words but is the same noise that lay in wait for me from the beginning: the monotone noise, the incessant noise, the stubborn noise, the hissing noise, the menacing noise, the calming noise, the far-off and familiar noise, the exciting and lethargic noise, the noise that fulfills me and leaves me empty, the persistent and lacerating noise of the sea. When I was a little girl I used to see the ocean at all the street crossings, but that has nothing to do with the novel that you are writing as if I were thinking about it, while I refuse to continue being your character and with an elegant or perhaps ridiculous leap I span the distance between the balcony and the sea, between my gaze and the sea, and remain lying at the foot of the promontory, while I softly moan knowing that no one hears me, during the lapse of a minimal instant that surely could be called an instant of agony, remembering that from the balcony I have looked out on the sea. And nevertheless I affirm that she, you, I have not moved from the balcony nor will move while I remember her and make you believe that you remember her, while someone, somewhere, one more time, formulates the words that in sequence, one by one, constitute this book beginning with "I am not here, I am on another beach . . ." and that someone, from the corner where she reads, begins to see the promontory and the ocean through the eyes of the redhead named Sabina. They advise me that at least the appearance of an ending, the fiction of a period, is indispensable. And I do put one here. But this is not the end, only the beginning.

Translated by Evelyn Picon Garfield

All the Roses

AURELIA GENTLY CARESSES the calendar page, runs her fingers along the numbers' raised surface, examines them tenderly, recognizing them. The yellow page has a silky consistency to it, almost velvety, and her finger slides along without a snag. *AUGUST 20, 1933*. The rest of the calendar pages in the back seem intact, unless, never having served as indicators of a specific moment, only the designated limits of each day and night, the assurance of unquestionable hours meant for everyone. No. That untorn yellow page suffices to suggest something like a limitless prolongation, a suspended duration forever true to itself that becomes confused with eternity, that fragile paper on which arrested temporality is condensed, where the frontiers of the past and the future are lost in the continuation of an interminable present that confounds memory and forgetfulness. To Aurelia it has always been August 20, 1933, but what happened, if something happened that day, has been erased definitively. There before the calendar every morning she only remembers that August 20th when all the others went away too quickly to even see the date, perhaps because something happened far away somewhere else, or very near in the city, that same city, something sinister or something that filled them with joy or probably something violent and irreversible like events that force people to leave everything and depart.

Suddenly Aurelia remembers that all the roses are going to die. All the rosebushes. Perhaps she has known it for some days or years. Or barely a second ago when she began to caress the disproportionate blue numbers on the calendar's yellow page. That strange realization is running through her unexpectedly like a chill that was a vague intuition at first and now obsesses her, penetrates and satiates her until she feels herself drained of everything but that imminent death, the inevitable agony of the moribund rosebushes.

Maybe if she could tear off that leaf, rip it up, destroy it, the rosebushes would stop dying. Maybe if she ran to fetch a pencil to cross out that number 20 with two enormous lines, Alda would no longer be driven mad, her slow death in the midst of madness would cease inside the closed room which she, Aurelia, did not wish to enter. The city would stop pursuing her relentlessly, would stop approaching the windows stealthily at night, Aurelia would cease whistling between the blinds ajar from a wind that would stop pressing on the roof of the house and lashing her with that implacable noise as if the sea were near, that noise you could cut with scissors or tear like you tear out a calendar page, because the noise is like paper, an enormous piece of paper that someone is constantly crushing in his hand. The city. The city that surrounds the house with that hoarse or piercing or whistling murmur, at times a crackling of an immense fire, perhaps the sound of the sun when it calcifies stones, a vibration that pulsates in the air outside and tries to break through the walls and blinds and slips into the protected shade where Aurelia barely trembles, remembering that the rosebushes are in danger and a secret curse burdens them, which she, and she alone, has foreseen. The city, the labyrinth voluntarily forgotten who knows since when. The city that is rendered benign, generous, desirable when it ceases being that desperate pressure, that sibilant, surreptitious presence that Aurelia tirelessly spies on with her ear to the wall just in case, and other superimposed cities become muddled in her mind: rivers among cypresses and bridges of an antique topaz color behind which rise towers and cupolas, white statues in the streets, columns, square patios full of flowers, small plazas lost forever at the turn of a corner, large squares down narrow stairways at the end of dark immemorial streets, white churches whose excessive beauty is superfluous and seems to fly loose from silent belfries to descend and rest on the atrium's tiled floor, fountains, gray stone streets and long, shiny sidewalks bordered by pine trees and palaces, many palaces with high terraces and layered gardens, palaces like this one, her house, identical to this one that someone moved, brought stone by stone, marble by marble, banister by banister, from some Florentine street, also brimming with heat and noise but ancient, dignified, too sober, to the city Aurelia wanted to forget, the feminine, tropical city, brimming over with colors and spirals, columns and cupolas in a garden of very tall palm trees, Caribbean pines and bougainvillea.

Aurelia is looking around and it is easy for her to return the house to its origins, to a muffled rumor, to a fresh, faraway autumn, to the antiquity of a street where she would be accompanied by others like her, the same not different, a stranger alongside houses crushed between balconies, colored window panes and plaster cornices. Then she can wipe away that other city, the real one that has now laid violent siege to the house, besieged by the noise and heat of too dense a presence, as if everything outside, beyond the stone walls were inhabited by a gigantic wild beast forever about to pounce, to sink its claws precisely into a weak spot, the most fragile part of the structure in order to provoke a noisy cave-in, the collapse of the palace into the great hall below which she contemplates from the second-floor balcony that surrounds it, for the floor below has no ceiling all along the hall up to the third story with its chandelier that will also fall down and shatter into a thousand glass shards.

Everything is so tranquil . . . The carved ceiling, the empty hall, the very white stairway with wide landings, the silent library books and the innumerable chairs, also mute, in the long dining room. Aurelia closes her eyes to feel the silence more, to permit herself to float in that vacant atmosphere that inhabits the house, to allow herself to remain empty, forgetful of everything. She likes to feel that emptiness. She can sink infinitely into that deep hollow that swallows her up sweetly and gently like an interminable, warm, aquatic funnel. It is a dizzying, intoxicating pleasure. Everything becomes tranquil and happiness intensifies. Until something shakes her, awakens her, forces her to open her eyes to look around, to question where she is, to sluggishly rest her heavy lidded glance on the still, dense objects, the mysteriously dense objects that mutely and incomprehensibly call to her.

She has forgotten everything but does not know what it is she has forgotten. What she ought to remember. No matter that at times she tries to remember, anxiously pursues memory, pretends to surround it, corral it, hound it, the way she senses that the foreign city surrounds the palace, lays siege to it and tries to conquer it. No matter that in the morning she wearily caresses the yellow calendar page. Nor that she softly repeats as in a litany the day, month, year, saint's name, the senseless sentence that is written below in very tiny letters. No matter that she asks Lucila, that she threatens to throw her out of the house if she does not tell her, does not help her to remember what she ought to remember, would remember if she were not bewitched, because perhaps they laid a curse on her and she is doomed like the rosebushes that are dying in the garden. Lucila. Lucila. Lucila must come. She must ask her how Alda is, how she is this morning. If she recognizes her when she enters the room with her meal to give her medicines, if she has asked for her, has asked why she never sees her, if she blames her. To ask Lucila, to imagine, to think that what she is imagining is what is happening at that precise instant there inside, in the room where only Lucila goes, where she does not want to go, Alda's room.

Alda's room is dark. It is always dark. Alda is alone. She spends long hours all alone. There is no one who keeps her company. No one. Not Lucila, because she goes in only to straighten up and several times a day to do first one thing and then another and then still another, because she, Aurelia, has ordered her to do so. She has sent her to do all that she herself could do, because Alda is her sister and it ought to be her duty, it is, it would be if all had not changed, if she herself did not have to take such care to protect herself from contamination, to continue living. Above all now (now?) that everyone has gone away. Since they left, Alda does not leave her room. Since that day she has never seen her walking around the house and both have remained alone, the other woman, Alda, a recluse in the room that faces the garden, that corner of the garden where the rosebushes are dying, and she, Aurelia, is obliged to search the house from one end to the other every day, morning, afternoon, sometimes night, because she knows something is going to happen if she fails to do so, and she has to count the steps while circling that interminable banister that surrounds the hall so that each time there will be the same amount of steps, not one more or less, and she must then go into the dining room and assure herself that all the glasses are in the cupboard, and check the tassels on the carpet and afterward cross the small reception room with its gilded furniture. The reception room where her other sister, the one who left, used to write letters all the time, as long as there were no visitors or they were not combing her hair or she was not playing that languid, marvelous music on the piano that is once again resounding, that Aurelia hears grow until it becomes confused with the muttered words and laughter, everything like one prolonged whisper of female voices, musically conjoined to the very intensely sweet melody of the piano. The maids serve tea while Aurelia moves from one chair to another, from one rocker to another so as to talk with everyone, because she does not want to miss anything and besides, she cannot stay still nor has ever been able to remain seated in one place for long. It is true that they are not her girlfriends but Alda's; no matter. She loves them, too, adores everyone and is delighted to go downstairs early, before they arrive, with her photograph album of the trip around the world, to show the photographs one by one, explaining them, illustrating with some anecdote those that were taken in unknown places, the unusual memory of something that happened where the photograph was taken, precisely at the moment it was taken or five minutes before or after, something trivial that only became significant by happening in relationship to the fact that someone, her husband or an unknown person who was passing by unexpectedly and whom they had asked to take the photo of the two of them together, had selected the place and the time to take a photograph and secondly, allowed himself to be chosen that way just to transmit something. Aurelia vaguely evokes each one of these possibilities upon discarding all the rest, with the exception of the afternoon reception, the guests, the music, the photograph album.

The album is here within arm's reach. She only has to take a few steps and open the top drawer of the chiffonnier to be able to embrace and caress it, the same way she caresses the numbers on the calendar. She has already stood up and run to look for it. She is as excited as if she were very much in love with someone at that moment. She calmly leafs through the pages without looking for anything in particular. Why? All the photos are the same. But besides, it is not necessary to get up. She will not get up. She has the album there on her lap, she always brings it with her for fear that if she puts it away, later on she will never again be able to remember where she has put it and she would have to cry over that loss forever, another among so many things she has lost. But none of that is true. The album is not in the chiffonnier nor on her lap. She does not have to go in search of it nor does she carry it with her everywhere but rather it rests, reclines, sleeps, awaits her, yes, waits for her always in the small hall, in Alda's reception room, the only thing on top of the piano and open to a page, the page where the photograph is, because all the other pages are empty, as Aurelia knows so well. The reception room, the piano, the album, the black page, the white page of the unknown woman's album, the portrait of a woman's profile, a woman who was or would be or could be Aurelia, her profile superimposed on another profile of stone with a pug nose as if it had been cut off by a sword's blow and underneath a few words written in sepia ink: "Axel Munthe's House, Anacapri."

Alda is breathing slowly, gasping, is almost losing her breath, she is going to suffocate. The throat is a small retractable orifice always in danger of closing off. And life, all of life can escape through the throat, can be imprisoned in the throat, depending on an unexpected instant in which any other sensation may disappear and the intensity, desire, need for a decisive effort may well up at that point and erase the rest. The throat can slowly shrink and small thorns, miniscule needles will continue to close off the tiniest opening that remains, more and more each time until it is obstructed forever and definitively impedes the flow of air. Then death arrives. Death is simple. One is always on the verge of death. What is so strange is that one can remain in this way for so long and not die. Not end up dying, not take that step, that small, gentle step surrounded by silence.

Alda.

Alda is breathing.

Breathing slowly.

She is about to suffocate.

Alda desperately rings the bell, the purple and white crystal bell etched with designs of leaves and flowers that was not there in her room before but on the long table in the long dining room completely surrounded by windows.

Alda is looking at the bell, but does not ring it. She touches it, of course, but only to caress it as if it were a frozen flower.

Alda has no bell. She has lost it. For a while (many years) she has kept it inside a drawer filled with linen sheets entirely covered by minute yellow flecks, and has forgotten it.

Alda is holding the bell in her hands, her two hands, she looks at it attentively as if it were a consecrated chalice, as if she wished to see something else and then without realizing it, drops it among the garden ferns, the ferns that cradle it gently under her window.

Alda should not do those things. She no longer knows what she is doing. She has no memory. She does not want to remember . . .

Alda is motionless. Motionless all the time. It is horrible to be that way, constantly immobile. Lying down. Looking at the ceiling. Without a single movement. Her back begins to hurt. At first it is easy to locate the pain, to know where it began. Afterward, not so. Afterward the pain is all consuming and there is nothing else. A pain that is not too strong, that one can bear, could almost enjoy that helps one to go on living.

No. She does not feel pain. She is lying down. She is not moving. But nothing hurts her. She does not feel anything. Only her tongue, thick in a mouth she cannot open. Swollen, large without any pain. Her tongue. Her mouth that she will never again be able to open (perhaps because she is dead?), her dry lips. Her teeth tightly shut against each other. Thirst. Infinite, interminable. The urge to wet one's lips with ice-cold water. The desire to yell for them to bring her water without wasting a moment: a large pitcher of water full of ice.

Alda is not in bed. She is not in pain. She is not thirsty. She is not going to suffocate. None of that is certain. Yes she is sick, but her illness is different. If she only knew the cause of Alda's illness so long ago, so very long ago!

Alda has strange dreams. She dreams without having slept. That is so. She never sleeps. She is always awake. Night and day.

And now she is not in her room, she is not seated in a corner in the shadows awaiting something.

She is looking at a photograph album, a thick album with a lilac-colored cover, embossed with small daisies, the profiles of blond girls and acanthus leaves drawn in gold leaf. She is slowly browsing through the pages, one by one, making an enormous effort each time as if her arm refused to move, as if it were made of lead. Her arm is weighted down and so are the aged photographs. Everything is enormous: album, photographs and never the sought-after face, pursued among small wicker tables and folding screens, palms and statues, mirrors and roses, always roses. The full album. With no empty space, with not one single free page in the middle of which one could place the solitary image of a woman's profile superimposed on the stone head's profile almost devoid of visible features, both the woman and the statue situated at the edge of a terrace as if resting at the same time on a fragment of sky and sea.

The album that Alda is looking at is too full. Full of pictures but without words. Without five words that transfix the instantaneous pose even better and more definitively, a pose that ought not be forgotten.

Alda is seated among the cushions on the small golden sofa in the reception room. She never moves. Everyone is looking for her. Everyone approaches her. Everyone wants to talk to her. Everyone is her friend. They praise her, spoil her, they ask her again like a hundred times before to tell the story about the trip around the world, to tell about Hong Kong and India, about the long voyage, the dances on the great ocean liner and that strange adventure they had in Pompeii. She talks almost softly, a little reluctantly as if not wanting to say too much or to be too generous, wisely spreading a veiled translucence over her words that only she is able to measure. Siegfried slowly travels upstream in the fog among forests full of mistletoe (she has always discovered and loved certain heroic, Wagnerian chords). Music moves her, transports her to a landscape of fog and humidity, of gigantic pines, ancient birches and pointed towers where valiant knights march to their deaths carrying the petals of a crumbled rose close to their hearts protected by thick iron armor. *Galloping, galloping, galloping. Valor on the wane, nostalgia is heartfelt* . . .

The entire palace vibrates, possessed by an intense and uncontrollable happiness. The cut crystal chandeliers vibrate, the mirrors surrounded by golden volutes, the two Titians that hang in the great ballroom, panels and tapestries between the staircase archways, and the steps tremble from the light, excited steps of the people who pass through the iron gate adorned with crystal, then ascend to the first landing and walk around the balcony on the floor above, contemplating those who are already gathered, who are already dancing below, then descend the other staircase to the reception room entrance and the terrace to partake almost violently of the festive euphoria.

Alda is looking at herself. She is contemplating herself in all the mirrors (that seem few to her for she would like to see her image reproduced a thousand times). She is dancing ceaselessly. She is having fun. She is twenty years old and is already married. She is twenty years old and has traveled worldwide. She has been happy. She loves noise, music, words and people. She moves through the house, stops for an instant in the dining room, her glance quickly caresses the purple and white glasses with initials engraved on the crystal, her own profile reflected at once in three mirrors. Her hands softly glide over her body, too thin, barely clothed by the irridescent chiffon, and the ring, the thick wedding band that was always too loose slides off noiselessly, losing itself in the carpet.

All about her the street, the breeze, the late afternoon, the city, the sea surround the palace like a small innocuous wave that crests with a pacific rhythm onto the beach. The high stone walls, the covered terrace on the last floor, the small shutters, too small for the tall gray walls, lose their rigidity, become malleable, are assimilated into the rich, dense, tropical foliage of neighboring houses, of plaster cornices, colored windows and infinitely intricate balconies.

Alda stops beyond the bridge, the old topaz-colored bridge, and looks out over the city above the variegated goldsmiths' shops and the intinerant salesmen's chatter. From there on the hill, the city recovers its symmetry, the impeccable order it had in primitive paintings.

Florence reverberates in the valley below, somewhat venerable, uniform, linear, ochre and gray, almost barely yellow without shadows, without shades, without secrets. And Alda transports it, substitutes it for her port city, shabby and at the same time generous and recondite but always disquieting, incessantly containing an ambiguous, imprecise risk. She will carry with her all that is remote, that serenity, that guarantee of eternal life, that amulet to ward off all that enters the houses and destroys them, saltpeter, termites, and all that penetrates human beings and pierces them, rendering them empty and useless, suitable for being gathered up by death. So the serious cinquecento dwelling abandoned the Via della Vigna Nuova forever.

And now the palace is here, unharmed and solid, while the rosebushes she had planted in the garden have become diseased, lost their sap and are going to die. The palace remains unaffected while a strange, invisible plague has begun to devour the rosebushes' most vulnerable shoots. Something was wrong from the beginning. Something was missing. Perhaps it was when the first stone was placed in the middle of the space that had to be cleared of so much rustic, almost wild vegetation covering the enormous terrain set like an improbable island in the middle of the city. Or perhaps it was when they moved into the house, without first having it blessed so that it was truly theirs, that they wrested from it the spirit that was living there, the spirit that wanted to be included.

Alda caresses the calendar page, runs her fingers gently over the numbers' thick surface, she reexamines them tenderly, recognizing them. The yellow page is silky, almost velvety and her finger slides along unhindered. AUGUST 20, 1933.

The garden is invading the inner regions, violating the dwellings that had been forbidden, slipping under the doors like green, humid moss, the bed where small mushrooms grow uncannily from one day to the next; it is penetrating the hollow spaces where before the air flowed through between the windowpanes and the wall in the form of fragile, scented and sinuous creeping vines inundating the rooms with a sickeningly sweet, nocturnal perfume; it is slipping through the cracks that have barely begun to open up timidly between the ceiling of the ground floor and the floor above, and it is starting to lift up the mosaics and fiercely push in between the joints where the cement has already cracked and the stucco is peeling off the wall, leaving dark hollows, empty caves exposed: it is sliding surreptitiously through all these somber corners, improvised paths, as if guided by destiny, by an unavoidable design, ivy.

And here is where the palace ceases to be impregnable. At first the garden had that unkempt charm, a certain freedom that did not transgress the boundaries of decorum and moderation. Cypresses and palm trees, hydrangea and crotons, flamboyants and pines coexisted. Then the proliferation of climbing rosebushes and ivy, of ferns and asparagus, of all sorts of tubers, caladium, poincianas and oleanders, of wild grasses that closed off the lanes, the velvety, fleshy leaves that invaded the previously traveled paths, restored the garden that had been molded and fit and ordered, to a former state, one that dominated the extensive, uncultivated land devoid of any human habitat during the entire period it remained forgotten and surrounded by a thick wall of thistles and thorns. Only then, there was no longer the natural chaos that certain rustic but innocent landscapes have, untouched by man's spirit. The garden began to be inhabited by a soul, to live a life in need of nourishing itself more and more on the palace and those who lived therein.

Aurelia is closing her eyes, trying in vain to repeat to herself the empty date on the calendar, the date that could be a key to everything, to something, but hollow and foreign as it is, does not encompass any memory.

She ought to get up. Walk again ceaselessly. Search the entire palace again from top to bottom. Watch over all entranceways. Prevent the plants from penetrating. Close off all the hollows. The doors and windows. The highest shutters, the ones to the rooms on the top floor that no one ever used. Those, too. Because if she does not hurry up, the rosebushes' curse will come in through any one of those openings, through each one of them.

One must watch that the palace's soul does not escape, dissipate, disappear as do perfumes that are left exposed for too long. The house has been open too long. She has carelessly left it open. She has forgotten to close the doors from within, secure the bolts, close the latches, position the thick iron bars in their supports hidden among the curtains that announce it is more prudent to protect the strong carved doors with something extra that closes them off from all intruders. But it is not a question of intruders. Aurelia has already forgotten that there can also be intruders, strangers, thieves with an inexplicable cause capable of penetrating the abode where one lives. She does not fear that. She fears, is terrified by another more dangerous invasion, a spiritual one that has taken possession of the garden, obliges the rosebushes to die and the ivy to grow uncontrollably and to creep inside. One must close the doors, windows, shutters, blinds. One must drag along tables, the heaviest chests, the high-backed easy chairs, everything fit to be placed behind a door, everything that can block free passage.

Lucila, Lucila! Where can Lucila be? Why doesn't she come to help her! To talk to someone! If Lucila came, she could talk to someone. Has Lucila abandoned her, too?

Aurelia calls, shouts, and Lucila's name resounds exaggeratedly enormous, echoless, only exacerbatedly inflated by the void.

Lucila is not there. She, too, left years ago. Everyone has left. Everyone has abandoned her. She alone must protect herself.

She alone will close, is closing, there is very little left . . . will close off the exits and entrances forever and will leave no cracks. She has begun upstairs. One by one, the windows behind the blinds that ought to separate the dust from the library books. Afterward one floor down, the frames of the blinds without windows, the wooden shutters, the jalousies, in each of the rooms for guests, for guests of the guests, for acquaintances and strangers alike. Then the first floor, the ten dining room windows barely ajar; the four in each room, all undoubtedly closed, nervously touched from top to bottom by feverish fingers more difficult to control each time. Finally the livingroom, the reception hall, the ballroom, the windows that look out on the terrace, the doors that could be opened onto the small inner garden with no exit to the street. The door that closes off Alda's room, the room where those other doors are, the only ones that lead to the inner garden, the one with no exit to the street. The garden she always loved. The garden that was never hers. The garden where all the roses were, are, ought to be.

The door gives way docilely without resistance. The room smells of tepid humidity and confined flowers, like the odor of chapels and grottoes. One is submerged voluptuously in the greenery of ferns on all sides, taking over the mirror frame in the hazy light, in an uncanny peace, abysmal and intemporal. And there she remains, hypnotically contemplating the mirror. Gazing at herself, seeing Alda's image, her own image, the lost face at last barely recovered. Then her eyes close, burdened by a long, remote and strange fatigue, and something gently abandons her body forever.

Translated by Evelyn Picon Garfield

Nélida Piñón

Brazil

Nélida Piñón. (Photo courtesy of Ednalva Tavares.)

Nélida Piñón was born in Rio de Janeiro in 1937 of a Spanish father and a Brazilian mother. For a while she worked for the newspaper *O Globo* until she decided that journalism was incompatible with literature, and then as assistant editor of the literary magazine *Cadernos Brasileiros.* She taught university courses in Brazil and at Columbia University in New York. Since 1955 she has dedicated herself full-time to creative writing, publishing more than six novels and three collections of short stories, several of which have won literary prizes and have been translated into Spanish, French, English, and Polish.

In her first novels—*Guia-mapa de Gabriel Arcanjo* (The Archangel Gabriel's Guidebook) and *Madeira feita cruz* (The Wooden Cross)—she explores philosophical and religious questions about sin (sexual) and spirituality through myths and signs in a style that seems at once neo-baroque and surrealistic. Sensuality and mysticism are represented in the mystery and miracle of contemporary earthly versions of biblical symbols. Solitude and a hermetic language are constants.

In her short stories, from which our selections are taken, Piñón turns away from trying to clarify spirituality to a world where only the material and minute descriptions of the surroundings along with fragmentary sensations and posturing of individuals reflect the characters' state of mind. The language is still hermetic but now that is due in part to a "poetics of poverty," a paucity of vocabulary and many brief utterances that often lack verbs. This type of prose throws readers off guard with its juxtaposed antitheses, constant transformations, shifts, elliptical utterances, and lack of transitions, all of which result in tense dramatic phrasing that alternates with sensuous descriptive imagery.

Piñón's worlds are both aggressive and innocent, friendly and hostile, with atmospheres of primitive freedom and hedonistic sensuality. Characters relate to dark forces as their weaknesses and even physical and mental deformities are blatantly exposed. In stories such as "The New Kingdom" ("O novo reino"), characters escape from suffocating and oppressive human relationships into an animal world unfettered by servitude and humiliation. Piñón is fascinated by the unknown and by characters who are damned or illuminated. In stories such as "Bird of Paradise" ("Ave de paraiso"), she treats love with her typical strangeness and exaggerated intensity. Both short stories are from the collection *Sala de armas* (The Fencing Room).

267

Bird of Paradise

ONCE A WEEK he visited the woman. To keep passion alive, he used to say agitatedly. She believed him and greeted him with chocolate cake and pear liqueur made from fruit picked from her own garden. The neighbors used to comment on the strange meetings, but she loved him more each time. Imagining how difficult her life must be, his looks begged her forgiveness, as if assuring her how else can I love you.

He would eat the cake and refuse the rest. Even though she would insist. He's being polite, she thought, hiding in his shadow. Once she even prepared a surprise dinner for him. The meal smelled wonderful, as if the spices were fresh from China. The place settings and the provisions bought for a holiday gleamed in anticipation of the moment he would open his eyes wide with delight.

The man took it all in appreciatively. He had always considered her sensitive to harmony and grace. A confidence in her that was present from their first meeting: on the streetcar she had forgotten money for the fare, had glanced about without asking for help, he paid and said very softly I need help, too. She smiled and, surprised, he took her hand; she had agreed, and when he left her safe and sound at her door he promised to return the next day.

"Don't insist because I won't accept the dinner." He seemed so natural, like a fish admonishing the sea. She cried thinking that of all men, God had given her the most difficult one. It was the only weak moment in her love. The next day she received roses and the card inside simply said: love. She laughed, repentant, condemning her lack of control. She shouldn't have subjected him to such a test that he heroically rejected. On the next visit he made love to her with the passion of a homeless soul and repeatedly whispered her name.

Once he disappeared for three months without even a letter, a telegram or a telephone call. She thought now she would die. All about her the same table, the purple tablecloth she had ironed one long Saturday, the bed with white sheets she herself had washed avoiding too much bluing, the house that he stopped visiting without warning. She wandered through the streets and with every sight added:

"What's to become of a woman without her love story."

She had gone to high school in the city where she was born. She didn't want to be a teacher. Ever since childhood she wanted to get married. It was her only ambition. She feared someone else's children would drain off the energy her own flesh and blood deserved. The mother began to complain, they needed money. The father had lost his job, his age was becoming a problem. He ended up at the counter in his godfather's pharmacy. And the mother took in sewing. Meanwhile, the daughter would take care of the housework since she refused to teach. It was then she became fascinated with the kitchen. But the recipe for the chocolate cake came later: Norma showed up elegant in a yellow dress, asking for help with a flared skirt, a style discovered in a magazine from the corner newsstand. Although she thought Norma frivolous for insisting she accompany her to dances where boyfriends were easily available, she never admonished her. That was when she met the other woman, Norma's casual acquaintance. After their typing course, they both wanted to work for a North American company. They would visit the States later. Stroll along Fifth Avenue. Norma only thought about American servicemen. Sorry they no longer visited us as in wartime. The friend, listening, finally asked her:

"Do you want to come along?" She was referring to the job opening with the North American company. She shook her head no. She was ashamed to explain that she wanted to get married. It was easier and her heart longed for that.

"I know all that matters to you is a chocolate cake recipe," the other woman declared angrily.

This time she agreed, trembling. Demanding the recipe with paper and pencil in hand. And that the other woman call her mother to be sure of the ingredients haphazardly committed to memory. At home, because of their budget, she couldn't try it out. But she consoled herself: as soon as I have a lover, I'll surprise him. She was always comforted by the hope that the chocolate cake would be her husband's dessert. Sweets were only made for a lover to taste. That ingenuous quality moved Norma. Years later when they parted and she lost touch with her friends, her destiny was to withdraw from the world to preserve love; and Norma, touching her on the shoulder, told her, "This had to happen to you." She never saw her again.

Yet she wanted to explain, prove she was wrong. But Norma went off without glancing back, free as ever.

When he returned months later, he brought her gifts, covered her hair with kisses, the hair he said smelled heavenly, impressed on her the importance of the trip, he wasn't sorry he'd gone because of the pleasure of returning. She found the explanation kind. She ran into the kitchen, before he led her off to the bedroom. She outdid herself to achieve perfection with the necessary ingredients. She would not permit his love unless the cake awaited them afterward, especially on holidays.

He laughed, charmed by her extravagance, felt he had no right to protest. He also recognized freedom. He waited for her to finish. She came then as if assuring him I am ready for your difficult absence. She was always delicate about love and he appreciated her discretion. He would repudiate any aggressive approach by her that might forever damage the illusion of possessing her as if it were still the first time. Intuitively she hid her face in the pillow, quietly weeping. He shouted like King Arthur's servant:

"How delightful women are! How delightful they are!"

She interpreted the sense of this pronouncement and collected her tears surrendering modestly. She had never avoided such scenes. Sometimes they occurred anew the following week. He pretended not to notice that if repeated, charm would be threatened with exhaustion.

Everything was done to renew that charm. That's why he loved her so during those years. His fantasy also rested on novelty. Sometimes he disguised himself, false beard and moustache, different color hair. He would arrive slowly, allowing people time to be suspicious. And not so the neighbors might think she was deceiving him but because he enjoyed fooling them, laughing at them afterward.

Now she was submissively passionate. Already suffering his absence. On difficult days her love became anxious so that she consulted the calendar hoping it might be a chocolate cake day, when he would surely come. Until year's end the calendar recorded every visiting day. She never suggested a change in dates or greater devotion. She respected that system.

Nevertheless at the beginning of the month, he used to arrive earlier bringing money for household expenses and other necessities. He would throw it on top of the fruit bowl, even if it held bananas, pears and apples that she loved to imagine amid snow. She didn't know how to explain it, but eating apples made her feel like a fine French lady with imported kid gloves and a silk scarf on her head. The money would remain there until he left. After his departure, she would place it near the prayer book. Both yielded to ritual.

One day he said, "Let's go out right now since we've never been to the movies and I want to go with you before I die. Now is the time to heed my wishes." She cried with joy, embracing him.

"You're all mine! All mine!"

They went and didn't like it, he categorized the love episodes as obscene. She agreed, but was too happy to react strongly. They had some ice cream and he kept on complaining. She soiled her dress; at that moment he laughed, he liked her awkward gestures, the way she fumbled with little things.

Mother used to visit her two or three times a year. She still took in sewing. She discreetly asked about him, afraid of annoying her. Never understood that couple. In the church he forbade her to wear a wedding dress, alleging that nuptial attire ought to be appreciated solely by the groom. But he surprised her with a white dress, veil and crown when they were left alone in the room after the ceremony. The first night they were to enjoy together, she appeared before him dressed as in his dreams and he closed his eyes and opened them quickly to see if she was still at his side, the woman he loved. Moved, he spoke to her the way she understood: you're pretty, all that's missing is the priest to marry us again. And in the middle of the night when they made love, he asked her to remain in bed for he should be the one to hang up the wedding dress he had bought for her. He could imagine such things with no other woman, and she never forgot it.

When the mother visited, the daughter always asked about the father, how were they, never inviting her to stay, she who lived far away, traveling by train for hours to return home. On those short visits, the daughter never complained. She seemed delighted with her lot. There was never a happier woman. The mother sometimes wanted to ask: what time does he get home. Or prolong the visit so as to surprise him when he came for supper. But after four o'clock, the daughter became anxious, got up constantly under any pretext, pretended to be busy, he took up all her time she touchingly assured her. When leaving, the mother always repeated:

"Your house is beautiful."

Next week, he intuitively asked her, "Doesn't your mother ever come to see you?" She would act sad and whisper: I have only you in this world. He used to kiss her and as if asking forgiveness say, "I will return next Wednesday, does that please you?" She would smile, her face shining, her hair the way he liked it. Beginning to gray. He respected that, thinking: this one is pure, this one is pure.

One day he could hold back no longer. He arrived disguised, his last chance to confuse the neighbors. He carried a suitcase in each hand. She suffered that long journey in anticipation. She helped him as if he were tired, life exacting too much from him. She brought him ice water, lamenting the absence of a fountain in the garden; she could adorn it with stones, maybe a statue. The man drank. He removed the disguise that she had never once criticized. And feigning independence he said, loud enough for her to hear:

"The trial period is over. This time I came to stay."

Hiding her profound joy, the woman looked at the man, then immediately ran to the kitchen. No one surpassed her in chocolate cakes.

Translated by Evelyn Picon Garfield

The New Kingdom

THE GREEN LANDSCAPE, light throwing insects into relief. The father up front like a king. He slaughtered the pigs and always sat at the head of the table. His entourage consisted of two women. Despite carnal intimacy, the man and woman had only one daughter. Ugly and unappreciated, she followed them everywhere. After going to town, they returned through the woods, the best way home where they lived surrounded by trees.

From the start the daughter felt she was being followed. Without identifying the pursuer or preparing the father for the enemy. She and the mother feared that man's brutish nature, he used to tie up the animals with the agility of the wind. Few challenged his superiority in most undertakings. But that pursuer's stare sought her stomach, the fiery landscape. Protecting her belly, she went tripping along over the roots, walking with difficulty. Hope sprang from the body's island.

Her disappearance was noticed much later. The father still tried shouting: come, you ugly thing, you look more like a snake crawling on the ground. He took pleasure in exposing her ugliness, he condemned her clumsiness. He rummaged about everywhere, trying to get her back. He imagined her motionless, emulating a tree and stone, her secret nature. He always judged her to be the whim of an abused mother, an extravagance that he, the libertine, imposed on the family.

In the middle of the woods, where the daughter had disappeared, he believed there was an impenetrable region. There all nature seemed to him transformed under the effect of a seismic tremor. The girl was nowhere to be found. The displaced earth on the banks of the lake barely showed where animals recently fought. The mother tried to correct the husband's abuses. Her hesitant expression seemed to point to the waters. He shook her by the shoulders in search of the secret. The woman nevertheless made him see that by losing the daughter, he consented to the sand's purification.

They were obliged to mourn, and since the news had spread, to receive guests with coffee and cornbread. Years later, the first beings of a new species emerged in the woods, no doubt a recent cross between certain animals. Then hunters appeared hot on the trail of the animals reputed to exist there. But the woods covered half the territory, access was especially difficult, and they lacked information so as not to get lost on senseless short cuts.

Nooks, leaves, insects, and fruit were exhaustively investigated, until they found the first of these animals, with eyes, nose, even ears just like the hunters'. The animal certainly gave the appearance of the human race in bygone times, deviating by continuous evolution to secure its present form.

The animal proudly displayed evidence extinct in human beings: an enormous tail, a hard shell, and successive diamond-shaped incrustations. With those fingers and hands different from man's, they easily conquered the trees, no doubt they excavated the earth in search of food as in the days of the Chinese empire . . .

During that intense analysis, the hunters seemed to retreat to the beginnings of their apparent origins, their bodies aching all over from witnessing the advent of their own species.

Even when faced with that monstrosity, their own beauty guaranteed the perfection they had always sought, for that beast's nature outdid itself by not evolving. On the other hand, they intuited the dubious alchemy from which both resulted. So much so that the earth suddenly ceased to be theirs faced with that animal's antiquity, surely the first in the order of creation and from which all had originated.

It awakened the suspicion that the beast had allowed himself to be plucked like a flower. One more mountain animal raised so sweetly on milk and corn. And they were already revering him when a strange shape, adorned with vegetation, emerged from the lake's depths. It walked ashore with difficulty. It was experiencing an equilibrium occasionally mastered and recovered now that it was accustomed to the initial shock.

The soil is its habitat, the hunters said. For its human ties were visible although disguised by the foliage. Especially when the animals embraced, the two ugly, filthy things responded to a feeling that, if imitated by man, would have lost him in solitude. But notwithstanding the love that both suffered, the lake creature was getting ready to speak and confronted the men who were totally horrified that a disgusting thing like that would try to mimic them.

"He's mine," the lake creature stated in a vulgar way.

That effort awakened in the hunters the impetus to free it from such responsibilities. So it would never yield to speech again. When they removed the green vines, a female form became apparent, arable and vulnerable. Capable of adapting under water where she had made her dwelling; everyone was convinced of that now.

Faced with their prying, she rebelled: I'm not a slave. A secretion emanated from her body and attracted everyone, meanwhile renewing among them a familiarity full of taboos.

But it seemed strange to the animal that the woman, after having conceived him with the help of his father's opposing nature and having learned to assume the trappings of his world, would now return to this verbal artifice opposed by his race. The beast knew himself to be the product of opposing races, he partook of the limits of both without ever absorbing their resources completely. Sometimes, wanting to imitate the father, he practiced the mother's gestures. The nature of one and the other frequently failed in him. And even though now he wished the mother victorious, she became the unforgivably divisive force. It was true he had used her to be born, but such love ought not exist any longer. He also defended his kingdom, the hunt, his law. In that conflict one thought stood out in his mind, that the only worthwhile life was among carnivores and agile fish.

At that moment his precariously emerging conscience despised the woman's withdrawal from the human world as well as the race his father and she had given him by their spurious and illuminated union. He communicated his hesitancy with a severe look. No one stopped him when he went away. The woman still wanted to ask him to stay, but seeing herself suddenly alone, recovered the power of speech she used to abandon the territory where as queen she began an absurd race.

She still passionately wanted to demand her maritime land, she pointed her finger toward the waters. The temptation to give reasons was brief. She feared life among men, especially when they tied her up, insensitive to the protest hurled to the winds, a protest saved for her fatal hour.

The return home, the exaggerated procession, the townsmen cursing those who betrayed them in exchange for evil pleasure, everything ended up confounding the hunters. The man and woman also seemed aged. She shouted my daughter. The father trembled struck by fever. The daughter remained motionless in an improvised cage. Slavery denied her customary affection.

She doesn't remember that she is ours, despite her transformations, and the father added rudely: this is the daughter we lost, though she has changed into a monster and cannot or does not want to recognize us. In between the bars, the mother mumbled her secrets preserved in brine. She did not demand offical recognition from her daughter. She knew that she would remember them even though the human race was no longer of any use to her. Since that day on the way back from the city when she saw the daughter disappear in the water without confessing anything to the husband. The daughter was submerging, holding fast to a monstrous creature until she disappeared. Then the mother began to pray without understanding the motives that made the daughter love another kingdom with an exceptional feeling unknown to man. To the point of relinquishing the very body they, the mother and father, had offered by their union, the body that imitated theirs from birth. A similarity the daughter did not hesitate to wipe out until it was unrecognizable there in the lake's depths, and all for a love she served selflessly. The mother asked herself: then love is not the force that says I love you and even devotes itself to mining uranium, silver, and rare minerals, without ever explaining their use. For the first time she was doubting the love they all experienced without originality, always driving away innovators like lepers. Then the daughter's confidence pointed out that what I proudly do, mother, turns out all right, so much that I didn't even hesitate. Her present rejection was of someone who was visiting hell after having inhabited her animal lover's paradise.

Between them there were no telling glances that the old woman might later store away in her chest. The silent battle lasted hours. The old woman tried to reclaim contact, the husband dragged her home. In the twilight hours of a new day, the men were surprised by the empty cage. The knots untied, forced open by claws. The sun rose on the horizon alongside the woods.

Translated by Evelyn Picon Garfield

Luisa Valenzuela

Argentina

Luisa Valenzuela. (Photo courtesy of Sara Facio–Alicia
D'Amico.)

Luisa Valenzuela was born in Buenos Aires in 1938 and has become the most translated contemporary woman author from Latin America. Six of her novels and collections of short stories have been published by prestigious U.S. presses. She has been a journalist for major Argentinean newspapers and the recipient of a Guggenheim fellowship. Presently she conducts creative writing workshops at universities in New York City, where she has been a fellow of the Institute for the Humanities and distinguished writer-in-residence at New York University.

Her fiction often parodies the conventions of bourgeois society and is critical of its institutions, taboos, and social structures. By means of the written word, she searches with irony and humor for knowledge of the self and the other. In novels such as *El gato eficaz* (Cat-o-Nine-Deaths), her self-critical prose relies on puns and games that invent and demythify the serious role of language as communicator of truths. Surrealistic and at times dreamlike, fragmented scenes and metamorphic imagery are nevertheless very often based on tangible Latin American political realities of power and repression. In her latest novel *Cola de lagartija*, translated by Gregory Rabassa as *The Lizard's Tail*, she explores the life of President Juan Perón's controversial minister of public welfare, José López Rega, who was also advisor and confidant to President Isabel Perón. He was known as the Sorcerer and the power behind the right-wing terrorist group called the triple A (Anti-Communist Association of Argentina). Valenzuela, however, uses him as a fictionalized metaphor for the megalomaniac character of power and cruelty, and through him also explores language, eroticism, and Latin American religious rituals such as those of Umbanda.

This link between somatic/semantic eroticism and power of a political, social, and psychological nature underlies the three stories included here, from Valenzuela's latest collections. "I'm Your Horse in the Night" ("De noche soy tu caballo") and "Other Weapons" ("Cambio de armas") are taken from the collection *Cambio de armas,* published in an English translation by Deborah Bonner as *Other Weapons* (Hanover, N.H., 1985), and "Blue Water-Man" ("El fontanero azul") is our translation from the collection *Donde viven las águilas* (Where the Eagles Live).

281

Blue Water-Man

THEY POINTED HIM OUT to me; he's the water-man. I approached him because I like the sound of that word, not because of what that title means around here: the right to distribute rationed water according to whim. But I wasn't the one who lit the wick. Even though I got pretty close and even managed to touch him, as some say (there are witnesses for everything, there's always someone unscrupulous enough to tell the truth: imagination is withering away and nothing's left for the poor).

Water-man and all, it seems I managed to touch him, so the witnesses say. But I insist that I wasn't the one to light the wick. The idea of the uproar didn't even enter my mind.

Water-man. In appearance a respectable man, someone worthy of living in this village so full of respect for fallen leaves, for starving dogs, for what's already dying and also patiently awaiting its end: the human being.

(The cemetery has colored tombstones. The houses in this part of the world are made of clay; while we're above earth it's best that we blend into it.)

The water-man, on the other hand, was the only dustless one in this village; that's rather insulting.

Stone, dust and stone, all the streets climb up to the patch of light we call the market. Up there, the clean water-man shines with his white shirt, golden teeth and moustache. Below we walk around carrying water buckets from the river that's already drying up.

This happened a week ago on Sunday.

I didn't light the wick and I wasn't part of the uproar either.

He was super clean standing in the atrium to the ancient convent and I, as dirty as ever, dusty, with fingertips of a fresh, indigo blue that I'd been painting on the walls (my house is adobe like everyone else's; I was slowly painting it blue to tone it down: I wanted a bit of blue to imitate water). (And if more than one witness says I touched him well I probably did. Even though I felt that they were his hands on my body and not the unthinkable opposite.)

To be more exact it was Palm Sunday and he was in the atrium calculating profits. An infamous water-man, no doubt: for one hundred pesos he allowed the rich man's water tank to overflow, and let the neighbors go to hell. He was the spider in the web of pipes, god in the subterranean world of sewers.

(And to think that just by moving a finger, just by removing the cloak of greed and generously opening up the valves, he could have quenched the thirst of the entire village.)

A blue patch remained on his chest that Sunday—Palm Sunday— almost hidden beneath the white shirt, that's all.

And a week went by:

Monday—

I won't tell you where I got the ten pesos I brought him, but enough water flowed from my own spout so that my three turkeys and my neighbor's sow wouldn't die from thirst.

Tuesday—

The tourists left and I didn't even get one peso. But because of human nature (weak, weak, weak!!) I got him to let more water flow. I washed my underpants.

Wednesday—

In complete silence, I continued painting the front of my house blue. At nightfall I went to see him for a while. Both of the water-man's arms, his chest and part of his back were already blue.

Holy Thursday—

In vain we waited in the atrium for the performance of the Last Supper. Would there be no water even for this humble reenactment? It wasn't my idea; the man who dismounted in front of the door said: Even if it's the last one, after this supper, we have to wash the dishes. Where's the water? The show's over, brothers, you can go home.

Good Friday—

Logically it was everyone's Via Crucis, with a procession, prayers, dry lips and cracked skin. (The rich from the houses on high pass by and exchange hidden smiles with our water-man. His pockets are brimming and the rich have full pools, all the water they want. For us there's not even a drop of humidity left for tears).

Holy Saturday—

All's calm in the village and in my life. Just the water-man's left hand, face and one testicle are still flesh color. The rest of him is indigo, I can't imagine why. Only children are walking around the village to-day, and dogs, like dried-up skins staked out on four legs.

From my window I saw the truck arrive with the judas figures*— red devils with horns—and I confess that I said to myself: our judas is blue, we're more afraid of him, he's not made of papier-mâché, nor is he hollow inside; he's evil.

Without much effort, I also saw how they stuck firecrackers inside each figure's belly, hung a string of firecrackers around the neck and left the wicks in the horns. (But it's one thing to see and a very different thing to think of applying what you've seen.)

(They all saw it, for four centuries now they've known much better than me, for even though I come from so far away, I'm on their side. I

---

*In many Latin American countries, during Holy Week, lifelike figures of Judas are burned in the public squares.

swear it wasn't me, don't make the usual mistake, don't single out the stranger even as a blessing.)

(Your house's color, they told me afterward, and I shrugged my shoulders, is the color of his tombstone.)

And at eleven o'clock at night rattles called us to mass.
Easter Sunday—
At midnight, bells were clanging away. As if the village still had such spirit. At one o'clock they shot off flares and at two thirty the first rains let loose, putting an end to the long months of drought. What a welcome sight, what an oasis! At last we didn't need him . . . (It rained all night and morning until eleven o'clock mass and the people in the convent thanked the heavens for that solitary offering. And they prayed on their knees proudly showing the mud-covered soles of their feet.)

At noon the sun reappeared unaware of the bliss. And can they think that in the mist's suffocating web I could have summoned up enough strength to concoct the idea? In the midst of infernal heat and firecracker blasts? In the market square the pâpier-maché judas exploded into a thousand pieces, evil was disintegrating, the people knew it and rejoiced.

At five o'clock as the firecrackers piled up, the celebration began. I ran to the marketplace to see the men in the village dancing around heaps of bananas and mangoes, watermelon stands and clay pots. Dazzling colors sparkled like the trees' leaves washed by the rain. I was going to dance in line with the villagers dressed up as fine folk; velvet tunics, embroidered hats, lace and tinsel, white men's masks with pointed beards, white gloves. I wanted to participate in the celebration, become part of the brass music. Communion with the people, until I saw the water-man there (that son of a bitch).

Standing over the fountain in the middle of the market. His back turned to me, looking around (searching for me, I bet), already dressed in blue all over. The water-man, blue atop the dry fountain. That was too much, so even though my job wasn't finished—the left hand, the face and one testicle—I couldn't stop myself and fled, terrified. Seeing me run away, the inexpressive faces of the masks with eyes (what an idea!) followed my flight. And he was so indigo, so very irreverent.

I bought white paint with my last pesos (the house is more demanding than the stomach: I didn't want a house the color of the water-man, I wanted a pure home).

The judas burst open in the square as I painted to the rhythm of the firecrackers. My electric-blue house began to lose its energy and turned transparent, sky blue. I had almost repainted one whole wall when I heard the blast of a giant firecracker.

There was a pregnant pause, suspense in the air, when they arrived breathless with the news:

He had been the great judas, almost like the real one. When I reached the square the dancing had stopped and the masks' inhuman eyes were watching. There was the blue water-man, disemboweled, stuck on the fountain's highest point.

(Was there a stick of dynamite in his fly or a handful of firecrackers in his navel?)

But listen here, *I wasn't the one who lit the wick* as you can verify just by reading my statement carefully.

It was strange that his face and also one of his hands, palm up, were my transparent, sky blue color. Besides, I could swear that one testicle had turned sky blue, but it flew off with his guts and they never found it (the guts splattered the people from the houses on high who were at arms' length, seated right there at the only tables with nice tablecloths in the middle of the square, in the dancer's way, sipping their drinks in a dignified manner, showing off their embroidered shirts or their long dresses. It only splattered them a little but they stood up in disgust and took their golden children away from the ill-fated spectacle).

I, on the other hand, remained there to await the miracle: from the riddled belly of this judas figure, water would forever flow.

The village natives, as often happens, didn't expect that much. Blood flowed from the pierced belly, to the surprise of none and the joy of all. And the masked ones stuck their white-gloved hands in that blood and washed the perfectly white masks that covered their faces.

Water-man's blood: symbol of water. Perfect ablution.

Later they tried to treat me with too much consideration. They loved me and hated me and shouted my name. And I was so undeserving, so forsaken, while the blue water-man was gradually turning red so that even his color didn't belong to me anymore.

Translated by Evelyn Picon Garfield

Other Weapons

The Words

SHE DOESN'T FIND IT the least bit surprising that she has no memory, that she feels completely devoid of recollections. She may not even realize that she's living in an absolute void. She is quite concerned about something else, about her capacity to find the right word for each thing and receive a cup of tea when she says I want (and that "I want" also disconcerts her, that act of willing) when she says I want a cup of tea.

Martina attends to all her requests. And she knows that's her name because Martina herself has told her so, repeating it over and over until she managed to retain the name. As for herself, she's been told she's called Laura, but that's also part of the haze in which her life drifts by.

There's also the man: that one, him, the no-name she can call by any name that happens to cross her mind; they're all just as effective, anyway, and when the guy's around the house he answers even if she calls him Hugo, Sebastian, Ignacio, Alfredo or anything else. He seems to be around the house often enough to keep her calm, a little, stroking her shoulders and arms, in a progression not lacking in tenderness.

Then there are the everyday objects: the ones called plate, bathroom, book, bed, cup, table, door. It's exasperating, for example, to confront the one called door and try to figure out what to do. A locked door, yes, but there are the keys, on the ledge, within her reach, and the lock's easy to open, her fascination with the beyond, which she can't make up her mind to face.

She, so-called Laura, is on this side of the so-called door, with its so-called locks and its so-called key begging her to cross the threshold. But she can't; not yet. Facing the door, she thinks about it and realizes she can't, although no one appears to care much. Suddenly the so-called door opens and the man we will now call Hector walks in, proving that he also has his set of so-called keys and uses them quite freely. If she stares at him when he walks in—it's happened to so-called Laura before—she discovers that two other men arrive with Hector and stay outside the door, trying to look inconspicuous. She calls them One and Two, which sometimes gives her a sense of safety and other times makes a shudder run through her. Then she welcomes him knowing that One and Two are standing outside the apartment (apartment?) right outside the so-called door, maybe waiting or protecting him, and sometimes she can imagine that they're with her and that they escort her, especially when he stares into her eyes as if he were weighing out the memory of old things about her which she doesn't share in the least.

Sometimes her head aches, and that pain is the only thing that really belongs to her and that she can communicate to the man. Then he gets worried, both hoping and fearing that she'll remember something specific.

The Concept

Crazy she is not. At least she's sure of that, although sometimes she wonders and even asks Martina where she gets that concept of insanity and why she's so sure. But at least she knows, she knows she isn't, she isn't running away from reason or understanding; it's a general state of forgetfulness that doesn't feel altogether unpleasant. And by no means painful.

So-called anguish is another story: so-called anguish sometimes tightens the opening of her stomach and makes her want to shriek *a bocca chiusa,* as if she were whining. She says—or thinks—whine, and it's as if she could see the image of the word, a clear image despite the lack of clarity a word can have. An image that is undoubtedly charged with memories. (Where have all the memories gone? Where are they, going around knowing much more about her than she herself?) Something's hiding and sometimes she tries to reach a mental hand out to catch a memory on the wing, and that's impossible. It's impossible to have access to that corner of her brain where memory crouches, so she finds nothing: memory locked into itself as a defense.

The Photograph

The photograph is lying on the lamp-table as evidence. He and she, staring into each other's eyes with a just-married look about them. She's wearing a veil and, behind the veil, an absent expression. Whereas he has the triumphant look of those who think they've gotten somewhere. He almost always does—almost always when he's within her sight—he takes on that triumphant air of those who think they've gotten somewhere. Suddenly it turns off, suddenly, as if someone had hit a switch, it turns off, and the triumph turns into doubt or something far more opaque, hard to explain, unfathomable. That is: eyes open but with a sort of lowered curtain, hermetic eyes, staring but not seeing her at all, or maybe only seeing what she's lost on some curve along the road. What's been left behind and he won't get back because, deep down, the last thing he wants to do is get it back. But there was a road, that much she does know, with all the atmospheric conditions of the human road (the big storms).

Living like that, in the absolute present, in a world that's born every instant or at most was born a few days back (how many?) is like living in cotton wool: somewhat soft and warm, but with no taste at all. Not rough, either. There's little she can know about roughness in that completely soft, slightly rosy apartment, in the company of Martina, who talks ever so softly. But she senses roughness, particularly when he (Juan, Martin, Ricardo, Hugo?) holds her too tight, squeezing her more out of hatred than embracing her out of love or at least out of desire, and she suspects that there's something behind all of that, but the suspicion isn't even a developed thought, only a detail that crosses her mind, and then, nothing. Then a return to softness, to letting oneself be, and again the beautiful hands of Antonio or whatever his name is caressing her, his long, lax arms surrounding her body, holding her very close but not oppressing her.

The Names

Sometimes he seems very beautiful to her, particularly when he's lying down beside her and she sees the whole length of his body.

Daniel, Pedro, Ariel, Alberto, Alfonso, she calls him softly, caressing him.

More, he asks, and it's not clear whether he's referring to the caresses or to the sequence of names.

Then she gives him more of both, naming each part of his body for the first time, even the darkest corners. Diego, Esteban, José Maria, Alejandro, Luis, Julio, and the stream keeps on running; he smiles ever so peacefully, and it's not altogether sincere. Something's on edge behind that peace, something's crouching, ready to pounce at the slightest tremble in her voice when she pronounces a name. But her voice is monotonous, with no apparent feelings or hesitations. She recites like a litany: José, Francisco, Adolfo, Armando, Eduardo, and he can let himself slip into sleep feeling he's all of them to her, he fulfills all their roles. Except that all is equal to none, and she keeps on reciting even after she knows he's asleep, while playing with the listless, sad remains of the wonder of him. She recites names, exercising her memory with some delight.

He of countless names, the nameless man, sleeps and she can examine him as long as she pleases, until she's had her fill, which soon occurs. The nameless man seems to divide his time with her between making love to her and sleeping, and it's an uneven split: he spends most of the time sleeping. Relieved, yes. But what from? They barely ever talk, seldom do they have much of anything to say to each other: she can't even recall the good old times and he acts as if he already knew them or he didn't care much about them, which is about the same.

Then she gets up carefully so as not to wake him up—as if it were easy to wake him up once he'd fallen asleep—and walks around the room naked. Sometimes she goes into the living room without minding Martina and just stands there, staring at the door, the one with all the locks, asking herself whether One and Two are still there, sleeping in front of the doorway like guard dogs, whether they're only shadows and whether they could become friendly shadows to a strange woman.

She feels strange, foreign, different. Different from whom? From other women? From herself? So she runs back to the bedroom to look at herself in the big wardrobe mirror. There she is, all of her: rather sad, pointy knees; in general, not much is rounded. Then there's that long, inexplicable scar that runs down her back, that she can only see in the mirror. A thick scar, apparent to the touch, sort of tender even though it's already healed and doesn't hurt. How did that long seam get to that back that seems to have suffered so much? A beaten back. The word beaten, which sounds so pretty if you don't analyze it, gives her goose pimples. She stands there, thinking about the secret power of words, all for . . . no more, none of that, enough, don't go back to the obsession of the photograph. But she does return, sure she does; it's the only thing that really attracts her in that entire small, warm, foreign house. Completely foreign with pastel shades that she never could have chosen herself, although what would she have chosen? Less definite colors, probably; darker shades, like the color of his rod, so dark it's almost brown.

And in that otherwise foreign house, that personal element that's the least personal of all: the wedding picture. In it he's alert and she's wearing her finest absent gaze behind the veil. A subtle veil that only lights up her face from the outside and follows the line of her nose (the same nose she now sees in the mirror, which she touches but doesn't recognize at all, feeling like it had just appeared above her mouth a second before. The mouth is rather hard, made for a nose that wasn't quite so light).

Laura, may all our days be as happy as the day that brought us together. And the clearly legible signature: Roque. It's her in the picture, there's no doubt about it despite the veil. It's her, so-called Laura; therefore, he must be Roque. Something hard, like granite. It suits him, it doesn't suit him; not when he turns soft as grass and surrounds her.

The Plant

She already can remember something and most of all she finds it surprising. It's a happy recollection, with bitterness rising within her like a seed, hard to pin down: just the way memories should be. Nothing too distant, obviously, nor too emphatic. Just a little memory to cover her tenderly in her sleepless hours.

It's about the plant. That plant over there in the flowerpot with white lines on green leaves; beautiful, hieratic leaves, dark, much like him, made in his image even though Martina chose it. Martina is also dark and hieratic and everything's in its place—one leaf to the right, one to the left, alternating. He did choose Martina. She was probably custom-made for him, because if it had been up to her she would probably have chosen someone full of life, one of those women who sing while they sweep the floor. Whereas he chose Martina and Martina chose the plant after a long counsel and the plant arrived with a yellow flower, firm and beautiful, which luckily wilted, the way flowers should no matter how firm and beautiful they are.

Martina didn't fade; she just lifted an eyebrow or maybe two as a sign of surprise when Laura called her and said: I want a plant.

Laura knew the response to I want was usually more or less immediate: I want a cup of coffee, some toast, a cup of tea, a pillow, and whatever she wanted came a while later; it was that simple. But apparently asking for a plant was straying away from the usual patterns, and Martina didn't know how to react. Poor lady, what will she do with a plant, poor sick lady, silly old thing. To think that she could probably ask for more substantial, less disconcerting things. Something valuable, for example. But who knows; maybe one can't expect anything but demands from that man. Poor woman, all locked up. Poor idiot.

When the man arrived the following day, Martina took him aside and told him the lady wanted a plant.

"What kind of plant?"

"I don't know. She only said a plant. I don't think she wants any particular kind."

"What does she want a plant for?"

"Who knows. She could water it, see it grow. Maybe she misses the country."

"I don't want her to miss anything; it isn't good for her. Did she take all her medicine? There's no reason why she should be thinking about the country, really . . . What does she have to do with the country, I wonder? Well, go ahead, get her a little plant, if that will make her happy, but something that isn't too wild. Something nice and urban, if you know what I mean. Buy it in a good flower-shop."

They were in the kitchen, like so many other times, discussing things about the household, which apparently didn't concern Laura. But she heard the conversation by mistake—or maybe on purpose, trying to find something out, unwittingly attempting to understand what was going on.

In fact, when the plant finally arrived, it looked artificial, but it was alive and growing; the flower was already wilting, but that was also part of life. That, above all, was life: an agony from the very start with some splendor and a fair dose of sadness.

When was her splendor at its peak? Has the moment already passed, or is it about to come? The questions are asked absent-mindedly and dropped a second later, because that isn't the point. The only real problem is the one that comes up when she sees her image in the mirror by mistake and stands facing herself for a long time, trying to find herself out.

The Mirrors

It's an inexplicable multiplication, a multiplication of herself in the mirrors and a multiplication of mirrors—the most disconcerting. The last one to appear was the one on the ceiling, above the big bed, and he forces her to look at it and thus to look at herself, face up, legs spread. She looks at herself, first out of obligation and then out of pleasure, and she sees herself up there in the mirror on the ceiling, cast on the bed, upside down and far away. She looks at herself from the tips of her toes where now he is tracing a map of saliva; she looks at herself and, without acknowledging it altogether, travels up her own legs, her pubis, her navel, the surprisingly heavy breasts, a long neck and that face of hers which suddenly reminds her of the plant—living, but somehow artificial—and, unwittingly, she closes her eyes.

"Open your eyes," he commands, watching her watch herself in the mirror.

"Open your eyes and see what I do to you. It's going to be well worth seeing."

His tongue starts creeping up her left leg, drawing it, and she starts to recognize herself up there, she starts to know that leg is hers because she can feel it's alive under his tongue and suddenly the knee she sees in the mirror is also hers, and most of all the curve of the knee, so sensitive, and her thigh, and so would the space between her thighs if he didn't take a roundabout route stopping at her navel.

"Keep on looking!" and it's painful to keep on looking, and his tongue creeps up and he covers her, but tries not to cover her too much; he lets her see herself in the mirror on the ceiling, and she discovers her own nipples as they awaken, she sees her mouth open as if it didn't belong to her, but it does, it belongs to her, she feels that mouth, and from her neck the tongue that's tracing her reaches for her mouth, but only for a split second, without greed, just enough time to recognize her and then the tongue goes down again and a nipple twitches and it's hers, hers, and further down the nerves quiver, and the tongue's about to get there and she spreads her legs wide, as wide as she can and they're her legs although they're responding to an impulse she didn't order but that came out of her anyway, a deep shudder of delight, right at the edge of pain when his tongue reaches the center of pleasure, a shudder she would want to prolong shutting her eyes tight and then he shouts

"Open your eyes, you bitch!" and it feels as if he shattered her, as if he bit her inside—and maybe he did—that shout as if he were twisting her arm, breaking it, kicking her head in. Open your eyes, spit it out, tell me who sent you, who gave the order, and she shouts such an intense, deep *no* that her answer is silent in the space they're in and he doesn't hear it, a *no* that seems to shatter the mirror on the ceiling, that multiplies and maims and destroys his image, almost like a bullet shot although he doesn't perceive it and both his image and the mirror stay there, intact, impervious, and she, exhaling the air she'd kept in, whispers Roque, his real name, for the first time. But he doesn't hear that either, as distant as he is from so much trauma.

The Window

Alone again, in her usual state. The other dimension is an accident, he is an accident in her life despite her being able to give him all kinds of names. She's alone, as it should be, nice and calm. Sitting by the window with a sterile white wall facing her eyes and who knows what that wall may be hiding. It may be hiding him.

The window has a wood frame painted white and the wall out there is also white, with several dribbles of soot from the many rains. She figures it must be on the fifth or the sixth floor, but she can't lean out because the window doesn't have a knob and only he can open it, when he's there. It doesn't matter. She doesn't need fresh air, and if she leaned out she'd feel dizzy from the height and wouldn't be able to control it. Suddenly she imagines him strolling through the streets with an oval window knob in his pocket, a knob like a weapon to squeeze in his fist and hit with.

Weapon, street, fist? Why does she think about things like that? The notion of a street isn't really what she's most concerned about. However, the notion of a weapon . . . A weapon in the street, a time bomb, him walking down the street when the time bomb that was waiting for him explodes. A loud boom and he walks down the dark street carrying the window knob in his pocket, an oval, heavy object, like a bronze egg and this window over here, a block, a window limiting a view instead of revealing one.

He on the other hand could reveal a few things to her, but the truth has little to do with him; he only says what he wants to say, and what he wants to say is never what she's interested in hearing. The truth may not be that important to him. He has those things, but other ones, too: the way he looks at her when they're together, as if he wanted to absorb her, stick her deep inside of him and protect her from herself. There's the slow ritual of undressing her, slowly to find her in each centimeter of skin that emerges behind each button he unfastens.

At times she suspects it could be what they call love. An indefinite feeling that grows like a short-lived heat source inside her, and which, on sublime occasions, flares up in flames. But nothing points out that it's really a question of love, not even the need that suddenly comes over her, the need for him to caress her. It's the only way she can feel that she's alive: when his hand caresses her or his voice threatens: move, slut. Tell me you're a bitch, a whore. Tell me how the others fuck you. Do they fuck you like this? Tell me how. Maybe that's just why, because of his voice that tells her about being somewhere else.

And sometimes she's tempted to answer: try it, call in those guys who are waiting outside the door. At least that way she'll know other men exist, other ones who can be fucked. But she prefers to keep thoughts such as those to herself, at least consciously, because then there's that dark area of her memory (memory?) which also keeps to itself and not precisely because it wants to.

The black pit of memory, sort of like a window looking onto a white wall with some stains. He's not going to explain anything, and, after all, what does she care? She only cares to be there, water her plant, which looks like plastic, put creme on her face, which looks like plastic, look out the window at a faceless wall.

The Colleagues

Then he's there again and there could be variations.

"Some friends of mine will be coming over tomorrow for a few drinks," he says, in a sort of offhanded way.

"Drinks?," she asks.

"Yeah, sure. Just a Scotch before lunch. They won't be staying very long, don't worry."

"Scotch?," she almost repeats, but holds back just in time.

"What friends?," she blurts out when she's trying to keep quiet. Maybe it's just as well; she may figure something out.

He deigns to answer. For once, he actually looks up and answers her questions, pretending she really exists:

"Well, they're not really friends. Just three or four colleagues, that's all, for a little while, for you to get a little entertainment."

Strange, so-called Laura thinks. Colleagues. A little entertainment, for me. Since when does he think of her that much? And then he lets out the most surprising statement of all.

"Look, I'm going to buy you a new dress. That way when you greet them you'll look cute and happy."

"Do I have to be happy with a new dress? Is a new dress really something?"

That's it. Just the kind of question he can't stand. Trying to make up for it, she adds:

"I'm glad your comrades are coming, anyway."

"Colleagues," he rectifies.

"All right, colleagues. I'll learn new names, I'll call you different names."

"Don't dream of it. They're all ugly names. I don't want to hear them. Besides, every now and then you could make an effort and call me by my real name, couldn't you? Just for a change, you know."

The following day he brings her the new dress which is indeed pretty and obviously expensive. She looks cute, smiling inside, and the colleagues with names that can't be repeated arrive all at once, marching in with a sort of martial step, and call her Laura as they shake her hand. She accepts theirs, bows her head when she hears the name Laura, accepting it, and he and his colleagues sit down in the armchairs and start to examine her.

Above all, those insistent questions about her health make her feel awkward and uncomfortable, and she doesn't quite understand why.

Are you feeling well now? Your husband told us you'd had some back problems. Your spine doesn't hurt anymore?

And those sentences uttered at random: you're very beautiful, you have a perfect nose . . .

She feels like she's being cross-examined. Their questions begin with "Do you think that . . . ," and she knows they really stand for the other, real question: "Do you think?" She tries to control herself as much as possible, not wanting to fail this first examination although she doesn't really know why she's thinking about cross-examinations and other exams, nor why she should care about the idea of passing or failing. She accepts a drink—just a drop (don't drink too much, it may not mix well with your medicine, he whispers almost tenderly), and she turns her head when someone calls her Laura and listens attentively.

". . . it was the time they put the bombs in the Palermo headquarters, remember?," one of them said, and, naturally, he turned to her to ask the question.

"No, I can't remember. Actually, I can't remember anything."

"Yes, when there were the guerrillas up North. You're from Tucumán, aren't you? How can you not remember?"

No-name, his gaze fixed on his glass, interjected:

"Laura doesn't even read the papers. She doesn't care much about what happens beyond these four walls."

She looks at the others not knowing whether to feel proud or indignant. The others, in turn, look at her, but give her no hints to guide her behavior.

When his colleagues finally leave, after chatting for quite a while, she feels sort of empty and takes the new dress off, eager to undress. He stares at her with a look of approval of his own work. Suddenly she feels like vomiting, maybe because of that drop of whisky, and he hands her a different pill from the ones he usually has her swallow.

One and Two stay outside, as usual. She can hear them whispering in the hallway. Maybe they saw the guests down to the door and now have come back. Yes, indeed, she can hear them, and she knows they won't leave until he does. She'll be left alone again, as she should be, until he shows up again. It's just that recurrent; one guy inside and two outside, one inside of her, to be more specific, and the other two as good as inside too, sharing her bed.

The Well

The moments when she makes love with him are the only ones that really belong to her. They're truly hers, they belong to so-called Laura, to this body right here, the body she's touching, and that gives her shape, all of her. All of her? Could there be something more, something like being in a dark well and not knowing what it's about, something inside her, dark and deep, aside from her natural cavities, to which he has easy access? That dark, unattainable bottom in her, the here-place, the inner space enclosing all she knows and doesn't want to know, without really knowing it and she curls up, she rocks in the chair, and what falls asleep is her black well, like a soothed animal. But the animal is there, inside the well and by the same token is the well, and she doesn't want to urge it on for fear of its claws. Poor deep, black well of hers, mistreated, cast aside, abandoned. She spends long hours inside out like a glove, stuck inside her own inner well, in a womb-like darkness which is almost lukewarm, almost humid. Sometimes the sides of the well echo and it doesn't matter what they're trying to tell her although sometimes she does seem to receive a message—a whiplash—and she feels as though the soles of her feet were being burned and suddenly she crawls back up to her surface, the message is too much for her to bear, better to stay out of that black, vibrant well, better to move back into the candy-pink room which they tell her is hers.

He may or may not be in the room. Usually he isn't, and when she's alone she withdraws into herself; now she smiles at the many mirrors that send back some kind of recognition which she rejects outright.

Then he returns, and when he's tender the well turns into a little hole with a light at the end, and when he's cold and apprehensive the well opens up like a chasm and she feels tempted to jump, but she doesn't, because she knows that the void inside dark wells is worse than the void outside them.

Outside the well, there's a void with the one who would appear to be her man. With him and the little hole her well becomes and which she peeps through to spy on him, reticulate. Him behind the little hole, behind the juncture of cross-hairs that focus on him. Through the little hole-well she sees him as if it were through a sight and she doesn't like that at all. Which of the two is holding the rifle? Apparently she is; he's criss-crossed by the sight and she sees him that way but doesn't quite understand why and doesn't want to find out, either. He smiles from the other side of the sight and she knows she's going to have to let down her guard again. Let down the guard and lean her head down: things she gets used to, little by little.

The Whip

"Isn't this pretty?," he says to her as he unwraps the package. She watches sort of indifferently, until she sees a big, strong whip come out of the package, almost immaculate, almost innocent. Made out of raw-hide, stunning, with a wide grip and a narrow tip. She, who knows nothing about these things, who's forgotten about horses—if she ever had much to do with them in the first place—starts to scream desperately, howling as if she were going to be ripped apart or raped with the grip of this weapon.

Maybe that was exactly his intention after all—to come up with a substitute. Or maybe he'd dreamt about lashing her, or maybe . . . why not? Maybe he wanted her to beat him or rape him with the grip.

The woman's cries stop him in the middle of his secret fantasies. She sobs in a corner like a wounded animal; he'd better leave the whip for some other time. He picks up the piece of paper he'd thrown in the wastebasket, irons it out with the palm of his hand and wraps the whip up again, so as not to hear the cries.

"I didn't mean to upset you," he says, and it's as if she hadn't heard him, because his words are too out of character. "I'm sorry; it was a stupid idea."

He apologizes, which is hard to believe, but it really happens: forgive me, calm down, purr, purr, he says, like a cat and the idea of a cat envelops her in warmth and stops her convulsions on the spot. She thinks "cat", and walks away from him. From the corner where she'd hid away from him she takes off to the open area and there's a sky and there's a man she really loves—without a whip. A place where there's love, in other words. The sensation of love runs across her skin like a hand and suddenly that ghastly, overwhelming feeling comes over her: the loved one is dead. How can she know that he's dead? How can she be so sure of his death if she hasn't even managed to bring his features, his shape back to life? All she knows is that he was killed, and that she has to take the mission upon herself all alone, all the responsibility is in her hands when the only thing she would have wanted to do was die with the man she loved.

A complex structure of memories/feelings runs through her among tears, and then, nothing. Then she feels that she's been so close to the revelation, to the explanation. But it's not worth getting to the explanation through pain; it's better to stay like this, sort of floating, not letting the cloud clear. It's a soft, protective cloud she has to try to keep there so as not to collapse and suddenly fall into memory.

She sobs quietly and he runs his hand through her hair and says, in a saccharine voice:

"Don't think, don't torture yourself, come with me. That's better; close your eyes. Don't think. Don't torture yourself (let me torture you, let me be the master of all your pain, of your suffering; don't run away). I'm going to make you happier and happier every day. Forget that stupid whip. Don't think about it anymore. See? We're going to throw it away, I'm going to make it disappear so you don't worry more than you should."

He slowly walks toward the front door, crosses the living room with the whip (the package that now contains the whip) in his hand. He takes the keys out of his pocket—why doesn't he use the other set that's on the ledge, right at an arm's reach, she wonders—he opens the door and with a rather theatrical gesture he throws the package out, and it falls with a soft, rubbery sound. See? It's gone, he tells her, as if he were talking to a child. She mistrusts him like a child and knows it isn't; outside the door, One and Two are ready to receive whatever he throws out, ready to pounce on the package like birds of prey.

One and Two. She doesn't forget them; they're everpresent, despite their being so separate from her. As separate as those keys on the ledge, present and separate as the whip, simply because it elicited such despair.

There are her charges, the depth-charges that explode when she least expects them to because of one of those sparks. They explode out of sympathy, as they say, vibrating in unison or just the opposite: due to clashing vibrations.

The fact is that there is an explosion and she's left feeling disconnected, standing alone amid her own rubble, hit by the shock wave or something like that.

The Peephole

No, it isn't a new sensation, it's an old sensation from way back, from before, from the areas that were washed away. Almost a feeling, a strange awareness which only manages to disturb her: the notion that there's a secret. But what is it? There's something she knows but that she'd have to reveal. Something about herself that runs deep, something forbidden.

She tells herself: it's the same for all humans. And she even finds that thought disturbing.

What is being forbidden? Where does fear end, where does the need to know begin, or viceversa? The price of knowing the secret is death; what is hiding, what is that depth-charge waiting so deep down that it would be better not to even suspect it existed?

Sometimes he helps her by denying her help of any kind. By not helping he actually lends her a hand to open up her inner doors.

Wanting, not wanting to know. Wanting and not wanting to be, at the same time. On more than one occasion he's given her a chance to see herself in the mirrors and now he's about to give her a new, rather frightening chance to see herself in the eyes of others.

He slowly starts to undress her in the living room and the moment draws near. She doesn't quite understand how she knew it from the start—she was probably surprised when he started undressing her in the living room, not in the bedroom. He leans her down on the sofa, facing the front door, also undressing himself without saying a word, in a silent ritual apparently aimed at the eyes of others. Suddenly he gets up from the sofa and walks away, naked, to the door; he lifts the cover to the peephole—that tiny, rectangular brass cover—and leaves it open. Just that simple; an action with no apparent justification whatsoever. Then he hesitates, he hesitates before turning and walking back over to her, as if he didn't want to turn his back on the peephole, but face it, point toward it with his proud erection.

She can't see anything on the other side of the mesh peephole, but she can sense them, almost smell them; the eye of One and the eye of Two stuck to the opening, watching them, knowing what's about to come and licking their chops in advance.

Now he moves over slowly, brandishing his dark rod, and she curls up in a corner of the sofa with her legs folded and her head between her legs like an ambushed animal, but maybe not, none of that: not an ambushed animal but a woman waiting for something to break loose inside her, waiting for the man to be by her side and help her break it and also for those two out there to help, the ones who have one eye on all the feelings that run through her.

Lovemaking becomes cruel, elaborate, and extends over time: he seems to want to split her in two with thrusts from his hips and in the middle of a shudder he stops short, moves away and then dives into her again furiously, not letting her move, digging his teeth into her.

Sometimes she wants to escape from the earthquake that's come over her and tries to discover the eye on the other side of the peephole. At other times she forgets the eye, all the eyes that are probably out there, eager to watch her squirm, but he shouts a single word—bitch—and she understands that's the epithet around which he wants to weave the thick web of stares. Then she lets out a long groan, unwittingly, and he doubles his thrusts to turn her groan into a howl.

There aren't only eyes out there; there are ears, too. Maybe not only One and Two are out there. Out there.

What good are their eyes, ears, teeth, hands, when those men out there can't cross the line. Because of that line, drawing it out, he keeps on taking her with fury, without pleasure. He turns her, twists her, and suddenly he stops, steps back and stands up. He starts walking around the room like a caged animal, displaying the strength of his dissatisfaction. Roaring.

She thinks of the crowd of people watching out there—watching her—and she calls him back to her side, for him to cover her with his body, not for him to satisfy her. Cover herself with his body like a glove. A body—not her own, obviously not her own—she can use as a screen, as a mask to face others. Or maybe not: a screen so she can hide from others, disappear forever behind or under another body.

And what for, after all? She already disappeared quite some time ago; the others are always on the other side of the door with nothing but a minute peephole to catch a glimpse of her.

Communicate? None of that. Then she foresees, rather vaguely, as in a cloud, that the others—the ones out there—can only receive her warmth by proxy, through the man who's only there to serve as a bridge to the others, the ones out there.

Tired of bellowing, he goes back to her side and starts caressing her in a surprisingly different mood. She allows the caresses to invade her, to achieve their aim; she lets her last nerve respond to the caresses, lets the vibrations of those very caresses gallop through her blood and finally explode.

Then both bodies are cast upon the sofa and the peephole darkens as if it were missing the gleam of a stare.

A while later, Martina tip-toes in and covers them both with a blanket.

The Keys

Later on he leaves. He's always leaving; when she sees him standing up she always sees him from behind, walking towards the door, and his real goodbye is always the sound of the key closing the exit, locking her in.

She's no longer fooled by the keys, the other set, the ones on the ledge by the door; even though she hasn't tried them out, she knows they'll never fit the lock, they've been placed there as a trick or actually as bait and she'll be sorry the day she gets up her courage to touch them. So she doesn't even go near them, fighting the temptation to reach out and even talk to them as if they were friends. They're not really to blame for the trap they're setting up. She caught him more than once checking them out of the corner of his eye as he comes in, to make sure they were in the exact same position as before. Dust is collecting on the poor keys; Martina can only blow on them a little and brush them lightly with the feather duster as if they were made of the most delicate crystal.

When he leaves he also checks to make sure the keys are at their post, just a step away from the locks they don't belong to, and then he shuts the door and turns his key twice—the real one—leaving her, so-called Laura, free, once again, to sink into her deep, closed well.

The Voices

There's only the sound of the clock, the syncopated tick-tock, and it's like a presence. So many almost presences, then, and no real presence, no voice calling her to pull her away from herself.

Not that his voice doesn't call her often. Not that his voice doesn't call out her name, Laura, sometimes from afar (from the other room) or just shout right into her ear when he's on top of her, calling just for the hell of it, imposing his presence, her obligation to be there and listen to him.

It's always like that with him, Juan, Mario, Alberto, Pedro, Ignacio, whatever he's called. No sense in changing his name, because his voice is always the same, and so are his demands: she should be with him, but not too much. He wants her to be erased, a malleable woman that he can put together as he pleases. She feels like clay, pliable under his touch, and she doesn't want to be, she refuses to be pliable, changing, and her inner voices howl in rage and hit against the walls of her body while he molds her at leisure.

Every so often she's overcome by these sudden rebellious bouts which are closely related to another feeling called fear. And then, nothing: then the tide recedes leaving nothing but a wet, wind-swept beach.

She wanders barefoot down the wet beach trying to pull herself back together after the horror she felt when the tide was high. So many waves washing over her, but not clearing her thoughts. The waves come in and then leave a sterile line of salty driftwood, which only allows for an indefinite, milder form of terror. She wanders aimlessly down the wet beach, and at the same time she is the beach, her own beach is her refuge; it isn't clay, it's wet sand he'd like to shape as he pleases. She's moist sand for him to build castles like a child. Castles in the air.

Sometimes he uses his voice for these purposes and names her and names each part of her body in a doubtful attempt to reconstruct her.

That's the voice that sometimes calls her and can't break through her shell. Then there's the smile: his sort of strained smile. Only when he laughs—on those very rare occasions when he laughs—does something seem to awaken within her, and it isn't good. It's a deep pang, far removed from laughter.

So there isn't much of an incentive to call her to the surface and pull her out of her dark well. At any rate, nothing coming from outside the apartment, although suddenly something does, a doorbell ringing insistently snaps her back into the here and now. It's rare for that bell to ring like that; someone's desperately trying to be heard and he cautiously walks to the door to see who it is. She's on edge, a live wire, she hears the voices of others and doesn't try to understand them:

"I'm sorry. Colonel, there's an uprising. We had no other way to let you know. They rebelled. They're advancing towards your barracks with the tanks. Apparently the Third Regiment of Infantry is behind them. And the Navy. They're up in arms. Excuse me, Colonel, but we didn't know how to contact you."

He gets dressed in a hurry and leaves without saying goodbye, like so many other times. Only in more of a rush, and maybe forgetting to lock the door. But that's all. She's not concerned about any other details. Not even the voices she heard, which keep on resonating like an unexpected, hopeful sound which she doesn't try to interpret. Interpret? What for? Why should she try to understand something that's far beyond her meager capacity to understand?

The Secret (The Secrets)

She suspects—although she doesn't want to question it too much—that something that shouldn't be known is about to be revealed. For a long time, she's feared the existence of those secrets, so deeply entrenched that they no longer belong to her; they're altogether inaccessible.

Sometimes she'd like to delve into her secrets and feel them out, but she can't, none of that, better to leave them as they are: in unfathomably deep, stagnant water.

Then she feels like delving into food and she asks Martina for coffee with milk, cookies, fruit, and Martina probably thinks: poor lady, she's going to lose her figure, she can't stop eating and doesn't move, or at least not much. And the master isn't back yet.

However, neither Martina nor she mentions the master's absence, which is getting rather long. She doesn't want to—or can't—remember the voices she heard when they came to get him. Martina had gone to the pantry and didn't hear a thing.

When the master was in the house, Martina would usually step out to buy food, and now she doesn't know whether she should leave the poor crazy lady alone or wait one more day or leave forever. The master has left her enough money for her to feel free, and he may have gotten tired of the game; she should take off before it's too late and forget about it all.

These are Martina's problems. Not Laura's; she no longer even leaves the bedroom. She stretches out on the bed, toying with some kind of vague sensation all day long.

Colonel, she sometimes repeats to herself, and the word only evokes a piercing sensation in her stomach.

Much later, almost a week later, he finally comes back and snaps her out of a dream where she was walking on the waters of the secret and not getting wet.

"Wake up," he says, shaking her. "I have to talk to you. It's time you knew."

"Time I knew what?"

"Cut it out. You heard something the other day."

"If you think I care . . ."

"Alright, you probably couldn't care less, but I want you to know anyway. If not, everything will be left up in the air."

"Up in the air?"

"Up in the air."

"I don't want to know anything. Leave me alone."

"What do you mean, leave me alone? What is this about not wanting to know? Since when does Madam make decisions in this house?"

"I don't want to."

"Well, you're going to find out—everything. Much more than I'd thought of telling you. What is this, 'I don't want to know?' I'm not going to keep any secrets from you, whether you like it or not. And I'm afraid you're not going to like it one bit."

She wants to cover her ears with her hands, cover her eyes, wrap her arms around her head and hold on tight. But he opens up the briefcase he was carrying and takes out a bag that seizes her attention.

"Do you remember this handbag?"

She shakes her head vehemently, denying it, but her eyes say something else. Her eyes are alert, alive for the first time in ages.

"Look at what's inside. It may perk you up a little."

She sticks her hand into the bag but pulls it back out almost immediately, as though she'd touched the viscous skin of a toad.

"Go on," he insists. "Stick your hand in there, take it out, don't be afraid."

"No," her head shouts again. "No, no, no." She shakes it desperately, until it starts hitting the wall. She wants to beat her head against the wall.

He knows what to do in these situations. He slaps her across the face and shouts a command:

"Take it out, I say."

And then, softer:

"It doesn't bite, it doesn't scratch. It's a dead object. It only comes alive when you want it to. And you no longer do, isn't that so?"

"I don't want to, I don't want to," she whimpers.

And so as not to go through it all over again (the head against the wall, the slap) he sticks his own hand into the woman's handbag and takes out the object. He presents it to her in the palm of his hand, inoffensively.

"Here. You should recognize this gun."

She stares and finally takes it and starts to examine it, not really knowing what to make of it.

"Watch out. It's loaded. I never carry unloaded weapons. Even if they aren't mine."

She looks up at him, almost understanding, on the verge of what could easily be her own abyss.

"Don't worry, honey. You know and I know. And we're right here, together."

"No, no," she starts up again, shaking her head. Not as equals, not with that gun.

"Yes." He shouts, he almost howls. "Nothing can be perfect if you stay out there, on the other side of things, if you refuse to know. I saved your life, do you know that? I know it doesn't look that way, but I saved your life; they would have done you in just like your friend, your accomplice. So listen to me, and maybe you'll pop out of your sweet little dream."

The Revelation

His voice starts hammering, and it hammers, I did it to save you, bitch, everything I did, I did to save you, and you have to know that now we've come full circle, my task is fulfilled. She's curled up like a skein,

308

pressed against the wall discovering a dried-up droplet of paint, and he insists, I did it all alone, I didn't let them lay a hand on you, all alone, there with you, hurting you, tearing you up, beating you to break you, just like a horse, break your will, transform you, and she runs the tips of her fingers down the drop, pretending nothing has happened, she isn't listening, and he insists, you were mine, all mine, because you'd tried to kill me, you'd aimed at me with this very gun, remember? You must remember, and she thinks, sweet little drop, soft to the touch, while he talks and says I could have sliced you into little pieces, I only broke your nose, but I could have broken all your bones, my bones, all of them, anything; and her finger and the droplet become a single unit, a single sense of comfort, and he insists, you were shit, scum, worse than a slut, they caught you when you were aiming at me, you were waiting for the best angle, and she shrugs her shoulders, not because of him or because of what he's saying, but because of that droplet of paint that won't respond or change, and he won't stop, you didn't know me but you wanted to kill me anyway, you had orders to kill me and you hated me even though you didn't know me. Did you hate me? Better still, I'd force you to love me, to depend on me like a newborn baby, I've got my weapons, too, and there, with her, a dried droplet of tenderness, and beyond, the smooth, impenetrable wall, and he, unmoved, repeating: I've got my weapons, too.

The Ending

"I'm very tired; don't tell me any more stories, don't talk so much. You never talk so much. Come on, let's go to sleep. Come to bed with me."

"Are you crazy? Didn't you hear me? Cut it out. The game is over, isn't it? It's over for me, which means it's also over for you. Curtains. Get that into your head, once and for all. I'm splitting."

"You're leaving?"

"I sure am. Do you expect me to stay? We don't have anything left to say. It's over. But thanks, anyway. You were a good guinea pig; it actually was pleasant. So now, just calm down and everything will be over."

"Come on, stay with me. Come on to bed."

"Can't you see this can't go on? Enough; wake up. The party's over. Tomorrow morning they'll open that door, and you can walk out, stay, tell everyone, do as you please. I'll be long gone by then."

"No, don't leave me. Will you come back? Stay."

He shrugs his shoulders, like he has many times before, turns on his heels and heads for the door. She sees his back move away and feels like the fog is beginning to clear. She starts to understand a few things—what that black instrument is for, that thing he calls a gun.

She lifts it and aims.

Translated by Deborah Bonner

I'm Your Horse in the Night

THE DOORBELL RANG: three short rings and one long one. That was the signal, and I got up, annoyed and a little frightened; it could be them, and then again, maybe not; at these ungodly hours of the night it could be a trap. I opened the door expecting anything except him, face to face, at last.

He came in quickly and locked the door behind him before embracing me. So much in character, so cautious, first and foremost checking his—our—rear guard. Then he took me in his arms without saying a word, not even holding me too tight but letting all the emotions of our new encounter overflow, telling me so much by merely holding me in his arms and kissing me slowly. I think he never had much faith in words, and there he was, as silent as ever, sending me messages in the form of caresses.

We finally stepped back to look at one another from head to foot, not eye to eye, out of focus. And I was able to say Hello showing scarcely any surprise despite all those months when I had no idea where he could have been, and I was able to say

I thought you were fighting up north
I thought you'd been caught
I thought you were in hiding
I thought you'd been tortured and killed
I thought you were theorizing about the revolution in another country
Just one of many ways to tell him I'd been thinking of him, I hadn't stopped thinking of him or felt as if I'd been betrayed. And there he was, always so goddamn cautious, so much the master of his actions.

"Quiet, Chiquita. You're much better off not knowing what I've been up to."

Then he pulled out his treasures, potential clues that at the time eluded me: a bottle of cachaça and a Gal Costa record. What had he been up to in Brazil? What was he planning to do next? What had brought him back, risking his life, knowing they were after him? Then I stopped asking myself questions (quiet, Chiquita, he'd say). Come here, Chiquita, he was saying, and I chose to let myself sink into the joy of having him back again, trying not to worry. What would happen to us tomorrow, and the days that followed?

Cachaça's a good drink. It goes down and up and down all the right tracks, and then stops to warm up the corners that need it most. Gal Costa's voice is hot, she envelops us in its sound and half-dancing, half-floating, we reach the bed. We lie down and keep on staring deep into each other's eyes, continue caressing each other without allowing ourselves to give into the pure senses just yet. We continue recognizing, rediscovering each other.

Beto, I say, looking at him. I know that isn't his real name, but it's the only one I can call him out loud. He replies:

"We'll make it some day, Chiquita, but let's not talk now."

It's better that way. Better if he doesn't start talking about how we'll make it someday and ruin the wonder of what we're about to attain right now, the two of us, all alone.

"A noite eu so teu cavalo," Gal Costa suddenly sings from the record player.

"I'm your horse in the night," I translate slowly. And so as to bind him in a spell and stop him from thinking about other things:

"It's a saint's song, like in the *macumba*. Someone who's in a trance says she's the horse of the spirit who's riding her, she's his mount."

"Chiquita, you're always getting carried away with esoteric meanings

312

and witchcraft. You know perfectly well that she isn't talking about spirits. If you're my horse in the night it's because I ride you, like this, see? . . . Like this . . . That's all."

It was so long, so deep and so insistent, so charged with affection that we ended up exhausted. I fell asleep with him still on top of me.

I'm your horse in the night.

The goddamn phone pulled me out in waves from a deep well. Making an enormous effort to wake up, I walked over to the receiver, thinking it could be Beto, sure, who was no longer by my side, sure, following his inveterate habit of running away while I'm asleep without a word about where he's gone. To protect me, he says.

From the other end of the line, a voice I thought belonged to Andrés—the one we call Andrés—began to tell me:

"They found Beto dead, floating down the river near the other bank. It looks as if they threw him alive out of a chopper. He's all bloated and decomposed after six days in the water, but I'm almost sure it's him."

"No, it can't be Beto," I shouted carelessly. Suddenly the voice no longer sounded like Andrés: it felt foreign, impersonal.

"You think so?"

"Who is this?" Only then did I think to ask. But that very moment they hung up.

Ten, fifteen minutes? How long must I have stayed there staring at the phone like an idiot until the police arrived? I didn't expect them. But, then again, how could I not? Their hands feeling me, their voices insulting and threatening, the house searched, turned inside out. But I already knew. So what did I care if they broke every breakable object and tore apart my dresser?

They wouldn't find a thing. My only real possession was a dream and they can't deprive me of my dreams just like that. My dream the night before, when Beto was there with me and we loved each other. I'd dreamed it, dreamed every bit of it, I was deeply convinced that I'd dreamed it all in the richest detail, even in full color. And dreams are none of the cops' business.

They want reality, tangible facts, the kind I couldn't even begin to give them.

Where is he, you saw him, he was here with you, where did he go? Speak up, or you'll be sorry. Let's hear you sing, bitch, we know he

313

came to see you, where is he, where is he holed up? He's in the city, come on, spill it, we know he came to get you.

I haven't heard a word from him in months. He abandoned me, I haven't heard from him in months. He ran away, went underground. What do I know, he ran off with someone else, he's in another country. What do I know, he abandoned me, I hate him, I know nothing.

(Go ahead, burn me with your cigarettes, kick me all you wish, threaten, go ahead, stick a mouse in me so it'll eat my insides out, pull my nails out, do as you please. Would I make something up for that? Would I tell you he was here when a thousand years ago he left me forever?)

I'm not about to tell them my dreams. Why should they care? I haven't seen that so-called Beto in more than six months, and I loved him. The man simply vanished. I only run into him in my dreams, and they're bad dreams that often become nightmares.

Beto, you know now, if it's true that they killed you, or wherever you may be, Beto, I'm your horse in the night and you can inhabit me whenever you wish, even if I'm behind bars. Beto, now that I'm in jail I know that I dreamed you that night; it was just a dream. And if by some wild chance there's a Gal Costa record and a half-empty bottle of cachaça in my house, I hope they'll forgive me: I will them out of existence.

Translated by Deborah Bonner

Isabel Allende

Chile

Isabel Allende. (Photo © Peter Peitsch.)

Isabel Allende was born in Lima in 1942, and lived her early years in her native Chile, until shortly after the fall of her uncle Salvador Allende's government. Since 1974 she and her family have been living in Caracas, Venezuela. A journalist since the age of seventeen, she often writes humorous articles and portraits of society.

The author of three novels, Allende owes her international fame primarily to her highly acclaimed first novel, *La casa de los espíritus,* translated by Magda Bogin as *The House of the Spirits.* She began to write it in 1981 in order to reconstruct the world she left behind in Chile. It is a story that spans the history of her country from the beginning of this century to the fall of the Allende government, as told by the extraordinary women of the Trueba family. Many of the characters are modeled after Isabel Allende's own grandparents and other relatives. We have chosen several pages from the very beginning of the novel's English translation.

Virginia Woolf stated that history is the history of the male lineage, that we know little about women. Isabel Allende rectifies that skewed view in her depiction of four generations of women growing successively in a luminous ascendancy toward a dawning of their own worth and sociohistoric commitment. At the turn of the century Nívea is involved in a movement to give women the vote; her daughter Clara, through whose notebooks part of the story is told, instructs the peasant women in practical tasks while maintaining her independence from the most patriarchal figure in the novel, her husband Esteban Trueba; their daughter Blanca fights to end sexual discrimination and chooses to be a single mother; and Blanca's daughter Alba enters the political arena where she becomes a victim of torture.

With a masterful storytelling technique, full of pathos, humor and fantasy, Allende portrays fear and injustice, bravery and love in a novel quite different from another Latin American family saga with which it is often compared, García Márquez's *One Hundred Years of Solitude.* For although the two novelists excel in the imaginative flair with which they describe Latin American history, the female characters in Allende's novel are at the very center of a dynamic narrative that defies patriarchal despotism and sexual prejudices. On the other hand, García Márquez elevates the traditional, exploited roles of Latin American women, with their concomitant allusions to machismo, sexual abuse, and illegitimate children, and uses them as the backbone for women characters whose context of power lies within family, home, or sexual dependence. All of his characters, women and men, are solitary figures. On the other hand, at least some of Allende's women exact a revision of their traditional roles in the patriarchal society both inside and outside of that home and in so doing exhibit a certain kind of solidarity rather than solitude. Perhaps it is a solidarity seen in Allende's close ties to her own mother, the recipient of her daily letters in which she chronicles all kinds of events, the way her fictionalized Clara records in her notebooks a potpourri of domestic matters, politics, news about relatives, friends, and national figures, the everyday and the supernatural.

Rosa the Beautiful
[Selection from the novel
The House of the Spirits]

BARRABÁS CAME TO US by sea, the child Clara wrote in her delicate calligraphy. She was already in the habit of writing down important matters, and afterward, when she was mute, she also recorded trivialities, never suspecting that fifty years later I would use her notebooks to reclaim the past and overcome terrors of my own. Barrabás arrived on a Holy Thursday. He was in a despicable cage, caked with his own excrement and urine, and had the lost look of a hapless, utterly defenseless prisoner, but the regal carriage of his head and the size of his frame bespoke the legendary giant he would become. It was a bland, autumnal day that gave no hint of the events that the child would record, which took place during the noon mass in the parish of San Sebastián, with her wholy family in attendance. As a sign of mourning, the statues of the saints were shrouded in purple robes that the pious ladies of the congregation unpacked and dusted off once a year from a cupboard in the sacristy. Beneath these funereal sheets the celestial retinue resembled nothing so much as a roomful of furniture awaiting movers, an impression that the candles, the incense, and the soft moans of the organ were powerless to counteract. Terrifying dark bundles loomed where the life-size saints had stood, each with its influenza-pale expression, its elaborate wig woven from the hair of someone long dead, its rubies, pearls and emeralds of painted glass, and the rich gown of a Florentine aristocrat. The only one whose appearance was enhanced by mourning was the church's patron saint, Sebastián, for during Holy Week the faithful were spared the sight of that body twisted in the most indecent posture, pierced by arrows, and dripping with blood and tears like a suffering homosexual, whose wounds, kept miraculously fresh by Father Restrepo's brush, made Clara tremble with disgust.

It was a long week of penitence and fasting, during which there were no card games and no music that might lead to lust or abandon; and within the limits of possibility, the strictest sadness and chastity were observed, even though it was precisely at this time that the forked tail of the devil pricked most insistently at Catholic flesh. The fast consisted of soft puff pastries, delicious vegetarian dishes, spongy tortillas, and enormous cheeses from the countryside, with which each family commemorated the Passion of the Lord, taking every precaution not to touch the least morsel of meat or fish on pain of excommunication, as Father Restrepo had repeatedly made clear. No one had ever dared to disobey him. The priest was blessed with a long, incriminating finger, which he used to point out sinners in public, and a tongue well schooled in arousing emotions.

"There's the thief who steals from the collection box!" he shouted from the pulpit as he pointed to a gentleman who was busying himself with the lint on his lapel so as not to show his face. "And there's the shameless hussy who prostitutes herself down by the docks!" he accused Doña Ester Trueba, disabled by arthritis and a devotee of the Virgin del Carmen, who opened her eyes wide, not knowing the meaning of the word or where the docks were. "Repent, sinners, foul carrion, unworthy of our Lord's great sacrifice! Fast! Do penance!"

Carried away by vocational zeal, the priest had all he could do to avoid openly disobeying the instructions of his ecclesiastic superiors, who, shaken by the winds of modernism, were opposed to hair shirts and flagellation. He himself was a firm believer in the value of a good thrashing to vanquish the weaknesses of the soul and was famous for his unrestrained oratory. The faithful followed him from parish to parish, sweating as he described the torments of the damned in hell, the bodies ripped apart by various ingenious torture apparatuses, the eternal flames, the hooks that pierced the male member, the disgusting reptiles that crept up female orifices, and the myriad other sufferings that he wove into his sermons to strike the fear of God into the hearts of his parishioners. Even Satan was described in his most intimate perversions in the Galician accents of this priest whose mission in this world was to rouse the conscience of his indolent Creole flock.

Severo del Valle was an atheist and a Mason, but he had political ambitions and could not allow himself the luxury of missing the most heavily attended mass on Sundays and feast days, when everyone would have a chance to see him. His wife, Nívea, preferred to deal with God without benefit of intermediaries. She had a deep distrust of cassocks and was bored by descriptions of heaven, purgatory and hell, but she shared her husband's parliamentary ambitions, hoping that if he won a seat in Congress she would finally secure the vote for women, for which she had fought for the past ten years, permitting none of her numerous pregnancies to get in her way. On this Holy Thursday, Father Restrepo had led his audience to the limits of their endurance with his apocalyptic visions, and Nívea was beginning to feel dizzy. She wondered if she was pregnant again. Despite cleansings with vinegar and spongings with gall, she had given birth to fifteen children, of whom eleven were still alive, but she had good reason to suppose that she was settling into maturity, because her daughter Clara, the youngest of her children, was now ten. It seemed that the force of her astonishing fertility had finally begun to ebb. She was able to attribute her present discomfort to Father Restrepo when he pointed at her to illustrate a point about the Pharisees, who had tried to legalize bastards and civil marriage, thereby dismembering the family, the fatherland, private property, and the Church, and putting women on an equal footing with men—this in open defiance of the law of God, which was most explicit on the issue. Along with their children, Nívea and Severo took up the entire third row of benches. Clara was seated beside her mother, who squeezed her hand impatiently whenever the priest lingered too long on the sins of the flesh, for she knew that this would only lead the child to visualize with even greater accuracy aberrations that transcended reality. Clara was extremely precocious and had inherited the runaway imagination of all the women in her family on her mother's side. This was evident from the questions she asked, to which no one knew the answers.

The temperature inside the church had risen, and the penetrating odor of the candles, the incense, and the tightly packed crowd all contributed to Nívea's fatigue. She wished the ceremony would end at once so she could return to her cool house, sit down among the ferns, and taste the pitcher of barley water flavored with almonds that Nana always made on holidays. She looked around at her children. The younger ones were tired and rigid in their Sunday best, and the older ones were beginning to squirm. Her gaze rested on Rosa, the oldest of her living daughters, and, as always, she was surprised. The girl's strange beauty had a disturbing quality that even she could not help noticing, for this child of hers seemed to have been made of different material from the rest of the human race. Even before she was born, Nívea had known she was not of this world, because she had already seen her in dreams. This was why she had not been surprised when the midwife screamed as the child emerged. At birth Rosa was white and smooth, without a wrinkle, like a porcelain doll, with green hair and yellow eyes—the most beautiful creature to be born on earth since the days of original sin, as the midwife put it, making the sign of the cross. From her very first bath, Nana had washed her hair with camomile, which softened its color, giving it the hue of old bronze, and put her out in the sun with nothing on, to strengthen her skin, which was translucent in the most delicate parts of her chest and armpits, where the veins and secret texture of the muscles could be seen. Nana's gypsy tricks did not suffice, however, and rumors quickly spread that Nívea had borne an angel. Nívea hoped that the successive and unpleasant stages of growth would bring her daughter a few imperfections, but nothing of the sort occurred. On the contrary, at eighteen Rosa was still slender and remained unblemished; her maritime grace had, if anything, increased. The tone of her skin, with its soft bluish lights, and of her hair, as well as her slow movements and silent character, all made one think of some inhabitant of the sea. There was something of the fish to her (if she had had a scaly tail, she would have been a mermaid), but her two legs placed her squarely on the tenuous line between a human being and a creature of myth. Despite everything, the young woman had led a nearly normal life. She had a fiancé and would one day marry, on which occasion the responsibility of her beauty would become her husband's. Rosa bowed her head and a ray of sunlight pierced the Gothic stained-glass windows of the church, outlining her face in a halo of light. A few people turned to look at her and whispered among themselves, as often happened as she passed, but Rosa seemed oblivious. She was immune to vanity and that day she was more absent than usual, dreaming of new beasts to embroider on her tablecloth, creatures that were half bird and half mammal, covered with iridescent feathers and endowed with horns and hooves, and so fat and with such stubby wings that they defied the laws of biology and aerodynamics. She rarely thought about her fiancé, Esteban Trueba, not because she did not love him but because of her forgetful nature and because two years' absence is a long time. He was working in the mines in the North. He wrote to her regularly and Rosa sometimes replied, sending him lines of poetry and drawings of flowers she had copied out on sheets of parchment paper. Through this correspondence, which Nívea violated with impunity at regular intervals, she learned about the hazards of a miner's life, always dreading avalanches, pursuing elusive veins, asking for credit against good luck that was still to come, and trusting that someday he would strike a marvelous seam of gold that would allow him to become a rich man overnight and return to lead Rosa by the arm to the altar, thus becoming the happiest man in the universe, as he always wrote at the end of his letters. Rosa, however, was in no rush to marry and had all but forgotten the only kiss they had exchanged when they said goodbye; nor could she recall the color of her tenacious suitor's eyes. Because of the romantic novels that were her only reading matter, she liked to picture him in thick-soled boots, his skin tanned from the desert winds, clawing the earth in search of pirates' treasure, Spanish doubloons, and Incan jewels. It was useless for Nívea to attempt to convince her that the wealth of mines lay in rocks, because to Rosa it was inconceivable that Esteban Trueba would spend years piling up boulders in the hope that by subjecting them to God only knew what wicked incinerating processes, they would eventually spit out a gram of gold. Meanwhile she awaited him without boredom, unperturbed by the enormous task she had taken upon herself: to embroider the largest tablecloth in the world. She had begun with dogs, cats, and butterflies, but soon her imagination had taken over, and her needle had given birth to a whole paradise filled with impossible creatures that took shape beneath her father's worried eyes. Severo felt that it was time for his daughter to shake off her lethargy, stand firmly in reality, and learn the domestic skills that would prepare her for marriage, but Nívea thought differently. She preferred not to torment her daughter with earthly demands, for she had a premonition that her daughter was a heavenly being, and that she was not destined to last very long in the vulgar traffic of this world. For this reason she left her alone with her embroidery threads and said nothing about Rosa's nightmarish zoology.

A bone in Nívea's corset snapped and the point jabbed her in the ribs. She felt she was choking in her blue velvet dress, with its high lace collar, its narrow sleeves, and a waist so tight that when she removed her belt her stomach jumped and twisted for half an hour while her organs fell back in place. She had often discussed this with her suffragette friends and they had all agreed that until women shortened their dresses and their hair and stopped wearing corsets, it made no difference if they studied medicine or had the right to vote, because they would not have the strength to do it, but she herself was not brave enough to be among the first to give up the fashion. She noticed that the voice from Galicia had ceased hammering at her brain. They were in one of those long breaks in the sermon that the priest, a connoisseur of unbearable silences, used with frequency and to great effect. His burning eyes glanced over the parishioners one by one. Nívea dropped Clara's hand and pulled a handkerchief from her sleeve to blot the drop of sweat that was rolling down her neck. The silence grew thick, and time seemed to stop within the church, but no one dared to cough or shift position, so as not to attract Father Restrepo's attention. His final sentences were still ringing between the columns.

Just at that moment, as Nívea would recall years later, in the midst of all that anxiety and silence, the voice of little Clara was heard in all its purity.

"Psst! Father Restrepo! If that story about hell is a lie, we're all fucked, aren't we. . . ."

The Jesuit's index finger, which was already raised to illustrate additional tortures, remained suspended like a lightning rod above his head. People stopped breathing, and those whose heads had been nodding suddenly woke up. Señor and Señora del Valle were the first to react. They were swept by panic as they saw their children fidget nervously. Severo understood that he must act before collective laughter broke out around them or some divine cataclysm occurred. He grabbed his wife by the arm and Clara by the neck and walked out dragging them behind him with enormous strides, followed by his other children, who stampeded toward the door. They managed to escape before the priest could summon a ray of lightning to turn them all into pillars of salt, but from the threshold they could hear his dreadful voice of offended archangel. "Possessed . . . She's possessed by the devil!"

These words of Father Restrepo were etched in the family memory with all the gravity of a diagnosis, and in the years to come they had more than one occasion to recall them. The only one who never thought of them again was Clara herself, who simply wrote them in her diary and forgot them. Her parents, however, could not forget, even though they both agreed that demonic possession was a sin too great for such a tiny child. They were afraid of other people's curses and Father Restrepo's fanaticism. Until that day they had never given a name to the eccentricities of their youngest daughter, nor had it ever crossed their minds to ascribe them to satanic influence. Clara's strangeness was simply an attribute of their youngest daughter, like Luis's limp or Rosa's beauty. The child's mental powers bothered no one and produced no great disorder; they almost always surfaced in matters of minor importance and within the strict confines of their home. It was true there had been times, just as they were about to sit down to dinner and everyone was in the large dining room, seated according to dignity and position, when the saltcellar would suddenly begin to shake and move among the plates and goblets without any visible source of energy or sign of illusionist's trick. Nívea would pull Clara's braids and that would be enough to wake her daughter from her mad distraction and return the saltcellar to immobility. The other children had organized a system so that in case of visitors, whoever was closest would reach out and stop whatever might be moving on the table before the guests noticed and were startled. The family continued eating without comment. They had also grown accustomed to the youngest daughter's prophecies. She would announce earthquakes in advance, which was quite useful in that country of catastrophes, for it gave them a chance to lock up the good dishes and place their slippers within reach in case they had to run out in the middle of the night. At the age of six, Clara had foreseen that the horse was going to throw Luis, but he refused to listen and had had a dislocated hip ever since. In time, his left leg had shortened and he had to wear a special shoe with an enormous platform that he made himself. After that Nívea had worried, but Nana reassured her by telling her that many children fly like birds, guess other people's dreams, and speak with ghosts, but that they all outgrow it when they lose their innocence.

325

"None of them reach adulthood like that," she explained. "Wait till she starts to 'demonstrate.' You'll see how fast she loses interest in making furniture move across the room and predicting disasters!"

Clara was Nana's pet. She had helped at her birth and was the only one who really understood the child's eccentricities. When Clara had emerged from her mother's womb, Nana had cradled and washed her, and from that time on she had felt a desperate love for this fragile creature whose lungs were always full of phlegm, who was always on the verge of losing her breath and turning purple, and whom she had had to revive so many times with the warmth of her huge breasts because she knew that this was the only cure for asthma, much more effective than Dr. Cuevas's fortified syrups.

On that particular Holy Thursday, Severo was pacing up and down the drawing room worrying about the scandal his daughter had provoked at mass. He reasoned that only a fanatic like Father Restrepo could believe in satanic possession in the heart of the twentieth century, this century of light, science, and technology, a time in which the devil had finally lost his reputation. Nívea interrupted him to say that was not the point. The seriousness of what had happened was that if word of their daughter's powers reached beyond the walls of the house and the priest began his own investigation, all their neighbors would find out.

"People are going to start lining up to look at her as if she were a monster," Nívea said.

"And the Liberal Party will go to hell," Severo added, anticipating the damage to his political career that could be caused by having a bewitched child in the family.

Just then Nana shuffled in with her sandals flapping, in her froufrou of starchy petticoats, to announce that a group of men were out in the courtyard unloading a dead man. And so they were. A four-horse carriage had drawn up outside occupying the whole first courtyard, trampling the camellias, and getting manure all over the shiny cobblestones, all this amidst a whirlwind of dust, a pawing of horses, and the curses of superstitious men who were gesticulating against the evil eye. They had come to deliver the body of Uncle Marcos and all his possessions. A honey-voiced man dressed in black, with a frock coat and a hat that was too big for him, was directing the tumult. He began a solemn speech explaining the circumstances of the case, but was brutally interrupted by Nívea, who threw herself on the dusty coffin that held the remains of her dearest brother. She was shouting for them to lift the cover so she could see him with her own two eyes. She had buried him once before, which explained why she had room for doubt whether this time his death was real. Her shouts brought the servants streaming from the house, as well as all her children, who came as fast as they could when they heard their uncle's name echoing amidst the cries of mourning.

It had been two years since Clara had last seen her Uncle Marcos, but she remembered him very well. His was the only perfectly clear image she retained from her whole childhood, and in order to describe him she did not need to consult the daguerreotype in the drawing room that showed him dressed as an explorer leaning on an old-fashioned double-barreled rifle with his right foot on the neck of a Malaysian tiger, the same triumphant position in which she had seen the Virgin standing between plaster clouds and pallid angels at he main altar, one foot on the vanquished devil. All Clara had to do to see her uncle was close her eyes and there he was, weather-beaten and thin, with a pirate's mustache through which his strange, sharklike smile peered out at her. It seemed impossible that he could be inside that long black box that was lying in the middle of the courtyard.

Each time Uncle Marcos had visited his sister Nívea's home, he had stayed for several months, to the immense joy of his nieces and nephews, particularly Clara, causing a storm in which the sharp lines of domestic order blurred. The house became a clutter of trunks, of animals in jars of formaldehyde, of Indian lances and sailor's bundles. In every part of the house people kept tripping over his equipment, and all sorts of unfamiliar animals appeared that had traveled from remote lands only to meet their death beneath Nana's irate broom in the farthest corners of the house. Uncle Marcos's manners were those of a cannibal, as Severo put it. He spent the whole night making incomprehensible movements in the drawing room; later they turned out to be exercises designed to perfect the mind's control over the body and to improve digestion. He performed alchemy experiments in the kitchen, filling the house with fetid smoke and ruining pots and pans with solid substances that stuck to their bottoms and were impossible to remove. While the rest of the household tried to sleep, he dragged his suitcases up and down the halls, practiced making strange, high-pitched sounds on savage instruments, and taught Spanish to a parrot whose native language was an Amazonic dialect. During the day, he slept in a hammock that he had strung between two columns in the hall, wearing only a loincloth that put Severo in a terrible mood but that Nívea forgave because Marcos had convinced her that it was the same costume in which Jesus of Nazareth had preached. Clara remembered perfectly, even though she had been only a tiny child, the first time her Uncle Marcos came to the house after one of his voyages. He settled in as if he planned to stay forever. After a short time, bored with having to appear at ladies' gatherings where the mistress of the house played the piano, with playing cards, and with dodging all his relatives' pressures to pull himself together and take a job as a clerk in Severo del Valle's law practice, he bought a barrel organ and took to the streets with the hope of seducing his Cousin Antonieta and entertaining the public in the bargain. The machine was just a rusty box with wheels, but he painted it with seafaring designs and gave it a fake ship's smokestack. It ended up looking like a coal stove. The organ played either a military march or a waltz, and in between turns of the handle the parrot, who had managed to learn Spanish although he had not lost his foreign accent, would draw a crowd with his piercing shrieks. He also plucked slips of paper from a box with his beak, by way of selling fortunes to the curious. The little pink, green, and blue papers were so clever that they always divulged the exact secret wishes of the customers. Besides fortunes there were little balls of sawdust to amuse the children and a special powder that was supposed to cure impotence, which Marcos sold under his breath to passersby afflicted with that malady. The idea of the organ was a last desperate attempt to win the hand of Cousin Antonieta after more conventional means of courting her had failed. Marcos thought no woman in her right mind could remain impassive before a barrel-organ serenade. He stood beneath her window one evening and played his military march and his waltz just as she was taking tea with a group of female friends. Antonieta did not realize the music was meant for her until the parrot called her by her full name, at which point she appeared in the window. Her reaction was not what her suitor had hoped for. Her friends offered to spread the news to every salon in the city, and the next day people thronged the downtown streets hoping to see Severo del Valle's brother-in-law playing the organ and selling little sawdust balls with a moth-eaten parrot, for the sheer pleasure of proving that even in the best of families there could be good reason for embarrassment. In the face of this stain to the family reputation, Marcos was forced to give up organ-grinding and resort to less conspicuous ways of winning over his Cousin Antonieta, but he did not renounce his goal. In any case, he did not succeed, because from one day to the next the young lady married a diplomat who was twenty years her senior; he took her to live in a tropical country whose name no one could recall, except that it suggested negritude, bananas, and palm trees, where she managed to recover from the memory of that suitor who had ruined her seventeenth year with his military march and his waltz. Marcos sank into a deep depression that lasted two or three days, at the end of which he announced that he would never marry and that he was embarking on a trip around the world. He sold his organ to a blind man and left the parrot to Clara, but Nana secretly poisoned it with an overdose of cod-liver oil, because no one could stand its lusty glance, its fleas, and its harsh, tuneless hawking of paper fortunes, sawdust balls, and powders for impotence.

That was Marco's longest trip. He returned with a shipment of enormous boxes that were piled in the far courtyard, between the chicken coop and the woodshed, until the winter was over. At the first signs of spring he had them transferred to the parade grounds, a huge park where people would gather to watch the soldiers file by on Independence Day, with the goosestep they had learned from the Prussians. When the crates were opened, they were found to contain loose bits of wood, metal, and painted cloth. Marcos spent two weeks assembling the contents according to an instruction manual written in English, which he was able to decipher thanks to his invincible imagination and a small dictionary. When the job was finished, it turned out to be a bird of prehistoric dimensions, with the face of a furious eagle, wings that moved, and a propeller on its back. It caused an uproar. The families of the oligarchy forgot all about the barrel organ, and Marcos became the star attraction of the season. People took Sunday outings to see the bird; souvenir vendors and strolling photographers made a fortune. Nonetheless, the public's interest quickly waned. But then Marcos announced that as soon as the weather cleared he planned to take off in his bird and cross the mountain range. The news spread, making this the most talked-about event of the year. The contraption lay with its stomach on terra firma, heavy and sluggish and looking more like a wounded duck than like one of those newfangled airplanes they were starting to produce in the United States. There was nothing in its appearance to suggest that it could move, much less take flight across the snowy peaks. Journalists and the curious flocked to see it. Marcos smiled his immutable smile before the avalanche of questions and posed for photographers without offering the least technical or scientific explanation of how he hoped to carry out his plan. People came from the provinces to see the sight. Forty years later his great-nephew Nicolás, whom Marcos did not live to see, unearthed the desire to fly that had always existed in the men of his lineage. Nicolás was interested in doing it for commercial reasons, in a gigantic hot-air sausage on which would be printed an advertisement for carbonated drinks. But when Marcos announced his plane trip, no one believed that his contraption could be put to any practical use. The appointed day dawned full of clouds, but so many people had turned out that Marcos did not want to disappoint them. He showed up punctually at the appointed spot and did not once look up at the sky, which was growing darker and darker with thick gray clouds. The astonished crowd filled all the nearby streets, perching on rooftops and the balconies of the nearest houses and squeezing into the park. No political gathering managed to attract so many people until half a century later, when the first Marxist candidate attempted, through strictly democratic channels, to become President. Clara would remember this holiday as long as she lived. People dressed in their spring best, thereby getting a step ahead of the official opening of the season, the men in white linen suits and the ladies in the Italian straw hats that were all the rage that year. Groups of elementary-school children paraded with their teachers, clutching flowers for the hero. Marcos accepted their bouquets and joked that they might as well hold on to them and wait for him to crash, so they could take them directly to his funeral. The bishop himself, accompanied by two incense bearers, appeared to bless the bird without having been asked, and the police band played happy, unpretentious music that pleased everyone. The police, on horseback and carrying lances, had trouble keeping the crowds far enough away from the center of the park, where Marcos waited dressed in mechanic's overalls, with huge racer's goggles and an explorer's helmet. He was also equipped with a compass, a telescope, and several strange maps that he had traced himself based on various theories of Leonardo da Vinci and on the polar knowledge of the Incas. Against all logic, on the second try the bird lifted off without mishap and with a certain elegance, accompanied by the creaking of its skeleton and the roar of its motor. It rose flapping its wings and disap-

peared into the clouds, to a send-off of applause, whistlings, handker-
chiefs, drumrolls, and the sprinkling of holy water. All that remained on
earth were the comments of the amazed crowd below and a multitude of
experts, who attempted to provide a reasonable explanation of the miracle. Clara continued to stare at the sky long after her uncle had become
invisible. She thought she saw him ten minutes later, but it was only a
migrating sparrow. After three days the initial euphoria that had accompanied the first airplane flight in the country died down and no one gave
the episode another thought, except for Clara, who continued to peer at
the horizon.

After a week with no word from the flying uncle, people began to
speculate that he had gone so high that he had disappeared into outer
space, and the ignorant suggested he would reach the moon. With a
mixture of sadness and relief, Severo decided that his brother-in-law and
his machine must have fallen into some hidden crevice of the *cordillera,*
where they would never be found. Nívea wept disconsolately and lit
candles to San Antonio, patron of lost objects. Severo opposed the idea
of having masses said, because he did not believe in them as a way of
getting into heaven, much less of returning to earth, and he maintained
that masses and religious vows, like the selling of indulgences, images,
and scapulars, were a dishonest business. Because of his attitude, Nívea
and Nana had the children say the rosary behind their father's back for
nine days. Meanwhile, groups of volunteer explorers and mountain
climbers tirelessly searched peaks and passes, combing every accessible
stretch of land until they finally returned in triumph to hand the family
the mortal remains of the deceased in a sealed black coffin. The intrepid
traveler was laid to rest in a grandiose funeral. His death made him a
hero and his name was on the front page of all the papers for several
days. The same multitude that had gathered to see him off the day he
flew away in his bird paraded past his coffin. The entire family wept as
befit the occasion, except for Clara, who continued to watch the sky with
the patience of an astronomer. One week after he had been buried,
Uncle Marcos, a bright smile playing behind his pirate's mustache, appeared in person in the doorway of Nívea and Severo del Valle's house.
Thanks to the surreptitious prayers of the women and children, as he
himself admitted, he was alive and well and in full possession of his
faculties, including his sense of humor. Despite the noble lineage of his
aerial maps, the flight had been a failure. He had lost his airplane and

had to return on foot, but he had not broken any bones and his adventurous spirit was intact. This confirmed the family's eternal devotion to San Antonio, but was not taken as a warning by future generations, who also tried to fly, although by different means. Legally, however, Marcos was a corpse. Severo del Valle was obliged to use all his legal ingenuity to bring his brother-in-law back to life and the full rights of citizenship. When the coffin was pried open in the presence of the appropriate authorities, it was found to contain a bag of sand. This discovery ruined the reputation, up till then untarnished, of the volunteer explorers and mountain climbers, who from that day on were considered little better than a pack of bandits.

Marcos's heroic resurrection made everyone forget about his barrel-organ phase. Once again he was a sought-after guest in all the city's salons and, at least for a while, his name was cleared. Marcos stayed in his sister's house for several months. One night he left without saying goodbye, leaving behind his trunks, his books, his weapons, his boots, and all his belongings. Severo, and even Nívea herself, breathed a sigh of relief. His visit had gone on too long. But Clara was so upset that she spent a week walking in her sleep and sucking her thumb. The little girl, who was only seven at the time, had learned to read from her uncle's storybooks and been closer to him than any other member of the family because of her prophesying powers. Marcos maintained that his niece's gift could be a source of income and a good opportunity for him to cultivate his own clairvoyance. He believed that all human beings possessed this ability, particularly his own family, and that if it did not function well it was simply due to a lack of training. He bought a crystal ball in the Persian bazaar, insisting that it had magic powers and was from the East (although it was later found to be a part of a buoy from a fishing boat), set it down on a background of black velvet, and announced that he could tell people's fortunes, cure the evil eye, and improve the quality of dreams, all for the modest sum of five centavos. His first customers were the maids from around the neighborhood. One of them had been accused of stealing, because her employer had misplaced a valuable ring. The crystal ball revealed the exact location of the object in question: it had rolled beneath a wardrobe. The next day there was a line outside the front door of the house. There were coachmen, storekeepers, and milkmen; later a few municipal employees and distinguished ladies made a discreet appearance, slinking along the side walls of the house to keep from being recognized. The customers were received by Nana, who ushered them into the waiting room and collected their fees. This task kept her busy throughout the day and demanded so much of her time that the family began to complain that all there ever was for dinner was old string beans and jellied quince. Marcos decorated the carriage house with some frayed curtains that had once belonged in the drawing room but that neglect and age had turned to dusty rags. There he and Clara received the customers. The two divines wore tunics "the color of the men of light," as Marcos called the color yellow. Nana had dyed them with saffron powder, boiling them in pots usually reserved for rice and pasta. In addition to his tunic, Marcos wore a turban around his head and an Egyptian amulet around his neck. He had grown a beard and let his hair grow long and he was thinner than ever before. Marcos and Clara were utterly convincing, especially because the child had no need to look into the crystal ball to guess what her clients wanted to hear. She would whisper in her Uncle Marco's ear, and he in turn would transmit the message to the client, along with any improvisations of his own that he thought pertinent. Thus their fame spread, because all those who arrived sad and bedraggled at the consulting room left filled with hope. Unrequited lovers were told how to win over indifferent hearts, and the poor left with foolproof tips on how to place their money at the dog track. Business grew so prosperous that the waiting room was always packed with people, and Nana began to suffer dizzy spells from being on her feet so many hours a day. This time Severo had no need to intervene to put a stop to his brother-in-law's venture, for both Marcos and Clara, realizing that their unerring guesses could alter the fate of their clients, who always followed their advice to the letter, became frightened and decided that this was a job for swindlers. They abandoned their carriage-house oracle and split the profits, even though the only one who had cared about the material side of things had been Nana.

Of all the del Valle children, Clara was the one with the greatest interest in and stamina for her uncle's stories. She could repeat each and every one of them. She knew by heart words from several dialects of the Indians, was acquainted with their customs, and could describe the exact way in which they pierced their lips and earlobes with wooden shafts, their initiation rites, the names of the most poisonous snakes, and the appropriate antidotes for each. Her uncle was so eloquent that the child could feel in her own skin the burning sting of snakebites, see reptiles slide across the carpet between the legs of the jacaranda room-divider, and hear the shrieks of macaws behind the drawing-room drapes. She did not hesitate as she recalled Lope de Aguirre's search for El Dorado, or the unpronounceable names of the flora and fauna her extraordinary uncle had seen; she knew about the lamas who take salt tea with yak lard and she could give detailed descriptions of the opulent women of Tahiti, the rice fields of China, or the white prairies of the North, where the eternal ice kills animals and men who lose their way, turning them to stone in seconds. Marcos had various travel journals in which he recorded his excursions and impressions, as well as a collection of maps and books of stories and fairy tales that he kept in the trunks he stored in the junk room at the far end of the third courtyard. From there they were hauled out to inhabit the dreams of his descendants, until they were mistakenly burned half a century later on an infamous pyre.

Now Marcos had returned from his last journey in a coffin. He had died of a mysterious African plague that had turned him as yellow and wrinkled as a piece of parchment. When he realized he was ill, he set out for home with the hope that his sister's ministrations and Dr. Cuevas's knowledge would restore his health and youth, but he was unable to withstand the sixty days on ship and died at the latitude of Guayaquil, ravaged by fever and hallucinating about musky women and hidden treasure. The captain of the ship, an Englishman by the name of Longfellow, was about to throw him overboard wrapped in a flag, but Marcos, despite his savage appearance and his delirium, had made so many friends on board and seduced so many women that the passengers prevented him from doing so, and Longfellow was obliged to store the body side by side with the vegetables of the Chinese cook, to preserve it from the heat and mosquitoes of the tropics until the ship's carpenter had time to improvise a coffin. At El Callao they obtained a more appropriate container, and several days later the captain, furious at all the troubles this passenger had caused the shipping company and himself personally, unloaded him without a backward glance, surprised that not a soul was there to receive the body or cover the expenses he had incurred. Later he learned that the post office in these latitudes was not as reliable as that of far-off England, and that all his telegrams had vaporized en route. Fortunately for Longfellow, a customs lawyer who was a friend of the del Valle family appeared and offered to take charge, placing Marcos and all his paraphernalia in a freight car, which he shipped to the capital to the only known address of the deceased: his sister's house.

This would have been one of the most painful moments in Clara's life if Barrabás had not arrived among her uncle's things. Unaware of the commotion in the courtyard, she was led by instinct directly to the corner where the cage had been set down. In it was Barrabás. Or, rather, a pile of bones covered with a skin of indefinite color that was full of infected patches, with one eye sealed shut and the other crusted over, rigid as a corpse in his own excrement. Despite his appearance, the child had no trouble in identifying him.

"A puppy!" she cried.

The animal became her responsibility. She removed it from the cage, rocked it in her arms, and with a missionary's care managed to get water down his parched, swollen throat. No one had bothered to feed him since Captain Longfellow—who, like most Englishmen, was kinder to animals than to people—had dropped him on the pier along with all the other baggage. While the dog had been on board with his dying master, the captain had fed him with his own hand and taken him up on deck, lavishing on him every attention that he had denied Marcos, but once on land he was treated as part of the baggage. Without any competition for the job, Clara became the creature's mother, and she soon revived him. A few days later, after the storm of the corpse's arrival had died down and Uncle Marcos had been laid to rest, Severo noticed the hairy animal his daughter was holding in her arms.

"What's that?" he asked.

"Barrabás," Clara replied.

"Give him to the gardener so he can get rid of him. He might be contagious," Severo ordered.

But Clara had adopted him. "He's mine, Papa. If you take him away, I'll stop breathing and I promise you I'll die."

The dog remained in the house. Soon afterward he was running everywhere, devouring drape fringes, Oriental rugs, and all the table legs. He rapidly recovered from his terrible condition and began to grow. After he had had a bath, he was found to be black, with a square head, long legs, and short hair. Nana suggested cutting off his tail to make him more refined, but Clara had a tantrum that degenerated into an asthma attack and no one ever mentioned it again. Barrabás kept his tail, which in time grew to be as long as a golf club and developed a life all its own that led to lamps and china being swept from tabletops. He was of unknown pedigree. He had nothing in common with the stray dogs in the street, much less with the thoroughbred races that assorted families of the aristocracy were raising. The veterinarian was unable to pinpoint his origin and Clara decided that he was from China, because most of her uncle's baggage was from that distant land. The dog had a seemingly unlimited capacity for growth. Within six months he was the size of a sheep, and at the end of a year he was as big as a colt. In desperation the family began to question whether he would ever stop growing and whether he really was a dog. They suggested that he might be some exotic animal their uncle had caught in some remote corner of the world and that perhaps in his natural habitat he was wild. Nívea looked at his crocodile claws and his sharp little teeth and her heart leapt at the thought that if in one bite he could snap the head off any grown-up, it would be even easier for him to gobble up one of her children. But Barrabás gave no indication of ferocity. On the contrary he had all the captivating ways of a frolicsome kitten. He slept by Clara's side with his head on her feather pillow and a quilt up to his neck because he was very sensitive to cold, and later, when he was too big for the bed, he lay on the floor beside her, his horse's hoof resting on the child's hand. He never barked or growled. He was as black and silent as a panther, liked ham and every known type of marmalade, and whenever there was company and the family forgot to lock him up he would steal into the dining room and slink around the table, removing with the greatest delicacy all his favorite dishes, and of course none of the diners dared to interfere. Despite his docility, Barrabás inspired terror. Delivery men fled precipitously whenever he stuck his head out into the street, and once he caused a riot among the women who were lined up waiting to buy milk, startling the dray horse who took off like a shot, scattering milk pails every which way on the pavement. Severo had to pay for all the damage and ordered the dog tied up in the courtyard, but Clara had another fit and the decision was indefinitely postponed. Popular imagination and ignorance with respect to his past lent Barrabás the most mythological characteristics. It was said that he would not stop growing, and that if a butcher's cruelty had not put an end to his existence, he would have reached the size of a camel. Some people believed him to be a cross between a dog and a mare, and expected him to sprout wings and horns and acquire the sulfuric breath of a dragon, like the beasts Rosa was embroidering on her endless tablecloth. Tired of picking up broken china and hearing rumors of how he turned into a wolf when there was a full moon, Nana applied the same method she had used with the parrot, but the overdose of cod-liver oil did not kill the dog. It simply gave him a four-day case of diarrhea that covered the house from top to bottom and that she herself had to clean.

Translated by Magda Bogin

Bibliographies

Lydia Cabrera

Fiction

Cuentos negros de Cuba. Havana, 1940.

¿Por qué?: Cuentos negros de Cuba. Havana, 1948.

Ayapá: Cuentos de jicotea. Miami, 1971.

Cuentos para adultos niños y retrasados mentales. Miami, 1983.

Afro-Cuban Culture

El monte: Igbo finda, ewe orisha, vititi nfinda: Notas sobre las religiones, la magia, las supersticiones y el folklore de los negros criollos y del pueblo de Cuba. Havana, 1954.

Refranes de negros viejos. Havana, 1955.

Anagó: El yoruba que se habla en Cuba. Havana, 1957.

La sociedad secreta Abakuá, narrada por viejos adeptos. Havana, 1959.

Otán Iyebiyé: Las piedras preciosas. Miami, 1970.

La laguna sagrada de San Joaquín. Madrid, 1973.

Yemayá y Ochún: Las diosas del agua. Madrid, 1974.

Anaforuana: Ritual y símbolos de la iniciación en la sociedad secreta Abakuá. Madrid, 1975.

Francisco y Francisca: Chascarrillos de negros viejos. Miami, 1976.

La regla Kimbisa del Santo Cristo del buen viaje. Miami, 1977.

Reglas de Congo: Palo monte mayombé. Miami, 1979.

Koeko Iyawó, aprende novicia: Pequeño tratado de regla lucumí. Miami, 1980.

English Translations

"Turtle's Horse" and "Walo-Wila." In *From the Green Antillas,* edited by Barbara Howes, pp. 275–79. New York, 1966.

"Obbara Lies but Doesn't Lie," translated by Suzanne Jill Levine and Mary Caldwell, and "The Hill Called Mambiala," translated by Elizabeth Millet. In *Contemporary Women Authors of Latin America: New Translations,* edited by Doris Meyer and Margarite Fernández Olmos, pp. 147–57. New York, 1983.

"How the Monkey Lost the Fruit of His Labor," translated by Mary Caldwell and Suzanne Jill Levine. In *Other Fires: Short Fiction by Latin American Women,* edited by Alberto Manguel, pp. 200–205. New York, 1986.

Secondary Sources

Abrea, Juan, et al. *Homenaje a Lydia Cabrera.* New York, 1982.

Figueroa, Esperanza. "Lydia Cabrera: *Cuentos negros de Cuba.*" *Revista Sur,* no. 349 (July–December 1981): 89–97.

Guzmán, Cristina. "Diálogo con Lydia Cabrera." *Zona Franca* 3, no. 24 (May–June 1981): 34–38.

Hiriart, Rosario. "La experiencia viva en la ficción: Lydia Cabrera e Hilda Perera." *Círculo: Revista de Cultura,* no. 8 (1979): 125–31.

————. *Más cerca de Teresa de la Parra: Diálogos con Lydia Cabrera.* Caracas, 1980.

————. "En torno al mundo negro de Lydia Cabrera." *Cuadernos Hispanoamericanos,* no. 359 (April 1980): 433–40.

Jiménez, Onilda A. "Dos cartas inéditas de Gabriela Mistral a Lydia Cabrera." *Hispamérica* 12, nos. 34–35 (April–August 1983): 97–103.

Josephs, Allen. "Lydia and Federico: Towards a Historical Approach to Lorca Studies." *Journal of Spanish Studies: Twentieth Century,* no. 6: 123–30.

Levine, Suzanne Jill. "A Conversation with Lydia Cabrera." *Review: Latin American Literature and Arts,* no. 31 (January–April 1982): 13–15.

Montes-Huidobro, Matías. "Itinerario del Ebo." *Studies in Afro-Hispanic Literature,* nos. 2–3 (1978–79): 1–13.

Perera, Hilda. *Idapo: El sincretismo en los cuentos negros de Lydia Cabrera.* Miami, 1971.

————. "La Habana intacta de Lydia Cabrera." *Círculo: Revista de cultura,* no. 13 (1984): 33–38.

Sánchez, Reinaldo, et al. *Homenaje a Lydia Cabrera.* Miami, 1978.

Valdés-Cruz, Rosa. "Mitos africanos conservados en Cuba y su tratamiento literario por Lydia Cabrera." *Chasqui* 3, no. 1: 31–36.

————. "The Short Stories of Lydia Cabrera: Transpositions or Creations?" In *Latin American Women Writers: Yesterday and Today,* edited by Yvette E. Miller and Charles M. Tatum, pp. 148–54. Pittsburgh, 1977.

Willis, Miriam Decosta. "Folklore and the Creative Artist: Lydia Cabrera and Zora Neale Hurston." *College Language Association Journal* 27, no. 1 (September 1983): 81–90.

Armonía Somers

Fiction

"La mujer desnuda." *Clima,* no. 2. 1st ed. 1950; 2d ed. 1951.

El derrumbamiento. Montevideo, 1953.
La calle del viento norte. Montevideo, 1963.
De miedo en miedo (Los manuscritos del río). Montevideo, 1965.
La mujer desnuda. Montevideo, 1967.
Todos los cuentos 1953–67. 2 vols. Montevideo, 1967.
Un retrato para Dickens. Montevideo, 1969.
Muerte por alacrán. Buenos Aires, 1978.
Tríptico Darwiniano. Montevideo, 1982.
Sólo los elefantes encuentran mandrágora. Buenos Aires, 1986.
Viaje al corazón del día. Montevideo, 1986.

Other Works

Educación de la adolescencia: El adolescente de novela y su valor de testimonio. Mexico, 1957.
Ana Sullivan Macy: La forja en noche plena. N.p., n.d. [Signed Armonía Etchepare.]
Postscript to *Diez relatos y un epílogo.* pp. 113–54. Montevideo, 1979.

English Translations

"Madness," translated by Susana Hertelendy. In *The Eye of the Heart: Short Stories from Latin America,* edited by Barbara Howes, pp. 300–302. Indianapolis and New York, 1973.
"The Immigrant," translated by Anne Hohenstein. *Diana's Second Almanac,* 1980, pp. 4–35.
"The Fall," translated by Alberto Manguel. In *Other Fires: Short Fiction by Latin American Women,* edited by Alberto Manguel, pp. 10–23. New York, 1986.

Secondary Sources

Araújo, Helena. "Escritura femenina: Sobre un cuento de Armonía Somers." *Cuéntame tu vida,* no. 5 (1981): 19–24.
De Espada, Roberto. "Armonía Somers o el dolor de la literatura." *Maldoror,* 1st trimester (1972): 62–66.
Figueira, Gastón. Review of *La calle del viento norte. Books Abroad* (Summer 1964): 295.
Gandolfo, Elvio E. "Para conocer a Armonía Somers." *Clarín* 9 (January 1986): 1–3.
Garfield, Evelyn Picon. "Yo soplo desde el páramo: La muerte en los cuentos de Armonía Somers." *Texto crítico,* no. 6 (January–April 1977): 113–25.
———. "Armonía Somers." In *Women's Voices from Latin America: Interviews with Six Contemporary Authors,* pp. 29–51. Detroit, 1985.
———. "La metaforización de la soledad: Los cuentos de Armonía Somers." *Revista de la Universidad Nacional,* 2, no. 10 (December–January 1986–87): 25–30.
Glantz, Margo. "Djuna Barnes y Armonía Somers: ¿Tiene la escritura sexo?" *Sábado* (supplement to *Uno más uno*), 6 July 1980.
Rama, Angel. "Testimonio, confesión y enjuiciamiento de veinte años de historia y de nueva literatura uruguaya." *Marcha* (1960).
———. "La insólita literatura de Somers: La fascinación del horror." *Marcha,* no. 1, 188 (1963): 30.
———. "Mujeres, dijo el penado alto." *Marcha,* no. 1, 290 (1966).
———. *Cien años de raros.* Montevideo, 1966.
———. "La conciencia crítica." *Enciclopedia Uruguaya,* no. 56 (1969).

———. *La generación crítica 1939–1969*. Montevideo, 1972.

Rela, Walter. *Diccionario de escritores uruguayos*, pp. 124–27. Montevideo, 1986.

Rodríguez Villamil, Ana María. "Aspectos fantásticos en *La mujer desnuda* de Armonía Somers." *Río de la Plata*, no. 1 (1985): 147–63.

Visca, Arturo Sergio. "El mundo narrativo de Armonía Somers." In *Nueva antología del cuento uruguayo*. Montevideo, 1976.

Zum Felde, Alberto. *Indice crítico de la literatura hispanoamericana*. Vol. 2, *La narrativa*, p. 501. 2d ed. Madrid, 1964.

Elena Garro

Fiction

Los recuerdos del porvenir. Mexico City, 1963.

La semana de colores. Xalapa, 1964.

Andamos huyendo Lola. Mexico City, 1980.

Testimonios sobre Mariana. Mexico City, 1981.

Reencuentro de personajes. Mexico City, 1982.

La casa junto al río. Mexico City, 1983.

Plays

Un hogar sólido, y otras piezas en un acto. Xalapa, 1958.

La dama boba: Pieza en tres actos. Mexico, 1963.

El árbol. Mexico, 1967.

Felipe Angeles. Mexico, 1979.

English Translations

"The Lady on Her Balcony," translated by Beth Miller. *Shantih* 3, no. 3 (Fall–Winter 1976): 36–44.

"The Dogs," translated by Beth Miller. *Latin American Literary Review* 8, no. 15 (1979): 68–85.

"The Day We Were Dogs," translated by Tona Wilson. In *Contemporary Women Authors of Latin America: New Translations*, edited by Doris Meyer and Margarite Fernández Olmos, pp. 186–191. New York, 1983.

"It's the Fault of the Tlaxcaltecas," translated by Alberto Manguel. In *Other Fires: Short Fiction by Latin American Women*, edited by Alberto Manguel, pp. 159–78. New York, 1986.

Recollections of Things to Come. Translated by Ruth L. C. Simms, 2d ed. Austin, 1987.

Secondary Sources

Anderson, Robert K. "La cuentística mágico-realista de Elena Garro." *Selecta: Journal of the Pacific Northwest Council on Foreign Languages*, no. 3 (1982): 117–21.

———. "Myth and Archetype in *Recollections of Things to Come*." *Studies in Twentieth Century Literature* 9, no. 2 (Spring 1985): 213–27.

Callan, Richard J. "Analytical Psychology and Garro's *Los pilares de doña Blanca*." *Latin American Theatre Review* 16, no. 2 (Spring 1983): 31–35.

Carballo, Emmanuel. "La vida y la obra de Elena Garro." *Sábado* (supplement to *Uno más uno*) (24 January 1981), pp. 2–5.

Bibliographies

Cypess, Sandra Messinger. "Titles as Signs in the Translation of Dramatic Texts." In *Translation Perspectives II: Selected Papers, 1984–1985,* edited by Marilyn Gaddis Rose, pp. 95–104. Binghamton, N.Y., 1985.

———. "Visual and Verbal Distances in the Mexican Theater: The Plays of Elena Garro." In *Woman as Myth and Metaphor in Latin American Literature,* edited by Carmelo Virgillo and Naomi Lindstrom, pp. 44–62. Columbia, MO., 1985.

Dauster, Frank. "El teatro de Elena Garro: Evasión e ilusión." *Revista Iberoamericana* 30, no. 57 (January–June 1964): 81–89.

Duncan, Cynthia. " 'La culpa es de los tlaxcaltecas': A Reevaluation of Mexico's Past through Myth." *Crítica Hispánica* 7, no. 2 (1985): 105–20.

Earle, Peter G. "*Los recuerdos del porvenir* y la fuerza de las palabras." In *Homenaje a Luis Alberto Sánchez,* edited by Peter G. Earlè, pp. 235–42. Madrid, 1983.

Glantz, Margo. " 'Andamos huyendo Lola': El niño y el adulto se vuelven expósitos." *Sábado* (supplement to *Uno más uno*) (23 May 1981), p. 21.

Johnson, Harvey L. "Elena Garro's Attitudes toward Mexican Society." *South Central Bulletin* 40, no. 4 (Winter 1980): 150–52.

Méndez Ródenas, Adriana. "Tiempo femenino, tiempo ficticio: *Los recuerdos del provenir* de Elena Garro." *Revista Iberoamericana* 51, nos. 132–33 (July–December 1985): 843–51.

Miller, Beth, and Alfonso González. *26 autoras del México actual.* Mexico, 1978.

Mora, Gabriela. "A Thematic Exploration of the Works of Elena Garro." In *Latin American Women Writers: Yesterday and Today,* edited by Yvette E. Miller and Charles M. Tatum, pp. 91–97. Pittsburgh, 1977.

———. "*La dama boba* de Elena Garro. Verdad y ficción, teatro y metateatro." *Latin American Theatre Review* 16, no. 2 (Spring 1983): 15–22.

Østergaard, Ane-Grethe. "El realismo de los signos escénicos en el teatro de Elena Garro." *Latin American Theatre Review* 16, no. 1 (Fall 1982): 53–65.

Robles, Martha. "Tres mujeres en la literatura mexicana." *Cuadernos americanos* 246, no. 1 (January–February 1983): 223–35.

Verwey, Antonieta Eva. *Mito y palabra poética en Elena Garro.* Querétaro, 1982.

Clarice Lispector

Fiction

Perto do coração selvagem. Rio de Janeiro, 1944.

O lustre. Rio de Janeiro, 1945.

A cidade sitiada. Rio de Janeiro, 1948.

Alguns contos. Rio de Janeiro, 1952.

Laços de família. São Paulo, 1960.

A maçã no escuro. Rio de Janeiro, 1961.

A legião estrangeira. Rio de Janeiro, 1964.

A paixão segundo G. H. Rio de Janeiro, 1964.

Uma aprendizagem ou o livro dos prazeres. Rio de Janeiro, 1969.

Felicidade clandestina: Contos. Rio de Janeiro, 1971.

Água viva. Rio de Janeiro, 1973.

A imitação da rosa. Rio de Janeiro, 1973.

Onde estivestes de noite. Rio de Janeiro, 1974.

A via crucis do corpo. Rio de Janeiro, 1974.

A hora da estrela. Rio de Janeiro, 1977.

Um sopro de vida. Rio de Janeiro, 1978.

A bela e a fera. Rio de Janeiro, 1979.

Children's Literature

O mistério do coelho pensante. Rio de Janeiro, 1967.

A mulher que matou os peixes. Rio de Janeiro, 1968.

A vida íntima de Laura. Rio de Janeiro, 1974.

Quase de verdade. Rio de Janeiro, 1978.

Nonfiction

De corpo inteiro. Rio de Janeiro, 1975.

Visão do esplendor: Impressões leves. Rio de Janeiro, 1975.

Para não esquecer. São Paulo, 1978.

English Translations

The Apple in the Dark. Translated by Gregory Rabassa. New York, 1967.

"The Crime of the Mathematics Professor." In *Modern Brazilian Short Stories,* translated and edited by William Grossman, pp. 146–52. Berkeley, 1967.

Family Ties. Translated by Giovanni Pontiero. Austin, 1972.

"The Smallest Woman in the World" and "Marmosets," translated by Elizabeth Bishop. In *The Eye of the Heart,* edited by Barbara Howes, pp. 320–28. New York, 1973.

"The Solution," translated by Elizabeth Lowe. *Fiction* 3 (Winter 1974): 24.

"Temptation," translated by Elizabeth Lowe. *Inter-Muse* 1, no. 1 (1976): 91–92.

"The Man Who Appeared" and "Better Than to Burn," translated by Alexis Levitin. In *Latin American Literature Today,* edited by Anne Fremantle, pp. 165–71. New York, 1977.

The Passion According to G. H., a portion translated by Jack E. Tomlins. In *The Borzoi Anthology of Latin American Literature,* edited by Emir Rodríguez Monegal, vol. 1, pp. 779–92. New York, 1977.

"Excerpts from *The Foreign Legion,*" translated by Giovanni Pontiero. *Review, Center for Inter-American Relations* 24 (June 1979): 37–43.

"Sofia's Disasters," translated by Elizabeth Lowe. *Review, Center for Inter-American Relations* 24 (June 1979): 27–33.

"The Woman Who Killed the Fish," translated by Earl E. Fitz. *Latin American Literary Review* 11, no. 21 (Fall–Winter 1982): 89–101.

"A Full Afternoon" and "But It's Going to Rain," translated by Alexis Levitin. *Latin American Literary Review* 12, no. 24 (Spring–Summer 1984): 76–81.

"Pig Latin." Translated by Alexis Levitin. *Ms.* 13, no. 1 (July 1984): 68–69.

The Hour of the Star. Translated by Giovanni Pontiero. New York, 1986.

Secondary Sources

Borelli, Olga. *Clarice Lispector: Um esboço para un possível retrato.* Rio de Janeiro, 1981.

Brasil, Assis. *Clarice Lispector.* Rio de Janeiro, 1969.

Bryan, C. D. B. "Afraid to be Afraid." *New York Times Book Review,* 3 September 1967, pp. 22–23.

Bibliographies

Campedelli, S. Y., and B. Abdala, Jr. *Clarice Lispector.* São Paulo, 1981.

Cook, Bruce. "Women in the Web." *Review, Center for Inter-American Relations* 8 (Spring 1973): 65–66.

Fitz, Earl E. "Clarice Lispector and the Lyrical Novel: A Re-examination of *A maçã no escuro.*" *Luso-Brazilian Review* 14, no. 2 (Winter 1977): 153–60.

————. "The Leitmotif of Darkness in Seven Novels by Clarice Lispector." *Chasqui* 7, no. 2 (February 1978): 18–28.

————. "The Rise of the New Novel in Latin America: A Lyrical Aesthetic." *Inter-Muse* 2 (1979): 17–27.

————. "Freedom and Self-Realization: Feminist Characterization in the Fiction of Clarice Lispector." *Modern Language Studies* 10, no. 3 (1980): 51–61.

————. "Point of View in Clarice Lispector's *A hora da estrela.*" *Luso-Brazilian Review* 19, no. 2 (Winter 1982): 195–208.

————. "Uma bibliografia de e sobre Clarice Lispector." *Revista Iberoamericana* 50, no. 126 (January–March 1984): 293–304. [We are indebted to this excellent bibliography.]

————. *Clarice Lispector.* Boston, 1985. [We are indebted to this excellent (and only) book in English on Clarice Lispector.]

Foster, David William, and Virginia Ramos Foster, eds. *Modern Latin American Literature,* pp. 484–91. New York, 1975.

Goldman, Richard Franko. "The Apple in the Dark." *Saturday Review,* 19 August 1967, pp. 33, 48.

Hamilton, D. Lee. "Some Recent Brazilian Literature." *Modern Language Journal* 32, no. 7 (November 1948): 504–7.

Herman, Rita. "Existence in *Laços de família.*" *Luso-Brazilian Review* 4, no. 1 (June 1967): 69–71.

Jozef, Bella. "Chronology: Clarice Lispector," translated by Elizabeth Lowe. *Review, Center for Inter-American Relations* 24 (June 1979): 24–26.

————. "Clarice Lispector: La recuperación de la palabra poética." *Revista Iberoamericana* 50, no. 126 (January–March 1984): 239–57.

Lindstrom, Naomi. "Clarice Lispector: Articulating Women's Experience." *Chasqui* 8, no. 1 (1978): 43–52.

————. "A Feminist Discourse Analysis of Clarice Lispector's 'Daydreams of a Drunken Housewife.' " *Latin American Literary Review* 9, no. 19 (Fall–Winter 1981): 7–16.

————. "A Discourse Analysis of 'Preciosidade' by Clarice Lispector." *Luso-Brazilian Review* 19, no. 2 (Winter 1982): 187–94.

Lowe, Elizabeth. "The Passion According to C.L." (Interview with Clarice Lispector.) *Review, Center for Inter-American Relations* 24 (June 1979): 34–37.

Moisés, Massaud. "Clarice Lispector: Fiction and Cosmic Vision," translated by Sara M. McCabe. *Studies in Short Fiction* 8, no. 1 (Winter 1971): 268–81.

Número Especial Dedicado a la Literatura Brasileña. Revista Iberoamericana 50, no. 126 (January–March 1984): 129–40, 293–306, 314–17.

Nunes, Benedito. *O mundo de Clarice Lispector.* Manaus, 1966.

————. *Leitura de Clarice Lispector.* São Paulo, 1973.

Nunes, Maria Luisa. "Narrative Modes in Clarice Lispector's *Laços de família:* The Rendering of Consciousness." *Luso-Brazilian Review* 14, no. 2 (Winter 1977): 174–84.

Patai, Daphne. "Clarice Lispector and the Clamor of the Ineffable." *Kentucky Romance Quarterly* 27 (1980): 133–49.

Pereira, Teresinha Alves. *Estudo sobre Clarice Lispector.* Coimbra, 1975.

Sá, Olga de. *A escritura de Clarice Lispector*. Petrópolis, 1979.

Pontiero, Giovanni. "The Drama of Existence in *Laços de família.*" *Studies in Short Fiction* 8, no. 1 (Winter 1977): 256–67.

———. "Testament of Experience: Some Reflections on Clarice Lispector's Last Narrative *A hora da estrela.*" *Ibero-Amerikanisches Archiv* 10, no. 1 (1984): 13–22.

Seniff, Dennis. "Self-Doubt in Clarice's *Laços de família.*" *Luso-Brazilian Review* 14, no. 2 (Winter 1977): 199–208.

Griselda Gambaro

Fiction

Madrigal en ciudad. Buenos Aires, 1963.

El desatino. Buenos Aires, 1965.

Una felicidad con menos pena. Buenos Aires, 1968.

Nada que ver con otra historia. Buenos Aires, 1972.

La cola mágica. (Stories for children.) Buenos Aires, 1976.

Ganarse la muerte. Buenos Aires, 1976.

Dios no nos quiere contentos. Buenos Aires, 1979.

Lo impenetrable. Buenos Aires, 1984.

Plays

El desatino. Buenos Aires, 1965.

Los siameses. Buenos Aires, 1967.

El campo. Buenos Aires, 1967 and 1981.

Teatro: Las paredes, El desatino, Los siameses. Barcelona, 1979.

Nueve dramaturgos hispanoamericanos (Los siameses). Vol. 2. Ottawa, 1979.

Teatro: Nada que ver y Sucede lo que pasa. Ottawa, 1983.

Teatro I: Real envido, La malasangre, Del sol naciente. Buenos Aires, 1984.

Teatro II: Dar la vuelta, Información para extranjeros, Puesta en claro, Sucede lo que pasa. Buenos Aires, 1987.

Nonfiction

Conversaciones con chicos. Buenos Aires, 1977.

"Algunas consideraciones sobre la mujer y la literatura." *Revista Iberoamericana* 51, nos. 132–33 (July–December 1985): 471–74.

"¿Es posible y deseable una dramaturgia específicamente femenina?" *Latin American Theatre Review* (Summer 1980): 17–22.

English Translation

The Camp. In *Voices of Change in the Spanish American Theater,* edited and translated by William I. Oliver, pp. 47– 103. Austin and London, 1971.

Secondary Sources

Boorman, Joan Rea. "Contemporary Latin American Women Dramatists." *Rice University Studies* 64, no. 1 (1978): 69–80.

Carballido, Emilio. "Griselda Gambaro o modos de hacernos pensar en la manzana." *Revista Iberoamericana,* no. 73 (October–December 1970): 629–34.

Cypess, Sandra Messinger. "Physical Imagery in the Plays of Griselda Gambaro." *Modern Drama* 18, no. 4 (December 1975): 357–64.

———. "The Plays of Griselda Gambaro." In *Dramatists in Revolt: The New Latin American Theatre,* edited by George W. Woodyard and Leon F. Lyday, pp. 95–107. Austin, 1976.

———. "Titles as Signs in the Translation of Dramatic Texts." In *Translation Perspectives II: Selected Papers 1984–1985,* edited by Marilyn Gaddis Rose. Binghamton, N.Y., 1985.

Feiman Waldman, Gloria. "Three Female Playwrights Explore Contemporary Latin American Reality: Myrna Casas, Griselda Gambaro, Luisa Josefina Hernández. In *Latin American Women Writers: Yesterday and Today,* edited by Yvette Miller and Charles M. Tatum, pp. 75–84. Pittsburgh, 1977.

Foster, David William. "El lenguaje como vehículo espiritual en *Los siameses* de Griselda Gambaro." *Escritura* 4, no. 8 (July–December 1979): 241–57.

———. "The Texture of Dramatic Action in the Plays of Griselda Gambaro." *Hispanic Journal* 1, no. 2 (1979): 57–66.

Foster, Virginia Ramos. "The Buenos Aires Theater, 1966–67." *Latin American Theatre Review,* nos. 1–2 (Spring 1968): 58.

———. "Mario Trejo and Griselda Gambaro: Two Voices of the Argentina Experimental Theater." *Books Abroad* 42, no. 4 (Autumn 1968): 534–35.

Garfield, Evelyn Picon. "Una dulce bondad que atempera las crueldades: *El campo* de Griselda Gambaro." *Latin American Theatre Review* Supplement, no. 13-2 (Summer 1980): 95–102; augmented version in *Zona Franca* 3, no. 19 (July–August 1980): 28–36.

———. "Griselda Gambaro." In *Women's Voices from Latin America: Interviews with Six Contemporary Authors,* pp. 53–71. Detroit, 1985.

Giella, Miguel Angel. "Entrevista: Griselda Gambaro." *Hispamérica* 14, no. 40 (April 1985): 35–42.

Holzapfel, Tamara. "Griselda Gambaro's Theatre of the Absurd." *Latin American Theatre Review,* no. 3-2 (Fall 1970): 5–12.

Méndez-Faith, Teresa. "Sobre el uso y abuso de poder en la producción dramática de Griselda Gambaro." *Revista Iberoamericana* 51, nos. 132–33 (July–December 1985): 831–42.

Moretta, Eugene L. "Spanish American Theatre of the 50's and 60's: Critical Perspectives on Role Playing." *Latin American Theatre Review,* no. 2 (1980): 5–30.

Podol, Peter L. "Reality Perception and Stage Setting in Griselda Gambaro's *Las paredes* and Antonio Buero Vallejo's *La fundación.*" *Modern Drama* 24, no. 1 (March 1981): 44–53.

Elvira Orphée

Fiction

Dos veranos. Buenos Aires, 1956.

Uno. Buenos Aires, 1961.

Aire tan dulce. Buenos Aires, 1966.

En el fondo. Buenos Aires, 1969.

Su demonio preferido. Buenos Aires, 1973.

La última conquista de El Angel. Caracas, 1977.

Las viejas fantasiosas. Buenos Aires, 1981.

English Translation

El Angel's Last Conquest. Translated by Magda Bogin. New York, 1985.

Secondary Sources

Bastos, María Luisa. "Una escritora argentina: Elvira Orphée." *Zona Franca* 3, no. 44 (April 1967): 24–26.

———. "Tortura y discurso autoritario: *La última conquista de El Angel* de Elvira Orphée." In *The Contemporary Latin American Short Story,* edited by Rose S. Minc. New York, 1979.

Chacel, Rosa. "Un libro ciertamente nuevo." *Sur,* no. 245 (March–April 1957): 111–17.

Chevigny, Bell. "Ambushing the Will to Ignorance: Elvira Orphée's *La última conquista de El Angel* and Marta Traba's *Conversación al sur.*" In *El cono sur: Dinámica y dimensiones de su literatura,* edited by Rose S. Minc, pp. 98–104. Upper Montclair, N.J., 1985.

"Conversación con Elvira Orphée." *Zona Franca* 3, no. 2 (July–August 1977): 24–28.

Crespo, Julio. *"Aire tan dulce." Sur,* no. 307 (July–August 1967): 47–49.

Díaz, Gwendolyn. "Escritura y palabra: *Aire tan dulce* de Elvira Orphée." *Revista Iberoamericana* 51, nos. 132–33 (July–December 1985): 641–48.

Dujovne Ortiz, Alicia. "Los demonios de lo cotidiano." *La Opinión Cultural* 27 (November 1977): 10–11.

E. D. Review of *Dos veranos. Ficción,* no. 4 (November–December 1956): 192–94.

Garfield, Evelyn Picon. "Desprendida a hachazos de la eternidad: Lo primordial en la obra de Elvira Orphée." *Journal of Latin American Lore* 5, no. 1 (1979): 3–23.

———. "Elvira Orphée." In *Women's Voices from Latin America: Interviews with Six Contemporary Authors,* pp. 97–113. Detroit, 1985.

Justo, Luis. "Elvira Orphée y sus novelas." *Sur,* no. 315 (November–December 1968): 88–89.

Loubet, Jorgelina. "Lo cotidiano, el fulgor y el signo en la obra de actuales escritoras argentinas." *Zona Franca* 3, no. 20 (September–October 1980): 7–23.

Carmen Naranjo

Fiction

Los perros no ladraron. San José, Costa Rica, 1966.

Memorias de un hombre palabra. San José, Costa Rica, 1966.

Camino al mediodía. San José, Costa Rica, 1968.

Responso por el niño Juan Manuel. San José, Costa Rica, 1971.

Diario de una multitud. San José, Costa Rica, 1974.

Hoy es un largo día. San José, Costa Rica, 1974.

Ondina. San José, Costa Rica, 1983.

Nunca hubo alguna vez. San José, Costa Rica, 1984.

Estancias y días. With Graciela Moreno. San José, Costa Rica, 1985.

Sobrepunto. San José, Costa Rica, 1985.

Poetry

Canción de la ternura. San José, Costa Rica, 1964.

Hacia tu isla. San José, Costa Rica, 1976.

Misa a oscuras. San José, Costa Rica, 1976.
Mi guerrilla. San José, Costa Rica, 1977.
Idioma del invierno. San José, Costa Rica, 1978.
Homenaje a don nadie. San José, Costa Rica, 1981.

Nonfiction

Por Israel y por las páginas de la Biblia. San José, Costa Rica, 1976.
Cinco temas en busca de un pensador. San José, Costa Rica, 1977.
La mujer y la cultura: antología. Mexico City, 1981.

English Translations

"The Flowery Trick," translated by Corina Mathieu, "The Journey and the Journeys," translated by Marie J. Panico, and "Inventory of a Recluse," translated by Mary Sue Listerman. In *Five Women Writers of Costa Rica,* edited by Victoria Urbano, pp. 3–5, 6–12, 13–16. Beaumont, Tex., 1978.
"Ondina," translated by Elise Miller. *Fiction International* 16, no. 2:7–12.

Secondary Sources

Burdiel de López, María Cruz. "Estudio de tres cuentos de Carmen Naranjo." *Revista de la Universidad de Costa Rica* 41 (1975): 101–10.

Busette, Cedric. Review of *Ondina. Lector* 3, nos. 3–4.

Filer, Malva. "Carmen Naranjo: *Mi guerrilla." Alba de América* 3, nos. 4–5 (July 1985).

Garfield, Evelyn Picon. "Entrevista con Carmen Naranjo." *Letras,* nos. 11–12 (January–December 1986): 217–28.

———. " 'La luminosa ceguera de sus días': los cuentos 'humanos' de Carmen Naranjo." *Revista Iberoamericana* 53, nos. 138–39 (January–June 1987): 287–302.

Garzón Céspedes, Francisco. Review of *Sobrepunto. Universidad,* August 1985.

Mathieu, Corina. "Commentary on 'The Flowery Trick.' " In *Five Women Writers of Costa Rica,* edited by Victoria Urbano, p. 19. Beaumont, Tex., 1978.

Minc, Rose S., and Teresa Méndez-Faith. "Conversando con Carmen Naranjo." *Revista Iberoamericana* 51, nos. 132–33 (July–December 1985): 507–10.

Miranda Hevia, Alicia. *Novela, discurso y sociedad (Diario de una Multitud).* San José, Costa Rica, 1981.

Rojas de Ayub, María Elena. "Una novela de Carmen Naranjo: *Camino a medio día." Revista de la Universidad de Costa Rica* 34 (1972): 57–65.

Urbano, Victoria. "Carmen Naranjo y su voz plena en *La canción de la ternura." Káñina* 1, no. 2 (1977): 5–31.

———. "The Creative Philosophy of Carmen Naranjo." In *Five Women Writers of Costa Rica,* edited by Victoria Urbano, pp. 17–18. Beaumont, Tex., 1978.

Vargas, A., and R. Aura. "*Los perros no ladraron:* una novedad técnica en la novelística costarricense." *Káñina* 1, no. 2 (1977): 33–36.

Zúñiga, Virginia. Review of *Nunca hubo alguna vez. La Nación,* October 1984.

Marta Traba

Fiction

Historia natural de la alegría. Buenos Aires, 1951.
Las ceremonias del verano. Havana, 1966.

Los laberintos insolados. Barcelona, 1967.

Pasó así. Montevideo, 1968.

La jugada del sexto día. Santiago, 1969.

Homérica Latina. Bogotá, 1979.

Conversación al sur. Mexico City, 1981.

En cualquier lugar. Bogotá, 1984.

De la mañana a la noche (Cuentos norteamericanos). Montevideo, 1986.

Art History and Art Criticism

Art in Colombia. Washington, D.C., 1959.

La pintura nueva en Latinoamérica. Bogotá, 1961.

Seis artistas contemporáneos colombianos. Bogotá, 1963.

Los cuatro monstruos cardinales. Mexico City, 1963.

Historia abierta del arte colombiano. Cali, 1968.

Propuesta polémica sobre el arte puertorriqueño. San Juan, Puerto Rico, 1971.

La rebelión de los santos. San Juan, Puerto Rico, 1971.

En el umbral del arte moderno. San Juan, Puerto Rico, 1972.

Dos décadas vulnerables. Mexico City, 1973.

Mirar en Caracas. Caracas, 1974.

Los signos de vida. Mexico City, 1976.

La zona del silencio. Mexico City, 1976.

Los muebles de Beatriz González. Bogotá, 1977.

Los grabados de Roda. Bogotá, 1977.

Mirar en Bogotá. Bogotá, 1977.

Nonfiction

"La cultura de la resistencia." In *Literatura y praxis en América Latina,* pp. 49–80. Caracas, 1974.

Marta Traba, selección de textos. Bogotá, 1984.

"Hipótesis de una escritura diferente." In *La sartén por el mango,* edited by Patricia Elena González and Eliana Ortega, pp. 21–26. Río Piedras, Puerto Rico, 1984.

English Translation

Mothers and Shadow. Translated by Jo Labanyi. London, 1986.

Secondary Sources

Agosín, Marjorie. "Marta Traba." *Sin Nombre* 14, no. 3 (April–June 1984): 97–100.

Bayón, Damián. "El espléndido no conformismo de Marta Traba." *Sin Nombre* 14, no. 3 (April–June 1984): 92–96.

Benítez, Marimar. "Apuntes sobre los escritos de Marta Traba en Puerto Rico." *Sin Nombre* 14, no. 3 (April–June 1984): 123–26.

Chevigny, Bell. "Angel Rama and Marta Traba: A Latin American Odyssey Ends." *Nation,* 4 February 1984, pp. 126–28.

———. "Ambushing the Will to Ignorance: Elvira Orphée's *La última conquista de El Angel* and Marta Traba's *Conversación al sur.*" In *El cono sur: Dinámica y dimensiones de su literatura,* edited by Rose S. Minc, pp. 98–104. Upper Montclair, N.J., 1985.

Bibliographies

Cobo Borda, Juan Gustavo. "Spanish American Fiction, 1981." *Review, Center for Inter-American Relations* 31 (April 1982): 83–87.

———. "Marta Traba, novelista." *Cuadernos Hispanoamericanos,* no. 414 (December 1984): 121–30.

García Pinto, Magdalena. "Entrevista: Marta Traba." *Hispamérica* 13, no. 38 (August 1984): 37–46.

García Ramos, Reinaldo. "La novelista y sus veranos." *Casa de las Américas* 6, nos. 36–37 (May–August 1966): 190–94.

Garfield, Evelyn Picon. "Marta Traba." In *Women's Voices from Latin America: Interviews with Six Contemporary Authors,* pp. 115–40. Detroit, 1985.

Grossman, Edith. "In Memoriam." *Review, Center for Inter-American Relations* 32 (January–May 1984): 8.

Poniatowska, Elena. "Marta Traba o el salto al vacío." *Revista Iberoamericana* 51, nos. 132–33 (July–December 1985): 883–98.

Sola, María. "*Conversación al sur,* novela para no olvidar." *Sin Nombre* 12, no. 4 (July–September 1982): 64–71.

———. " 'Escribo como mujer': Trayectoria de la narrativa de Marta Traba." *Sin Nombre* 14, no. 3 (April–June 1984): 101–14.

Waller, Claudia J. "Light and Darkness in Marta Traba's *Los laberintos insolados.*" *Romance Notes* 14 (1972): 262–68.

Julieta Campos

Fiction

Muerte por agua. Mexico City, 1965.

Celina o los gatos. Mexico City, 1968.

Tiene los cabellos rojizos y se llama Sabina. Mexico City, 1974.

El miedo de perder a Eurídice. Mexico City, 1979.

Jardín de invierno. Vuelta 10, no. 115 (June 1986): 19–29.

Literary Theory and Criticism

La imagen en el espejo. Mexico, 1965.

Oficio de leer. Mexico, 1971.

Función de la novela. Mexico, 1973.

"¿Tiene sexo la escritura?" *Vuelta* 2, no. 21 (August 1978): 44–45.

La herencia obstinada. Mexico, 1982.

"Mi vocación literaria." *Revista Iberoamericana* 51, nos. 132–33 (July–December 1985): 467–70.

English Translation

"Story of a Shipwreck," translated by Beth Miller. *Review, Center for Inter-American Relations* 76, no. 18 (Fall 1976): 66–68.

Secondary Sources

Agüera, Victorio G. "El discurso de lo imaginario en *Tiene los cabellos rojizos y se llama Sabina.*" *Revista Iberoamericana* 51, nos. 132–33 (July–December 1985): 531–38.

Francescato, Martha P. "Un desafío a la crítica literaria: *Tiene los cabellos rojizos y se llama Sabina* de Julieta Campos." *Revista de Crítica Literaria Americana* 7, no. 13 (1st semester, 1981): 121–25.

Garfield, Evelyn Picon. Review of *Tiene los cabellos rojizos y se llama Sabina*. *Revista Iberoamericana* 46, nos. 112–13 (July–December 1980): 680–83.

———. "*Tiene los cabellos rojizos y se llama Sabina* de Julieta Campos: Una caída interminable en la inmovilidad." *Eco*, no. 248 (June 1982): 172–91.

———. "Julieta Campos." In *Women's Voices from Latin America: Interviews with Six Contemporary Authors*, pp. 73–96. Detroit, 1985.

Glantz, Margo. "Entre lutos y gatos: José Agustín y Julieta Campos." In *Repeticiones: ensayos sobre literatura mexicana*, pp. 70–74. Veracruz, 1979.

Martínez, Martha. "Julieta Campos o la interiorización de lo cubano." *Revista Iberoamericana* 51, nos. 132–33 (July–December 1985): 793–98.

Miller, Beth. "Julieta Campos: La escritura es un modo de organizar la vida." *Los Universitarios* (1974): 6–8.

———. "Julieta Campos" and "Entrevista con Julieta Campos." In *Mujeres en la literatura*, edited by Beth Miller, pp. 118–27. Mexico City, 1978.

Miller, Beth, and Alfonso González. *26 autoras del México actual*. Mexico City, 1978.

Pacheco, José Emilio. "Novela de la conciencia y conciencia de la novela." *Plural*, no. 35 (August 1974): 72–73.

Rivero Potter, Alicia. "La creación literaria en Julieta Campos: *Tiene los cabellos rojizos y se llama Sabina*." *Revista Iberoamericana* 51, nos. 132–33 (July–December 1985): 899–908.

Rodríguez Nebot, Joaquín. "Una herencia y su historia." (Review of *La herencia obstinada*.) *Revista de la Universidad de México* 38, no. 20 (December 1982): 42–43.

Verani, Hugo J. "Julieta Campos y la novela del lenguaje." *Texto Crítico* 2, no. 4 (1976): 132–49.

Nélida Piñón

Fiction

Guia-Mapa de Gabriel Arcanjo. Rio de Janeiro, 1961.
Madeira feita cruz. Rio de Janeiro, 1963.
Tempo das frutas. Rio de Janeiro, 1966.
Fundador. Rio de Janeiro, 1969.
A casa da paixão. Rio de Janeiro, 1972.
Sala de armas. Rio de Janeiro, 1973.
Tebas do meu coração. Rio de Janeiro, 1974.
A força do destino. Rio de Janeiro, 1978.
O calor das coisas. Rio de Janeiro, 1980.
A república dos sonhos. Rio de Janeiro, 1984.
A doce canção de Caetana. Rio de Janeiro, 1987.

English Translations

"Brief Flower," translated by Gregory Rabassa. In *The Triquarterly Anthology of Contemporary Latin American Literature*, edited by José Donoso, pp. 309–16. New York, 1961.

"Big-Bellied Cow," translated by Gregory Rabassa. *Mundus Artium* 3, no. 3 (Summer 1970): 89–96.

"Adamastor," translated by Giovanni Pontiero. *Shantih* 3, no. 3. (1976): 20–23.

"Bird of Paradise," translated by Giovanni Pontiero. *Review, Center for Inter-American Relations*, no. 19 (Winter 1976): 75–78.

Excerpts from *House of Passion*, translated by Gregory Rabassa. In *The Borzoi Anthology of Latin American Literature*, edited by Emir Rodríguez Monegal, vol. 2, pp. 793–98. New York, 1977.

"Adamastor," translated by Giovanni Pontiero. In *Contemporary Women Authors of Latin America: New Translations*, edited by Doris Meyer and Margarite Fernández Olmos, pp. 235–40. New York, 1983.

Secondary Sources

Bins, Patrícia. "Nélida Piñón: O Escritor e uma voz a mais a denunciar e combater as realidades incompatíveis com o homem." *Minas Gerais, Suplemento Literario* 19, no. 941 (13 October 1984): 2–3.

Campos, Maria Consuelo Cunha. "O romance da nova república." *Minas Gerais, Suplemento Literario* 20, no. 962 (9 March 1985): 5.

Crespo, Angel, and Pilar Gómez Bedate. "Nélida Piñón, de *Guia mapa a Tempo das frutas.*" *Revista de Cultura Brasileña* 7, no. 24 (March 1968): 5–27.

Guimarães, Dénise A. D. "Uma Poética de autor, leitura de um texto de Nélida Piñón." *Estudos Brasileiros*, no. 9 (June 1980): 39–56.

Hoki Moniz, Naomi. "*A casa da paixão:* Etica, estética e a condição feminina." *Revista Iberoamericana* 50, no. 126 (January–March 1984): 129–40.

Issa, Farida. "Entrevista con Nélida Piñón." *Nueva Narrativa Hispanoamericana* 3, no. 1 (January 1973): 133–40.

Medina, Cremilda. "Embarque no sonho nesta república em mutação." *Minas Gerais, Suplemento Literario* 20, no. 964 (23 March 1985): 8.

Nunes, Maria Luisa. Review of *O calor das coisas*. *Revista Iberoamericana* 50, no. 126 (January–March 1984): 326–27.

Ornelas, Joseph. "El mundo simbólico y filosófico de *Madeira feita cruz* de Nélida Piñón." *Nueva Narrativa Hispanoamericana* 3, no. 1 (January 1973): 95–102.

Pontiero, Giovanni. "Notes on the Fiction of Nélida Piñón." *Review, Center for Inter-American Relations*, no. 19 (Winter 1976): 67–71.

Rodriguez Paulino, Maria das Graças. "*Fundador:* A subversão do mito." *Cadernos de Lingüística de Teoria da Literatura* 2 (December 1979): 71–75.

Secco, Carmen Lúcia Tindo. "A metáfora da traiçao em João Alphonsus e em Nélida Piñón." *Minas Gerais, Suplemento Literario* 14, no. 789 (14 November 1981): 11.

Zagury, Eliane. "Sobre *Tempo das frutas* de Nélida Piñón." *Revista de Cultura Brasileña* 7, no. 24 (March 1968): 61–65.

Luisa Valenzuela

Fiction

Hay que sonreír. Buenos Aires, 1966.

Los heréticos. Buenos Aires, 1967.

El gato eficaz. Mexico City, 1972.

Aquí pasan cosas raras. Buenos Aires, 1975.

Como en la guerra. Buenos Aires, 1977.

Libro que no muerde. Mexico City, 1980.

Cambio de armas. Hanover, N.J., 1982.

Donde viven las águilas. Buenos Aires, 1983.

Cola de lagartija. Buenos Aires, 1983.

Nonfiction

"I Was Always a Bit of a Rebel." In *Artists in Exile,* edited by Jane Katz, pp. 59–70. New York, 1982.

"The Word That Milk Cow." In *Contemporary Women Authors of Latin America: Introductory Essays,* edited by Doris Meyer and Margarite Fernández Olmos, pp. 96–97. New York, 1983.

"La mala palabra." *Revista Iberoamericana* 51, nos. 132–33 (July–December 1985): 489–91.

"Dangerous Words," "Dirty Words," "In Search of My Own Backyard," and "Little Manifesto." In *Luisa Valenzuela Number. Review of Contemporary Fiction* 6, no. 3 (Fall 1986): 9–21.

English Translations

Clara: Thirteen Short Stories and a Novel. Translated by Hortense Carpentier and J. Jorge Castello. New York and London, 1976.

Strange Things Happen Here. Translated by Helen Lane. New York and London, 1979.

"The Best Shod" and "A Story about Greenery," translated by Helen Lane. *Ms* 7, no. 12 (June 1979): 60–61.

"Three Stories from *Strange Things Happen Here,*" translated by Helen Lane. *Review, Center for Inter-American Relations* 24 (1979): 44–53.

"The Censors," translated by David Unger. *City 8* 1, no. 8 (1980): 8–10.

"Papito's Story," translated by David Unger. *City 8* 1, no. 8 (1980): 66–68.

"The First Feline Vision" from *El gato eficaz,* translated by Evelyn Picon Garfield. *Antaeus,* no. 48 (Winter 1983): 75–78.

"Generous Impediments Float Down the River," translated by Clementine Rabassa. In *Contemporary Women Authors of Latin American: New Translations,* edited by Doris Meyer and Margarite Fernández Olmos, pp. 245–48. New York, 1983.

The Lizard's Tail. Translated by Gregory Rabassa. New York, 1983.

"The Efficient Cat" from *El gato eficaz,* translated by Evelyn Picon Garfield. *River Styx,* no. 14 (January 1984): 87–89.

Other Weapons. Translated by Deborah Bonner. Hanover, N.H., 1985.

"From *The Motive:* A Novel-in-Progress," translated by Cynthia Ventura. *Review of Contemporary Fiction* 6, no. 3 (Fall 1986): 22–24.

"My Deadly Doctorate" from *El gato eficaz,* translated by Evelyn Picon Garfield. *Review of Contemporary Fiction* 6, no. 3 (Fall 1986): 7–8.

"Springtime" from *El gato eficaz,* translated by Evelyn Picon Garfield. *Formations* 3, no. 1 (Spring 1986): 1–3.

Secondary Sources

Araújo, Helena. "Valenzuela's *Other Weapons." Review of Contemporary Fiction* 6, no. 3 (Fall 1986): 78–81.

Callejo, Alfonso. "Literatura e irregularidad en *Cambio de armas* de Luisa Valenzuela." *Revista Iberoamericana* 51, nos. 132–33. (July–December 1985): 575–80.

Cook, Carole. "*Strange Things Happen Here:* Twenty-six Short Stories and a Novel." *Saturday Review,* 23 June 1979, p. 80.

Bibliographies

Cortázar, Julio. "Luisa Valenzuela." *Review: Latin American Literature and Arts,* no. 24 (1979): 44.

Fores, Ana M. "Valenzuela's *Cat-o-Nine Deaths." Review of Contemporary Fiction* 6, no. 3 (Fall 1986): 39–47.

Francescato, Martha Paley. "*Cola de lagartija:* Látigo de la palabra y la triple P." *Revista Iberoamericana* 51, nos. 132–33 (July–December 1985): 875–82.

Garfield, Evelyn Picon. "Muerte-Metamorfosis-Modernidad: *El gato eficaz* de Luisa Valenzuela." *Insula,* nos. 400–401 (March–April 1980): 17, 23.

———. "Luisa Valenzuela." In *Women's Voices from Latin America: Interviews with Six Contemporary Authors,* pp. 141–65. Detroit, 1985.

———. "Interview with Luisa Valenzuela." *Review of Contemporary Fiction* 6, no. 3 (Fall 1986): 25–38.

Gautier, Marie-Lise Gazarian. "The Sorcerer and Luisa Valenzuela: Double Narrators of the Novel-Biography, Myth-History." *Review of Contemporary Fiction* 6, no. 3 (Fall 1986): 105–8.

Glantz, Margo. "Luisa Valenzuela's *He Who Searches." Review of Contemporary Fiction* 6, no. 3 (Fall 1986): 62–66.

Grossman, Edith. "To Speak the Unspeakable." *Review, Center for Inter-American Relations* 32 (January–May 1984): 33–34.

Hicks, Emily. "That Which Resists: The Code of the Real in Luisa Valenzuela's *He Who Searches." Review of Contemporary Fiction* 6, no. 3 (Fall 1986): 55–61.

Josephs, Allen. "Sorcerers and Despots." (Review of *The Lizard's Tail.) New York Times Book Review,* 2 October 1983, pp. 15, 26.

Maci, Guillermo. "The Symbolic, the Imaginary and the Real in Luisa Valenzuela's *He Who Searches." Review of Contemporary Fiction* 6, no. 3 (Fall 1986): 67–77.

Magnarelli, Sharon. "Gatos, lenguaje, y mujeres en *El gato eficaz* de Luisa Valenzuela." *Revista Iberoamericana* 45, nos. 108–9 (July–December 1979): 603–11.

———. "Humor and Games in *El gato eficaz* by Luisa Valenzuela: The Looking-Glass World Revisited." *Modern Language Studies* 13, no. 3 (1983): 81–89.

———. "Juego-fuego de la esperanza (En torno a *El gato eficaz* de Luisa Valenzuela)." *Cuadernos Americanos* 247, no. 2 (1983): 199–208.

———. "Censorship and the Female Writer—An Interview-Dialogue with Luisa Valenzuela." *Letras femeninas* 10, no. 1 (Spring 1984): 55–64.

———. "*The Lizard's Tail:* Discourse Denatured." *Review of Contemporary Fiction* 6, no. 3 (Fall 1986): 97–104.

Martínez, Zulma Nelly. "*El gato eficaz* de Luisa Valenzuela: La productividad del texto." *Revista canadiense de estudios hispánicos* 4 (1979): 73–80.

———. "Luisa Valenzuela's 'Where the Eagles Dwell': From Fragmentation to Holism." *Review of Contemporary Fiction* 6, no. 3 (Fall 1986): 109–15.

Marting, Diane. "Female Sexuality in Selected Short Stories by Luisa Valenzuela: Toward an Ontology of Her Work." *Review of Contemporary Fiction* 6, no. 3 (Fall 1986): 48–54.

Morello-Frosch, Marta. "*Other Weapons:* When Metaphors Become Real." *Review of Contemporary Fiction* 6, no. 3 (Fall 1986): 82–87.

Mull, Dorothy S. "Ritual Transformation in Luisa Valenzuela's 'Rituals of Rejection.' " *Review of Contemporary Fiction* 6, no. 3 (Fall 1986): 88–96.

Wilson, S. R. Review of *Aquí pasan cosas raras. Latin American Literary Review* 9, no. 18 (Spring–Summer 1981): 67–69.

———. Review of *Cambio de armas. Latin American Literary Review* 12, no. 24 (Spring–Summer 1984): 82–84.

Isabel Allende

Fiction

La casa de los espíritus. Barcelona, 1982.
De amor y de sombra. Barcelona, 1984.
Eva Luna. Barcelona, 1987.

Nonfiction

"La magia de las palabras." *Revista Iberoamericana* 51, nos. 132–33 (July–December 1985): 447–52.

English Translations

The House of the Spirits. Translated by Magda Bogin. New York, 1985.
Of Love and Shadows. Translated by Magda Bogin. New York, 1987.

Secondary Sources

Agosín, Marjorie. "Isabel Allende: *La casa de los espíritus.*" *Revista Interamericana de Bibliografía—Inter-American Review of Bibliography* 35 (1985): 448–58.

Aguirre, María Elena. "Isabel y sus espíritus. " *Carola,* no. 51 (9 April 1984): 23.

Badra, Nadia F. "Una historia de amor desvela a Isabel." *Gente,* 29 April 1984, pp. 3–4.

Coddou, Marcelo, ed. *Los libros tienen sus propios espíritus.* Veracruz, 1986.

Eberenz, Rolf. "La imaginación como libertad: *La casa de los espíritus* de Isabel Allende." *Iberoamericana* 8, nos. 22–23 (1984): 102–8.

Freixas, Ramón. Review of *La casa de los espíritus. Quimera,* no. 28 (February 1983): 69.

Magnarelli, Sharon. Review of *The House of the Spirits. Latin American Literary Review* 14, no. 28 (July–December 1986): 101–4.

Marcos, Juan Manuel. Review of *La casa de los espíritus. Revista Iberoamericana* 51, nos. 130–31 (January–June 1985): 401–6.

———. "Isabel viendo llover en Barataria." *Revista de Estudios Hispánicos* 19, no. 2 (May 1985): 129–37.

Medwick, C. "The Amazing Isabel Allende." *Vogue,* March 1985, p. 506.

Peña, Mónica. "Isabel Allende y sus espíritus," *APSI,* no. 153 (October 1984).

Rodríguez Fernández, Mario. Review of *La casa de los espíritus. Atenea,* no. 448 (1983): 270–73.

Rojas, Mario A. "*La casa de los espíritus* de Isabel Allende: Un caleidoscopio de espejos desordenados." *Revista Iberoamericana* 51, nos. 132–33 (July–December 1985): 917–26.

Romero, Graciela. "Isabel Allende: Diez años de soledad." *Mundo,* no. 12 (November 1983): 28–29.

Shapiro, H. "Salvador's Niece Builds a House of the Spirits from the Ashes of Exile." *People Weekly,* 10 June 1985, pp. 145–46.

Smith, Amanda. "Publishers Weekly Interviews: Isabel Allende." *Publishers Weekly,* 17 May 1985, pp. 119–20.

Zamudio, Alfredo. "Isabel Allende: A vivir con alegría." *Hoy,* no. 385 (December 1984): 31–33.

Evelyn Picon Garfield is professor of Spanish and Comparative Literature and associate dean of the College of Liberal Arts and Sciences at the University of Illinois at Urbana-Champaign. She received her A.B. from the University of Michigan, her M.A. from Washington University, St. Louis, and her Ph.D. from Rutgers University. She has previously taught at Wayne State University, Brown University, and Montclair State College. Dr. Garfield is the author of Women's Voices from Latin America: Interviews with Six Contemporary Authors, ¿Es Julio Cortázar un surrealista?, Julio Cortázar, Cortázar por Cortázar, *and numerous articles, and coauthor with I. A. Schulman of* "Las entrañas del vacío": Ensayos sobre la modernidad hispanoamericana *and* Poesía modernista hispanoamericana y española (Antología).

The manuscript was prepared for publication by Christina Postema. The typeface for the text is Times Roman. The typefaces for the display are Caslon and Times Roman. The book is printed on 55-lb. Glatfelter text paper and bound in Holliston's Roxite Vellum.

Manufactured in the United States of America.